HOOVERING UP THE HOLY CARPET

~ AN ARTIST'S LIFE AND TRAVELS ~ VOLUME 2: NEW CENTURY TRAVELS

LINDA ALVIS

For Siobhan with love

HOOVERING UP THE HOLY CARPET
An Artist's Life and Travels ~ Volume 2: New Century Travels

First published 2022 by Alvis Fine Art

Paperback ISBN 978-1-9160106-4-2
Ebook ISBN 978-1-9160106-5-9

British Library Cataloging in Publication Data

A CIP catalogue record for this book is available from the British Library.

To my brother John

CONTENTS

Preface   1

Introduction   2

1. Cornwall   3

2. Northumberland   5

3. Italy (2000)   10

4. China (2001)   16

5. Ten Countries (2002)   41
    The Baltic
    Prague

6. The Amalfi Coast (2003)   62

7. The Balloon Festival (2003)   68

8. Colonial Friends (2003)   71

9. Andalucia (2003)   73

10. The Concorde, Bristol (2003)   79

11. Munich (2003)   82

12. London Exhibitions and the Ukraine (2004)   85

13. Canada and Alaska (2004) 102

14. Canada Again (2005) 129

15. Singapore and Australia (2006) 143

16. Broken Bones and India (2007) 194

17. New Zealand and Australia (2008) 227

18. Postscript (2013) 257

19. The Fracture (2007) 261

Also by Linda Alvis 262

Cover Images 263

Acknowledgements 264

PREFACE

This book could easily be retitled 'Travels with Mother' as she features so prominently, gamely agreeing to be included in most of my travels. However, 'Hoovering Up the Holy Carpet' is most appropriate as I may never have started my painting journey in pastels, that most tricky of mediums, without meeting with Peter Clay again and hearing his famous phrase.

I hope this story will inspire my readers to be brave in their artistic endeavours and possibly travel to wonderful places... or just enjoy accompanying me on the journey.

Introduction

The Millennium was upon us and, as always on New Year's morning, I wondered what the year would bring. How strange it felt, coming to terms with a brand-new century. I went downstairs and was stopped in my tracks by a most beautiful and dramatic sky. Light poured through clouds onto a frosted, misty landscape. It was quite stunning, and I immediately got my pastels out and recorded this miraculous morning. Luckily, I finished it in one go, as a short time after, leaning over the bannister, I almost knocked myself out on an iron support. I felt ill for hours, and had to have a very quiet day. New Year's Day 2000 was stunning, in every sense of the word.

***

Photographs relating to this book can be found on my website at www.alvisfineart.co.uk/books.

My paintings and further award-winning poems, inspired by these travels, can be found in the poetry book *Dawn Rising.*

CORNWALL

F OR SEVERAL YEARS DURING the summer months, I took the long train journey from Bristol to Penzance to visit my old friend, the great artist Joan Edwards. What a wonderful sight, skirting the shore, looking over to St Michael's Mount and chugging into Penzance Station, the distinctive long building at the very end of the line. It was always the start of an enchanting and inspirational visit. Joan and her late husband Don had been my next-door neighbours in Flax Bourton, and on Don's retirement from the British Aircraft Company in Filton they retired to the Penwith Peninsula. Joan had been a Pascoe, and with her Cornish roots the lure of Cornwall and its wonderful light was irresistible to her and gentle Don. At the age of thirteen she had won a scholarship to the Bristol College of Art but, as with so many of her age, the war intervened and she eventually found herself in a drawing office. After the war she married Don, became a teacher of art, and had their son David, who proved to be a very intelligent little boy. Joan then put aside her own art career and continued teaching to be able to send David to Clifton College.

The move to Cornwall provided Joan with the time and in-spiration for her complex, beautiful work. On many occasions we ambled along the cliff paths and into the delightful cove at Penberth to collect pebbles, driftwood and seaweed for Joan to study back in her light and airy studio. I was so envious of such a professional working space and loved just sitting there, absorbing the atmosphere and admiring Joan's work. The thatched cottage and studio, perched within sight and sound of the sea, was a sublime place, filled with classical music from early morning to late at night. It generously provided me with many opportunities to rest and recharge my batteries, before returning home brimming with knowledge and ideas.

We made frequent visits to the Tate St Ives. Full of light and reminiscent of a lighthouse, it stands proudly overlooking the coast and the distinctive yellow rooftops of the town. Joan introduced me to the works of many famous St Ives artists, and, of course, the sculptures of Barbara Hepworth. We visited her garden and studio, which remains as she left it with her tools laid out on the work bench. We peered admiringly through the glass wall separating us from her actual workshop.

Later I produced a little oil painting from a photograph I took of Joan intently studying a rather phallic Hepworth sculpture at The Tate. I was given permission to reproduce it, but I was asked to mention the Tate in the title, which of course I was delighted to do. However, as a subtitle, I just had to call it 'Private View'. I made some greetings cards of the image and couldn't resist sending it as a get-well greeting to an aunt who was recovering from a hysterectomy.

Dear Joan. What a wonderful friend and mentor. It pains me now to remember her, frail, lonely and delicate with age, unable to paint because of failing sight and lack of confidence. She has a huge body of unique work, and may one day surely be discovered as a national treasure.

NORTHUMBERLAND

T HEN THERE WAS ALWAYS my beloved Northumberland, visiting every year without fail. But as time passed, all those dear loved ones, dozens of them, were no longer there, of course. John and I are one of the 'canny bairns' no more. My grandmother's death in her seventies was my first huge loss, though she lived long enough to see and enjoy baby David. I was expecting James when she died of a heart attack, with poor Grandad at her side. The end of a great love story

Converted into two flats now, the house in Roxburgh Terrace looks the same from the outside today, but is just a shell of its former magnificence. The heart has gone. Mum and Dad continued to visit for many years, staying with Grandad and Auntie Ella who kept the downstairs flat, whilst the boys and I had bed and breakfast nearby. So I had my usual 'fix' of the accent and bracing Northumbrian air.

When the boys were young, we always visited at Easter when the weather was usually bitter. The worst year we experienced was during the perishing winter of 1981 when we moved into Beaconsfield Road. We were off 'Up North' for my cousin Avenell's wedding to Bryan on 19th December at St George's Church in Cullercoats, overlooking Tynemouth Long Sands. Getting all three boys into the car and comfortably settled was usually a challenge, but that year it was a nightmare. Heavy snow and freezing conditions made packing up difficult, and every time the car door shut, it froze.

Eventually ready for the off, we were passed by a group of people trudging through the snow. 'Where are you going?' they asked. When I replied, 'Northumberland', they just shook their heads in disbelief and wished us the best of luck.

I tucked the boys into sleeping bags and, ever mindful of my physio training, we did 'exercises' every hour to keep warm and eventually made quite good progress. The motorways were clear enough, and I shall never forget passing Chester-Le-Street in County Durham when the last slab of snow slid off the car bonnet. We had travelled 300 miles by then, and it had taken that long to dislodge the final persistent chunk!

Grandad, a darling, mild man, lived to the ripe old age of 94, but as Dad always said, 'smoking got him in the end.' Poor Dad was soon to follow, and Auntie Ella eventually sold up and moved into sheltered housing in nearby Monkseaton.

Auntie Joyce moved to a little flat in Cambo Place, North Shields, and I continued staying with her as years went by and the boys gradually flew the nest. We had some lovely trips around Northumberland, and as her weakening heart started to fail I did all the driving. What a fabulous county. It never fails to overwhelm me with its stark beauty and wildlife, numerous castles built to keep the marauding Scots at bay, and most striking of all, vast empty beaches stretching as far as the eye can see.

We both loved the Northumbrian Pipes, and when we heard that the Northumbrian Pipers Society met once a month in Morpeth Chantry we decided to visit. The pipes are quite heavenly, and Joyce and I sat transfixed in the upper room as about twelve pipers played their evocative traditional pieces. The pipes make such a beautifully breathy sound, and being in the same room was a delight. We would have had to sit at the end of the street to comfortably hear twelve Scottish pipers performing together.

In 2000, Colin Ross, chairman of the Northumbrian Pipers, invited me to visit him in his home. I was so excited as he actually made pipes, and was then the official pipe-maker to the Duke of Northumberland. He lived within walking distance of Cambo Place, and I shall never forget sitting in his workshop, hearing a master play.

Colin allowed me to take photographs so I could eventually paint his portrait. As we talked, I mentioned my portrait of Donald Patrick Sinclair, the Barra boatman, and to my amazement they actually knew each other. Colin and his Scottish wife owned a holiday cottage on Barra, and right next door to Donald.

One memorable day Auntie Joyce's friend Jean offered to drive us up to the Woollen Mill at Otterburn, and then on to Kielder Forest. I was always pleased to visit Otterburn as Mum and Dad had bought one of the Mill's famous pram rugs for David way back in 1968, and I knew the Queen always had one for her children. The Mill is so lovely, set amidst fields of sheep and in the most glorious countryside. We had our cuppa in the cafe, then proceeded to the store to enjoy a look around, enveloped in the all-pervading warm smell of spun wool and lanolin, before setting off for Kielder.

'You must see the chalets at Kielder,' Jean told us. 'They have everything you could want for a holiday.'

Arriving at the Forest and surrounded by birdsong, we came across a group of very well-appointed timber chalets nestling among pine trees and overlooking Kielder Water. What a perfect holiday home, and how cosy to return there after a hard day's trek. It is here, if you are lucky, you can find an abundance of wildlife, including red squirrels, osprey, and otters.

Returning to the car, I came across a gate and peered over it to see netted compounds, and what looked like an owl on a pole. I found a notice: 'Kielder Forest Bird of Prey Centre', but sadly, being February, it was closed. Suddenly a man appeared and, never one to miss an opportunity, I asked if we could have a quick peep round. My luck was in. The gate was opened and the man, Ray Lowndon, who ran the centre, invited us in. He proceeded to put on a large leather gauntlet and brought out a handsome peregrine falcon, which warily perched on the thick hide. This was a female with a damaged wing, being cared for at the centre and kept for breeding. The next bird was quite the most amazing sight. A magnificent female steppe eagle, found on the loose in the countryside, had been rescued and brought to the centre. She wore a red hood, and her huge talons tightly gripped the gauntlet. It was quite something to sense the rapport and understanding between this man and his bird. I took many photos, which I eventually used for a portrait. Ray is squinting into the sun as the eagle, unable to see, her head covered by the hood, seemed conscious only of him. Their eyes weren't visible, but I had to capture that moment of pride and trust.

'I can't let you handle the large birds, but would you like to hold a little owl?' Ray asked. I couldn't get the gauntlet on quick enough! It was large and very stiff, but soon, there on my arm, was this tiny, exquisite bird. I stroked its head and marvelled at its sweet softness, a rare and unforgettable moment.

Back home I produced a series of paintings, including Ray's portrait and the 'Little Owl', placed against a starlit night sky. The picture was quickly snapped up by a friend, Ruth, who said, 'It is perfect except for one thing. There are spots on the background.'

'Do you mind?' I retorted, having done some homework on the matter. 'Those are stars and that is the Northern night sky in February.' We both laughed.

The new Millennium brought a second wedding. David married Katie in the famous heavily-panelled church of St Leonards, Old Warden in Bedfordshire and their reception was held in a marquee in the grounds of Shuttleworth College. Katie's family lived on the estate, and as a child Katie had played in its beautiful grounds. It was all so personal and appropriate for both sides of the family, as David's father John had studied agriculture at the College in the 1960s.

Choosing my hat for the wedding had been an interesting experience. Mum and I decided to visit the Royal Academy in London for the day, and we also popped into Fortnum and Mason opposite for a quick peep at the hats. 'We are only looking,' we told ourselves. Famous last words! We both found absolutely perfect creations, but mine was really much too pricey. I enjoyed parading around, and then, as I was taking it off, a smiling assistant came over and declared, 'You must have that hat. It is quirky. I shall reduce it for you.' The reduction was very large, and Mum decided to make it her treat, and then bought a slightly more modest one for herself. This was to be a lovely family wedding, with relations and friends from all over the British Isles, and the hat turned out to be just perfect on a really perfect day.

The setting for the marquee was idyllic, with peacocks strutting and calling, later roosting in the surrounding trees. But the high point was a large ice sculpture, a Vodka Ski Louge which was enjoyed with abandon by guests young and old. Most of us remember it well! David had originally wanted sculptures of male and female forms, but I am glad to say Katie put her foot firmly down. It was around the time of the Clinton-Lewinsky episode, and really wouldn't do!

ITALY (2000)

THE FOLLOWING WINTER, MUM and I decided to have a change of scene and booked 'A Tuscan Christmas'. The promised delights of Vinci, Florence, and Siena were too attractive to resist. Unfortunately our plane was late arriving, but our coach was waiting, and very shortly we found ourselves on the motorway between Florence and Rome. It was rush hour, and, on this Friday before Christmas, one of the busiest days of the year. As darkness descended we were still on the road, and beginning to think we would never arrive at our mountain top hotel. At last, the turning for the village of Gavinana appeared and we all sighed with relief; but too soon, as our journey was by no means over. The long, winding road took us up and up the mountain, and after about twenty minutes I felt decidedly travel sick. Not wanting the embarrassment of being ill in front of a lot of people I didn't know, I thought about one of my paintings, 'Saunton Sands', which I had given to Rob and Bernice for their wedding present; and so, in my head, I started to compose a poem about love. It was a massive effort for such a short verse, but it worked; although a close-run thing, pins and needles having taken over by the time we reached the family-run Hotel Franceschi. We were most warmly welcomed, and I gladly took our room keys for a little 'lie down'. The window of our bedroom directly overlooked the narrow village street, and the church opposite was almost within touching distance.

That night I was woken by a strange noise. It seemed at first like a duck quacking and, in my imagination, I could just see the poor thing, walking along the dark and narrow street, in and out of small pools of light, as the sound gradually increased and then faded away.

Relieved, as peace descended, I settled down but very soon the 'quacking' started again! With a bit of a 'hurrumph' up I got and looked out of the window, but there was nothing to be seen, certainly nothing feathered, and then it dawned on me, the sound was very much closer and actually in the room. Now it was more like a rubber band twanging. First a large rubber band then a small one, with quite distinct and different 'twangs'. I moved over to the telephone near Mum's bed. Surely it was that. But no, leaning over her very soundly sleeping figure I had found the source. She was snoring! You can get quite tetchy in these circumstances and, being a very light sleeper, I resolved to have single rooms whenever possible on future trips!

The next morning broke clear blue and very cold for our visit to Vinci, birthplace of the genius Leonardo. In the museum dedicated to the great man's work, we marvelled at his inventions. One of our party, an engineer, pointed to a page in Leonardo's workbook showing his drawing of an instrument which is used to this day. Amongst designs of helicopters, tanks, and tools were the most beautiful and intricate drawings. The feverish brain of this son of Vinci and a peasant girl must have been an almost terrifying enigma to simple townspeople in the 15th century.

Coming out of the museum, we found refuge from the bitter cold in a small restaurant. Not really hungry, we each ordered a hot chocolate, hoping this steaming drink would warm us up. The eagerly awaited concoction arrived, luckily with spoons as, attempting our first sip, we realised this 'drink' wasn't going anywhere without assistance. It was hot and almost solid, and ambrosial.

Well-warmed and satisfied, we proceeded to our next stop, the Villa Capezzana. Home of a local Conte and Contessa, it is superbly situated on the hills of Carmignano, directly overlooking Florence and Pistoia. It was still very cold, but with the sky a beautiful blue we gazed happily over the Tuscan Hills, its vineyards and olive groves. In the cantina of the villa, we sampled local wine and olive oil before enjoying a lunch of local produce. It was an enchanting afternoon.

That evening we were taken to a 'typical Tuscan restaurant'. It was here that Mum's knee problems began. To reach the restaurant, we had to climb a village street by pulling ourselves up on a rope. It was very hard work, and quite a relief, especially for a struggling Mum, to reach our supper, which was indeed ample. Her knees never quite recovered.

The next day dawned a dull, cold Christmas Eve, and our destination was Siena. Stretching over three hills, this beautiful Tuscan town, encircled by ramparts, has the famous fan-shaped square, the elegant Piazza del Campo, at its heart. Here the frantic Palio horse race takes place once a year. We visited the magnificent cathedral, and on my own I walked into the Palazzo Pubblico, and, finding some steep, intriguing stairs, walked up to a pair of glass doors. They opened automatically, and I found myself on a balcony with extensive views over the town. It was a wonderfully solitary moment, but with no one else around I hoped the doors would open again for me to get down. I took a series of photographs of the tall terracotta dwellings all crowded together on the hills, and then, of course, the doors opened again and down I went. Where was everyone? How strange and rather perfect to enjoy such a view on my own.

In the palazzo I found the impressive Martini fresco dating from 1328. The last time I saw this image was on a tapestry hanging in my brother's house in Long Ashton. I had always admired it, and to see the whole illustrious original was quite a special moment.

The day was bitter and after a rather much too long lecture on Siena standing right in the middle of the cold and windy Piazza, we were glad to return to our mountaintop hotel and a warming supper. Being Christmas Eve, we were to witness a torch-lit procession through the main square, followed by midnight mass in the church opposite. I wondered whether I should go, as it would mean getting into bed well after midnight, when, at that time, my bedtime was around 8 'o clock. I couldn't resist, and joined villagers young and old, with some of our group, in the crowded church. Eventually feeling exhausted, I gave in and returned to the hotel just a few steps opposite.

I had made a terrible mistake, and should have known better. At 4 am I awoke with a devastating migraine. This was going to be the end of Christmas Day for me. I quickly took the migraine pill, but it was pointless. The next twenty-five hours were spent in agony, with waves of pain and sickness so violent it made my nose bleed. Even talking was difficult, but I signalled Mum to go off and enjoy herself. She couldn't do anything for me, and I was best left on my own. She left at noon for what was evidently a superb multi-course Christmas lunch, and I didn't see hide nor hair of her for five hours. They were eating all that time! I was happy for her though. I wouldn't want her to have missed it.

At five o'clock in the evening Madame Franchesci's daughter arrived with some clear consommé. I just managed to sip the soup, but was unable to eat the warm homemade bread roll. Ah well, that was my Christmas lunch, but I was glad Mum was able to have such a lovely time. She loved her food, and I think it was a pretty spectacular banquet.

So Christmas Day passed me by, but thank goodness I had recovered enough for our Boxing Day visit to Florence. If I had to have a migraine, 25th December was the best day to endure it. Florence was, of course, magnificent and unmissable! Oh, the relief of feeling better and immersing myself in the wonders of this fabulous city. After a conducted tour we filtered off on our own. Mum and I enjoyed a coffee on the Ponte Vecchio after admiring the tantalising shops, and finished with an essential visit to the Uffizi.

The Uffizi is a superb and most manageable gallery to walk around. I found the marvellous Bronzino, Piero della Francesci and Pollaiuolo originals of portraits I had copied at school in the 1950s, and suddenly experienced quite a wave of nostalgia. Then there were the icons. I had never been too keen on these, or mediaeval altar pieces, until I watched a series of programmes on restoration and gilding by the masterly Neil MacGregor, then Director of the National Gallery. I had immediately been hooked, and now enjoyed scrutinising these works of art. The high point of our visit was the Botticelli gallery. To this day I am still in awe of these beautiful paintings at the Uffizi. Botticelli's execution of feet and hands are unbelievably exquisite, and so fresh. What a joy to look on such beauty.

Our final day came too soon and it was freezing. Rain poured down and the sky pressed in on us with a grey foreboding. Nevertheless, we proceeded with our visit to the mediaeval market town of Pistoia, where I managed to buy pieces of the local Pecorino cheese to take home as presents. Originally a fortified Roman city, the town was interesting enough and well worth a visit with its ancient streets, the green and white marble cathedral housing an impressive silver altarpiece, and four gates built by the wealthy Medici family. However, we were all very damp and cold, and couldn't wait to get back to the warmth of our hotel for lunch. There was Madam Franchesci waiting for us with her famous Ribollita, the hearty rustic soup, and we fell upon it with almost unseemly relish. It was the most perfect meal for a cold, soggy day. As the rain gradually eased off we walked around the hilly town, imagining how the ski slopes would appear with the approaching snow. Ahead of the snow, we left for home the next day, stopping at a motorway service station for lunch. Feeling a little wary, we were surprised to find more of a Fortnum & Mason experience than in the average English services. We tucked into fresh pasta and admired the delicatessen before boarding our coach for the last leg to Bologna Airport and home.

The new century heralded my introduction to the Friends of the Royal West of England Academy, and being keen to support local arts I readily joined. In the autumn a members' portrait exhibition was to be held at the RWA, and I decided to submit my three northern portraits. To my great delight, all three were accepted: Colin Ross, the Northumbrian piper, Ray Lowndon and his steppe eagle from Kielder, and dear Donald Patrick Sinclair from Barra. During the exhibition, an Academician from the North of England was heard to say, 'I'd like to meet the man who painted that.' He was referring to Colin Ross. I felt quite proud, and not at all upset he thought a man had painted the portrait!

CHINA (2001)

I HAD ALWAYS WANTED to visit India, but Mum was not so keen. China was her dream, and to see the Yangtze before it was due to be flooded in 2003. My brother John had been to China a few years before and had loved it, but I felt nothing could beat my experience of Vietnam. Mum would be 81 in October, so when in March I found a rather interesting tour scheduled for that October, we decided to book up. Flying to Shanghai and finishing in Beijing by way of Xi'an and, unusually, a ten-day cruise on the Yangtze, it looked perfect. Yangtze cruises were often only three to five days long, so I hoped ten days would be more relaxing and certainly more interesting.

Mum was very enthusiastic and I immediately tried to book, only to find the cruise for October was already full.

'Oh dear,' I told the representative on the phone. 'Mum is 80, and it is her dream to see the Yangtze. Never mind.'

'Ring back first thing Monday morning. One booking is only provisional, and if they haven't come back by then you shall have the cabin. We open at 9am, but if you ring at 8.30 I will be here.'

We spent an anxious weekend with Mum trying not to be disappointed, and, when Monday morning arrived, at 8.30 on the dot I made the call.

'We knew it was you, Mrs Alvis. Those people haven't come back, so the cabin is yours. We wouldn't dream of letting anyone else have it.' How wonderful. We were thrilled, and started to plan for the following October.

In the meantime, we had another wedding to look forward to. Rob was to marry Bernice in St Albans that summer.

Rob's godfather was Malcom Widdecombe, dear friend and vicar of SS Philip and Jacob church in Bristol, and we all wanted him, with Meryl, his wife, to be involved in the proceedings. The invitation was sent for them to join us in St Albans for the whole wedding weekend, staying at the Hatfield Jarvis, famously originally known as the Comet Hotel, where the reception was to be held. They accepted.

Choosing yet another, quite different, outfit for the occasion was going to be difficult. My original choice looked much too staid and not at all 'me', so I searched for the 'right thing'. One afternoon I found myself looking at an interesting ensemble in the window of a boutique in Whiteladies Road. Before I knew it, I was inside the shop being invited to try it on. How could I refuse?

The outfit, a black linen bolero over a long, slim blue-grey dress with a palm tree motif, felt just right, but choosing a hat to match was to prove extremely difficult. After fruitless searching, my brother offered to take me to John Lewis in The Mall shopping centre on the outskirts of Bristol. Mum came along and we spent a long morning 'trying on'. Nothing seemed suitable, until, at last, I spied something: a wondrous creation in lilac and pale blue. It rose from my smallish crown in a curlicue of net ribbons, with a large butterfly nestling in its rear swirls. A millinery confection, with shades of Carmen Miranda. Ooh, I wasn't really sure, but it was fun and certainly suited the outfit – and, I have to admit, it was me – but possibly just a little too exotic?

I was suddenly aware of a small crowd gathering, eventually growing to about twenty people. I soon realised the object of their interest was me. Mothers with their children looked on, and men were smiling as Mum gave the 'thumbs up'. John quietly laughed to himself. The decision was made after an elderly lady declared, 'That's the one for her.'

As the great day approached, I began to have some misgivings. Not knowing Bernice's family too well at that time, I wondered if I had made an embarrassing mistake. I started to warn people that the hat might seem a bit 'over the top', but I decided to go ahead and wear it anyway.

Sitting in the church in Colney Heath, waiting for the marriage service to start, David approached.

'I don't know what you are worried about, Mother. You look lovely.' So kind of him, and with great relief I was then able to relax and enjoy a happy day. Many of the guests had fun with that hat, and during the reception several ladies tried it on, as did the Best Man and even Grandpa Alvis. It suited them all!

October and our trip to China came soon enough, but by then the world had been traumatised by the events of 9/11, as it became known. This catastrophic sequence of events in New York changed everything, and the world became quite a different place.

We decided to have the luxury of flying business class. Mum, already a little plump, was coming up to 81, and at her age a long-haul flight needed to be as comfortable as possible. I tagged on, of course, and enjoyed the massive difference this elevation provided.

On 18th October we boarded a Lufthansa flight for Shanghai, changing planes in Frankfurt where we experienced 'The Lounge' for the first time. After that, there could be no going back. Peace, comfort, food, and space in abundance. I slipped into it as to the manor born. Sadly, Mum had a different experience. Nipping off to the loo, she mistakenly left the private lounge and eventually found the more public convenience. Some 20 minutes later, a search was in progress. Mum was eventually found, and it dawned on me then that I was going to have to keep a very close eye on her from now on. Losing her in a European airport was one thing, mislaying an elderly parent in China would definitely be something else!

This wasn't anything to do with age; poor Mum never had a good sense of direction. As long as she was moving it didn't seem to matter which way she was going. I came to experience this on many occasions.

Arriving at dawn in Shanghai, we found we had been beaten to it by George Bush, who, together with his extensive retinue, had taken up residence in our planned hotel, described as 'the stunning, high-rise, JC Mandarin'. Uncannily empty, the city streets were guarded by the military, and top security measures were much in evidence. Messrs Bush and Putin had hit town for APEC: the Asia-Pacific Economic Cooperation.

We were driven to our new hotel, the perfectly adequate and very comfortable, but rather soulless, Shanghai East Asia. Here we met our leader and guide, the gentle and kindly Edward Tong, and, quite unexpectedly, another group of fellow travellers from North America. We didn't know it then, but over the next seventeen days we were to become a tight-knit family group, and indeed, life-long friends with some. Lunch that day was chicken soup, a delicacy with, if you were lucky to find it, a chicken foot! The dish contained peanuts which were extremely soft, hopefully signalling that the chicken feet had been well boiled up. I found this very encouraging as I was 'lucky'.

China proved to be a revelation. We were whisked to a tranquil Jade Buddha Temple to light prayer candles, and then taken on a less tranquil tour around a carpet factory where we were subject to intense, indeed frenetic, marketing. I really didn't need a rug or carpet and, unlike some, managed to escape slightly unnerved but, luckily, empty-handed.

That evening we were transported to a local theatre for a performance by young acrobats. This was colourful and impressive, but I wondered how hard these very young people had to work, and whether, with their strained smiles, they were really happy in their task?

Looking out of the hotel window early the next morning, I was transfixed by the sight of crowds of people on the large forecourt, some performing Tai Chi, with others practising a sort of theatrical and very disciplined sword dancing. A most serious business, it seemed. I was beginning to appreciate the Chinese psyche, so different from our own.

This was the day of our visit to the Heavenly Gardens. We piled into our coach, with Edward in attendance, and after a fascinating drive arrived in the beautiful town of Suzhou. The walk to the gardens was precarious, as we were besieged by groups of street vendors with sunhats, hair ornaments and fruit; all very pleasant but quite insistent. In a large enclosed complex, the delightful gardens rejoiced in names such as 'The Humble Administrators Garden' and 'Garden of The Fishermen's Nets'. Initially staying in a tight group, we marvelled at the scenes before us: pavilions, lanterns, lotus beds and throngs of people, all Chinese. A sea of black heads.

Suddenly I found myself in a small, separated group, luckily with Edward, but we were quite lost. The rest of the group, including Mother, was nowhere to be seen. I knew she had been with two Scottish ladies the last time I saw her, so she should be safe. After some difficulty, even for Edward, we found the way out and made our way to the coach. The rest of the group straggled back and the coach filled up, but one seat remained empty. Mum hadn't returned. My heart started pounding. I had lost my Mother! I should have remembered the Frankfurt airport incident.

Our new friend Kevin, from Alberta, immediately made for the coach door, with me quickly following. Stopped by Edward, who didn't want to lose anyone else, we returned to our seats as he and the local guide set off to retrieve poor Connie. It took some time. Evidently, Mum had turned her back to buy some fans for my three daughters-in-law and her group had meandered off, not realising she had stopped. It was our first day in Shanghai and we had not really bonded with the group yet, but by the next day we became a tight family group, and this situation would not have happened. Meanwhile, kindly elderly Chinese ladies came to Mum's rescue. Offering her a drink of water, they found a young girl who could speak English and understand her predicament. Luckily, at that very moment, Edward spotted her and, waving his red flag, managed to attract her attention. She was relieved to be found but, unlike me, hadn't been at all worried.

Staying very close together, our next stop was the silk factory. Legend has it that silk was first found here in Suzhou when a silkworm cocoon fell into a vessel of boiling water. I found the aroma of simmering cocoons to be quite strong but pleasant, not unlike boiled rice. We were taken though the whole process of silk thread production, and eventually channelled into the shop, of course! I had been very taken with what the Chinese called 'comforters'. These are duvets made completely of silk, even including the filling which is made up of the finest silk thread sheets layered one on another. I had to have one, plus a bright red silk cover with pillowcases to match.

At the embroidery institute we marvelled at intricate artistry. Exquisite landscapes, flowers or animals were being embroidered on to transparent nets. These were absolutely perfect, front and back, with no evidence of loose threads or stray stitches. We stared in admiration. Luckily these creations were priced way beyond our means, being mainly gifts for foreign dignitaries and royalty.

That evening we left the hotel for our ship, the *Victoria 3*, and the start of our Yangtze adventure. The original plan was to sail from The Bund, Shanghai's famous waterfront; but as George Bush was in town, the security measures forced us to take a weary four-hour drive to the next landing area up river. We piled into the coach, each given a bag of bananas, crisps and biscuits to keep us going, and off we went.

It was dark when we reached *Victoria 3*, and we had to navigate precarious wooden walkways down to the landing stage at the water's edge. As we approached the ship we were welcomed by strange piercing songs. It was quite surreal, and I am ashamed to admit that Mum and I, clinging together, made our way over the gangplank with rictus smiles to stop us from bursting out laughing at the shock and stridency of the noise. But this was a courteous Chinese welcome for honoured guests and so we kept very stiff upper lips, until we reached our cabin where we fell about.

We set sail for Yangzhou during a delicious late supper. How I loved the Chinese diet. Each night I could hardly wait my turn as the rotating server on each table offered dishes of tofu, vegetables and plain rice. Ah, the rice! So delicious, and so perfect.

Yangzhou, an ancient capital at the foot of the Purple and Gold Mountains, seemed a dreamy place with its slender boating lake and lovely flower beds. At the park entrance we came across vendors with barrows of sugarcane waiting to be pressed into juice. Fellow travellers munched away, but I decided not to partake – 'just in case'. Mum just tutted. She would have been first in the queue.

Back on board for lunch, we sailed on down river towards Nanjing. Here we could walk up to the impressive Sun Yat-Sen Mausoleum, surrounded by gorgeous green forests, high up in the mist. This venerable gentleman was a Chinese revolutionary, first president and founding father of the Republic of China, as well as a medical practitioner.

The more able of us climbed up to the Mausoleum on a vast stone stairway of exactly 392 steps (when this was built, the population of China was believed to be 392 million). It was an invigorating and lovely experience.

Our last destination before dinner was the highly illuminated Confucious Garden, and what a sight it was. A noisy, music-filled, neon-lit playground with lanterns, a lake with boats bobbing and, of course, many shopping booths. It was spectacular and quite unlike anything we had experienced before. I was suddenly aware we were not alone. Peter, the pearl expert from our boat, had obviously been given the task of making sure we didn't get lost. He was a most pleasant shadow, and we were never out of his sight.

Back on board we were welcomed by rows of smiling staff for the Captain's Party. Stiff upper lips to the fore once more as we were addressed by the Captain's representative (Captain, evidently, was busy navigating the treacherous river). As we sat at our tables an officer, flanked by his staff, marched into the dining room and stood to attention in front of us. Arms stiffly at his side, he veritably barked out his speech as if at a political rally. We suddenly felt guilty. What crime had we committed? Then it dawned; this dear man was greeting us in traditional fashion as his important and most honoured guests. Events like this bring home just how important it is to travel. Otherwise, how can we possibly understand and appreciate other cultures which often appear so alien?

Peter, the pearl merchant, gave a lecture and opened huge oyster shells in front of us, winkling out pearls of various shapes and sizes. It was fascinating and many of us rather fancied a visit to his small on-board shop. At the end of his talk, he proceeded to give some of us a pearl. Although standing at the back of the group, I was one of the happy recipients. One of the Scottish ladies also had one, but gave me hers as she said she wouldn't know what to do with it. Somehow, by the end of the evening, I had acquired three beautiful pearls. Wanting to do something special with them, I decided to have them made into rings for each of my daughters-in-law.

The following day, a twelve-hour trip had been arranged to Mount Huangshan, the Yellow Mountain, in a famous tea-growing area. Passing through a Bonsai Village, we had a 'loo' stop. It was here we finally, and totally, bonded. After sharing basic toilet facilities, with only half a door and where our heads and feet were on display, we became a family. Some cheeky person even took a photograph of me sitting there!

On arrival at the foot of Mount Huangshan, we were told our lunch would be halfway up the mountain. To reach sustenance, we had to take a fifteen-minute cable car ride into the clouds, and then a further climb of around a hundred steps. I tried to persuade Mother to keep with the small group who had decided to stay at the foot of the mountain. However, lunch being very important to Mum, she was determined to go. Bamboo walking sticks were handed out.

Mount Huangshan is a most famous mountain in China, and its fabulous landscape has attracted scholars and influenced traditional Chinese painting over the centuries. We could see why. Our cable car ride swept spectacularly up through the clouds, giving us a taste of breath-taking views as we emerged into the higher reaches. After a long fifteen minutes of swaying and lurching, the cable car arrived halfway up the mountain and, stepping out, we proceeded to tackle some steep steps. Mum went ahead, aided by her essential stick, but obviously found it difficult. However, soldiering on, we arrived at lunch, which was definitely worthwhile. I was beginning to appreciate how well the Chinese diet suited me. Lots of light soups, tofu, vegetables, and that lovely rice.

After lunch we had the option of a walk around the mountain. I eagerly took up the challenge and, leaving Mum with Kevin and his mother, Rae, off I went. This was certainly no exercise for an eighty-year-old. In fact, even for me it was terrifying at times. Incredible as the views were, the walk was precipitous, and anyone with the slightest touch of vertigo would have been drawn over the edge into the sheer drop of many thousands of feet. I clung to the cliff face and continued along the steep, narrow paths. One way only, it was impossible to turn back, with no room for two on the path.

Scenery appeared as traditional Chinese paintings. I was surrounded by domed mountain tops encircled by swirling mists with trees clinging to them, pointing gracefully heavenwards. It was so beautiful, and I would have to try to reproduce it if I ever managed to return safely home. I was glad to have taken the challenge, but after inching my way down was most relieved to reach the restaurant.

Mum's knees were beginning to play up, and by the time we reached the boat she was in a lot of pain. Climbing to the Tuscan restaurant at Christmas had triggered off some arthritis that was now greatly exacerbated by the final effort up Mount Huangshan. Luckily the ship's lady doctor was trained in Western and Chinese medicine, so we joined the group waiting outside her consulting room. It was an orderly queue, which also included Rae. Poor Mum. I stayed with her to make sure she had the appropriate help. Dr Huang was a kind and attentive lady who administered suitable advice and also acupuncture which seemed to give relief. She then prescribed something called 'Moxibustion'... at a cost of 29 dollars. Rae also left the surgery with her 'Moxibustion' box. Having never seen or even heard of such a strange implement before, it was at this point I thought to myself, 'there's one born every minute.'

Dr Huang also took Tai Chi classes, and I decided to join up as soon as possible.

Dinner that evening was a birthday celebration, and this included Mum, who was to be 81 in a few days' time. She had her cake, a Chinese scroll, and 'Happy Birthday' sung with gusto by the crew and fellow passengers. Rae and Kevin shared our table, and I offered to give Rae the same knee massage I had promised Mum, and also to look at how to use the 'Moxibustion' kit.

After dinner Rae arrived at the cabin with her boxed set, plus Kevin's cigarette lighter. The wooden Moxibustion implement had an opening through which a cigar-shaped herb item was to be inserted and then set alight. But first, a rubber paddle at one end had to be stroked along the lower leg, followed by the same procedure with the other domed end. It all ended in helpless hysterics. Using the paddle and dome as advised, we just couldn't take it seriously; and anyway, we failed to properly ignite the 'cigar', despite many attempts. It was obviously damp from the river atmosphere. The result was a cabin filled with scorched herb fumes, and one which of course Rae could eventually leave for her fragrant, smoke-free room; but only after my proper physio massage. It brought to mind the hilarious sketch by the comedian Bob Newhart, with his account of the introduction of cigarettes from America by Sir Walter Raleigh. We laughed so much that the occupants of the two adjoining cabins told us next morning they had heard us and wished they could have joined in to share the fun. Our neighbours on one side were two Scottish ladies, cousins Hannah and Mary, and on the other was the delightful Lilian Neuberger, who we had first met on the plane coming over.

The following day's offering was a long and tortuous trip into the countryside to see the scenic Mount Lushan, and included a visit to Mao's country cottage. Only thirty-six miles, but with four hundred bends. Travel sickness pills would be dispensed, but any sufferers were best advised to stay behind. I felt as if I might have a migraine starting, probably due to Moxibustion fumes, so I opted out. Mum, still in pain, also decided to stay behind, and off the little band went without us.

Those who remained could visit the local town Juijang. This was a fascinating venture into a market town where local farmers brought their goods to sell on the streets. It was the only place where we were regarded with some suspicion, although it was non-threatening; just a little unnerving. The indoor market was quite something. Pungent, colourful and exotic, it was definitely a different experience for western eyes, and at times quite 'eye-popping'. On one stall, scales held two of the tiniest feathered creatures you could ever see, possibly ducklings. Hardly weighing anything at all, perhaps they were just being stored as they were much too small to escape from the slippery smooth pan and kept toppling over. Walking around another stall I stopped abruptly, having nearly trodden in a heaving net of large toads. On a shelf above, eager stretching turtles stared from an over-full aquarium. It was actually a bustling, rather cheerful place with friendly vendors, but we were glad to get out into the air again.

Suddenly we came across a very smart tea shop, which seemed quite incongruous amongst the mayhem of the town. Here, the manager and his two smiling assistants offered us various teas to sample. With our choices beautifully packed in ornate tins and boxes, we left, me with fresh, white leaf Mount Huangshan tea, and returned to the boat. Meanwhile I was pleased to hear from Mum, who had also enjoyed her own little excursion, having been carried off the boat and up the harbour steps in a fireman's lift by the manager and a member of the crew, then escorted around the town and local school. Evidently much was made of a toothpaste statue and the manager insisted she had her photo taken in front of it. It had been a wonderful time for her, so all was well. The Mount Lushan party arrived back on board later in the afternoon, and we set sail for Wuhan. I didn't ask if anyone had been travel sick.

That evening, after dinner, we were treated to a fashion show, accompanied by music and dancing by the staff, modelling traditional costumes from various Chinese dynasties and minority groups. The girls, all so young and beautiful, wore most exquisite Suzhou silk gowns and, gliding gracefully, were reflected in the highly polished floor. At 8am the next morning, we left the ship for the fabulous Hubei Provincial Museum of Wuhan. Displaying treasures unearthed from the tomb of Prince Yi, and dating from 433 BC, it was a privileged view of intricate and beautiful objects. These included musical instruments and an immense set of large bronze bells. We were treated to a concert of ancient traditional music in a darkened auditorium where replica bells were played. Not having internal clappers, they were physically struck as dancers, with five-foot long sleeves to their gowns, performed their stately routines. It was a moving experience and I edged closer to the stage, sitting on steps in the dark, quite immersed in the occasion.

On returning to the boat, we learnt that we were to be joined by new passengers, making a full house. They indeed arrived, a large group of excited Americans, and the reaction of our own transatlantic group was interesting to say the least. To our amusement, they made it known we were their 'English', to be kept away from the invaders who were definitely lowering the tone.

I have to say the noise level certainly rose at dinner, and a newly arrived Chinese American lady serenaded Mother with English bar songs, such as 'Roll out the barrel'- the complete version! We, a small English group, were a minority, and held in some esteem after our support of the USA after the 9/11 atrocity.

That evening, our dear leader Edward introduced us to the delights of Mahjong. We became obsessed by the game, and Mother was determined to buy her own set as soon as possible. We were so keen that on our return home, with a new set acquired for us by Edward, we joined a weekly Mahjong group at the Museum of East Asian Art in Bath.

Yeuyang was our next destination. Here we found the highly-carved Yueyang Pagoda overlooking the vast Dongtong Lake. Some of us climbed up to enjoy the view over the lake, which was slowly being obscured by encroaching mist. Dongtong Lake was prone to severe flooding, and indeed a few years after our visit, television news was full of the latest major episode, which was so sad to see.

Before returning to the boat we were taken a little way into the countryside, where pretty young girls from the Miao ethnic minority entertained us. They wore wide silver metal headdresses, tasselled metal plaques around their shoulders, silver belts over rich blue tunics, with long, heavy and very colourful woollen skirts. They danced, sang, and played pipes, unlike anything we had experienced before. After, we, of course, bought some replica dolls to remind us of the occasion.

Our next entertainment was a talk on Tai Chi. It sounded just the thing for me, and every morning I joined a disciplined little band for these most wonderful exercises. Seemingly quite gentle, but controlled and quite difficult movements gave us a top-notch work out. Completely hooked, we all ordered a video so we could maintain the addiction at home.

The mists of Yueyang increased, and next day, as we approached the Gezhouba Dam, our gateway to the Yangtze Gorges, the weather turned foggy and wet. Slowly passing a western style, large red brick church situated right next door to a tall pagoda, we entered Gezhouba Lock, and for twenty minutes, as the waters rose, we watched and were watched by curious passers-by and a few chickens.

It was still misty, but as the rain gradually stopped, we approached Xiling Gorge with its steep sides and waterfalls. A few heavily laden barges overtook us as we slid past terraced lower slopes, steep hills and waterfalls. It was a taste of things to come. We moored at Sandouping village for a tour of the dam.

The heavens opened again, and this time the taps stayed full on for the whole foggy visit. This could have been a pretty miserable experience, but we wanted to see such an important project which would soon change forever the Yangtze, and, of course, the lives of many people. The constant pelting rain and mist made it difficult to see the actual dam workings but, amidst the din, we climbed viewing platforms to get a good idea of this vast undertaking and its massive progress. We were relieved to eventually reach a bright, modern demonstration building where we could see plans and progress, as well as a model of the then endangered Yangtze dolphin, which, I believe, is now no more.

Returning quite sodden to the boat, a kind young hairdresser led me to her salon and dried me off with her beautifully warm and powerful hairdryer.

After lunch we entered Xiling Gorge, still in persistent drizzle, but in no way did it reduce the impact of such magnificence.

The Gorge cliffs towered above us and led our sights to soaring mountain tops and, every so often, markers showed the two levels of proposed flooding. Red banners and graffiti in Chinese were evident pleas for reprieve from the devastation to come. We watched farmers and their families at work on the land. They stopped and waved, their children calling to us over the water. After generations working their land, they would be uprooted and moved elsewhere without appeal. It was a sad thought. As we left the Gorge, we passed the delightfully named 'Fragrant Stream Village'. However, as we progressed on through the gorges, it was evident to me that the flooding would be more like slum clearance on a grand scale. Dwellings and towns on the lower slopes were in a poor, neglected state – decidedly scruffy, in fact. Cleanliness and prosperity higher up the mountain sides was all too obvious.

That evening, the ship's artist Zhen Siumeng gave us a demonstration of his work. Using two brushes and ink, he produced a simple yet delightful picture of bamboo, and showed us how important the red 'chop' or seal is in the design. We learnt how pictures can have many 'chops'; the first being the artist's name, the others being that of subsequent owners. Such perfect provenance.

We later found Zhen Siumeng to be a karate expert, as he wowed the ladies with his expertise. 'Body like a panther,' said Mum!

Anchoring overnight at Badong, we pushed on to the second gorge and Wushan. Wu, the second Gorge, had the usual abandoned houses and markers as before, as well as typical steep terraces and waterfalls. We arrived at Wushan after breakfast, where we found the usual scruffy abandoned lower levels, and a bright new town on the upper slopes.

At last, a gloriously sunny day dawned, and we boarded a small motorised sampan for our excursion into the Daninghe River and the lesser gorges. The current was terribly strong, and our journey took almost five hours. At one point the two accompanying boatmen took to their oars, and really strained to keep the sampan going up stream. Two at a time, we were invited to sit at the front of the sampan, and as my turn came, the men started to heave at the oars, becoming almost horizontal in their effort against the current. Seemingly as one, and without any signal, they broke into a quiet song in time to the rhythm of their oar strokes. I felt quite moved.

Along this turbulent river we glimpsed hanging caves, stalactites, ancient walkways and bridges, with the usual monkeys, and children excitedly waving from the banks. How much of these irreplaceable treasures would be left after the flooding, I wondered?

When we reached our destination we just turned about and, incredibly, on the fierce current, it took only an hour to whizz back to Wushan. I then remembered a boat passing us on its return as we had laboured on upstream. A young man stood at its head, pointing forward with a flag as he enjoyed the bracing race back. In the late afternoon *Victoria 3* entered the final gorge, Qutang, and we were at last rewarded with a golden sky and a gorgeous red sunset.

The mountain city of Wangxian was our next morning stop: a friendly place, colourful and bustling, with a busy market and cheerful inhabitants. After a short but impressive acrobatic show by lithe young bodies in the local theatre, we walked around the market, then returned back on board for the last stage of our voyage. We spent the afternoon on deck enjoying the scenery, which was the usual decrepit lower reaches of the Yangtze, but opening up to the more magnificent higher levels. We chatted and watched the staff flying kites which, of course, could be purchased from the onboard shop. All good things come to an end, and our voyage would soon end. Tomorrow we would be disembarking at Chongqing.

Our final dinner included the Captain's farewell speech, plus lots of champagne. It was a happy and noisy finale. Dear Peter, the pearl merchant, suddenly appeared, and to my surprise he bowed and gave me another gift: an oval pink pearl with a ring attachment, ready for hanging on a chain. It was so beautiful, and I treasure it to this day.

We were warned that our final river destination, the city of Chongqing, was the most polluted in China, and how true! The next morning, through a blanket of heavy yellow mist, the high-rise buildings of upper Chongqing loomed into sight. Our voyage would soon be over and we were all rather subdued, despite being nowhere near the end of our holiday. We still had Xi'an and Beijing to look forward to, but we were leaving our cosy home for the mysterious unknown.

Greeted by porters, all shouting and desperate for work, we made our way up the walkways to the city. Surprisingly, above the fumes, Chongqing was a delightful, busy and very large modern city. First stop was lunch in a superb local restaurant specialising in spicy Szechuan cuisine; not so much spicily hot as gorgeously aromatic. Memorably, we were presented with a pyramid of small red peppers and chicken, but warned not to eat the peppers. They were for flavour and decoration only. I wonder how many unsuspecting diners in the past bravely waded through explosive peppers. It was the most delicious and special of all the meals we had enjoyed so far in China. Live fish awaited selection in their tanks at the entrance, but I stuck to the house menu. Later we visited a bamboo garden and panda zoo, where small red, as well as the usual black-and-white pandas ambled sleepily about. The fastest pandas were battery-operated toys found on sale every few steps. The Scottish cousins, Hannah and Mary, bought one for Mum as a birthday present for the next day.

I was excited to find we were to visit the Chongqing Art Institute, where, sitting on benches, we were given a lecture on traditional scroll paintings by the resident professor. Some were huge, and I could see why giant brushes were absolutely essential. Walking round the galleries, I was confronted by surprisingly modern and exciting paintings, the most striking being a pair of ultra-realistic pure white horse heads; quite stylised, but marvellously executed, one on red and one on a green background. Each part of the frame was a different colour – yellow, red, green and blue. It certainly worked and I was fixated by it, and inspired. On my return home I couldn't wait to try my hand at contemporary takes on traditional Chinese themes.

This was a short but nevertheless delightful interlude, and soon we were at Chongqing airport for the one-hour flight to our next destination, Xi'an. This flight was very Chinese, extremely interesting, and rather fun. Despite being just one hour's duration, we were still served a hot, homely meal of noodles and pickles. Mum, Rae and I squashed together in a row built for tiny Chinese ladies, removed the foil covers from our meals, and tucked in. Kevin, being a little larger, was enjoying more space at the front of the plane.

At Xi'an airport we were whisked away to the luxurious Sheraton for a three night stay. That evening we were taken out for supper and a cabaret. It was the only thing I didn't really enjoy. Colourful and beautifully performed by gorgeously clad, unsmiling dancers, it seemed to me to be all too contrived. Everyone else appeared to love it, and Mum accused me of being snobby. However, I had so appreciated the true traditional performances we had previously seen on the boat and in Wuhan. I was more excited about our planned visit to the Peking Opera further up the line in Beijing.

During the cabaret evening, an African-American man appeared on the stage and was courteously introduced to the appreciative audience. It was the Mayor of Los Angeles on a diplomatic visit, so the performance was obviously a great honour.

A city tour was scheduled for the following day and, with the sun slowly filtering through, off we went into this misty, magical place. My main memory is of delicious early morning light and masses of chrysanthemums. We were taken to the usual tourist sites –

the impressive Wild Goose Pagoda and Bell Tower en route to a jade factory where, as usual, we ended up in the shop. I had to admit, it was all rather gorgeous, and I succumbed. A large, cleverly carved horse in 'jade' (which was green soapstone, but attractive nevertheless) took my eye. Auntie Ella had recently and most generously given her four nieces and nephews some money. 'Buy something nice for yourself,' she had said. I felt this was the very thing. The transaction was made, along with arrangements for shipping home, and I left quite happily. 'Jade' the horse has become a much-loved addition to the home, and the children always give her a pat when they visit. Sometimes I find sweet papers in her mouth!

We were all looking forward to the Terracotta Warriors site and eagerly entered the large compound with its pavilions and pits. We were not disappointed. What marvels. Forming only part of the tomb of the first Qin Emperor, and dating from around 221 BC, the pits are almost a mile from the actual burial mound, with more warriors and army paraphernalia from that time still being excavated.

We were given tickets for each pit. These tickets were to be punched at each entrance and, as a group, we entered the first one. Leaning on the barrier, we looked down onto a wondrous sea of individual figures. Each pit revealed chariots, horses, pots, some figures broken, some toppled over, but mainly whole, and all with individual, unique faces. What a sight. Mum, Lilian and I chatted together and moved around the enclosure, only to find we had lost our group. They were absolutely nowhere to be seen. Keeping close together, we then sped from one pit to another, our tickets now looking lacelike with holes 'punched' so many times. We tried not to panic, but this was a vast area and we wondered if we were even missed? Where was our group? Would we get the promised noodle lunch? As we exited one of the pits for the umpteenth time, we scanned the area.

'I think I can see Kevin,' said Mother. Such relief. Kevin, well over six feet tall and towering over the rest of the group, was quite a landmark. We sidled up and nonchalantly re-joined our fellow travellers, who had only just begun to miss us.

After a tasty noodle lunch, we visited the pits again. Mum, Lilian and I had already visited them several times, of course, but we weren't complaining and this time kept very close to the group. An amazing surround-sound film show of a battle ended the tour. It was a most impressive and realistic performance, where we could just believe we were in the thick of the action as horses and warriors thundered around us. Finally, and as always, we were led to the shop where a smiling old man was signing books. This was the peasant farmer who, with other villagers in 1974, had come across the very first pit as they were drilling wells in search of water. He smiled a lot, his well-digging days long behind him. Of course, we bought the book.

Before our afternoon flight to Beijing, we spent our last morning in Xi'an visiting a costume museum which also had superb wall paintings. One especially took my eye. It depicted cattle in the same format as the wonderful geese mural in the Cairo Museum. We had to make do with our own photographs here, hoping the light was good enough, as no postcards, or anything else, were available for sale. No shop here!

Next, was a multi-course lunch of fifteen dishes, no less – but all with dumplings! We enjoyed exotic dumpling scenes being produced before our eyes, in various shapes, sizes, fillings and colours. Some were highly decorated, even one with penguins on an iceberg. We were quite 'dumplinged out' by the end.

An hour and a half flight took us north to Beijing. Suddenly the temperature was noticeably cooler. When the luggage arrived at our hotel, we quickly unpacked warm jackets and jumpers to be well prepared for our first outing the following morning.

The day dawned bright and cold for our early start to Tiananmen Square. It was definitely one of those places which, knowing its violent history, had a strange atmosphere. A huge portrait of Mao Zedung watched over the square, where tourists, foreign and Chinese, plus the usual hawkers of postcards and kites, milled around, as white police surveillance vans continually patrolled the perimeter. Kevin pretended to whisper subversive comments, so we kept well away from him and bought an eagle kite. Paradoxically, Tiananmen means 'Gate of Heavenly Peace'.

The Forbidden City was our next stop, and in its complex of ancient red-walled and yellow-roofed buildings we had a glimpse of Peking's Imperial past. Fascinating stuff! Until the downfall of the final Qing dynasty, soon after the death of the Dowager Empress Xixi in 1908, only the Imperial family and those on official business were allowed here. In 1911 Tiananmen Square and the Forbidden City became the headquarters and parade ground of the new Republic.

A leisurely afternoon was spent in the grounds of the Summer Palace. Built on a hill, the palace is set in a beautiful park, and with its large lake, Lake Kunming, had been developed for the sole use of the Imperial family and their attendants where they could escape the heat of Beijing. However, it was now rather cool as we walked through the famous Long Corridor, with its highly-painted scenes of gods and battles. A dragon boat waited for us at the lakeside and we climbed on board to enjoy a serene cruise, although wisely huddling inside the ornate cabin to shelter from the cold air. Despite the blue sky, it was bitter, and we were mostly unprepared for this change in temperature, feeling it keenly when we disembarked. Coincidentally, and close at hand, hawkers awaited our arrival. With piles of cosy fleece jackets, a steal at only $10 each, they did a roaring trade.

A final curiosity was the large marble imperial boat, seemingly tethered to the bank but actually fixed to the bottom of the lake. The Dowager Empress had lavished great sums of money from navy funds on its refurbishment. We were only allowed to admire from a distance.

One thing I really wanted to find in Beijing was a small piece of an original door panel. So many old houses were being torn down, and these beautifully carved wooden decorative panels were just ripped out and dumped. Louise Brown had found one a few years previously and had given it to her parents, Mollie and Sandy. Having always admired it, I had hoped to find one myself, but with no luck so far.

The afternoon was rounded off by a visit to a cloisonné factory. We watched the whole process, from original design to finished article. After delicate painting on metal surfaces, and then being fired at high temperatures, they became quite exquisite pieces. There were bowls, vases and jewellery, all produced in basic surroundings. A beautiful girl with big eyes and graceful hands painted a large bowl from pigments laid out before her in an array of plastic dishes, saucers and basins. It was like an intensive playgroup with sophisticated results. Finally, in the shop, we made our purchases, mine being a pair of jade and cloisonné earrings to be worn that night at the Peking Opera.

After a spicy supper, served with a multitude of other dishes on the usual rotating Lazy Susan, we walked from the restaurant through a dark oriental garden to the 'theatre'. This was a homely affair, and indeed looked as if the family of actors actually lived there. Taken through an untidy dressing room where the actors were preparing themselves for the performance, we felt rather embarrassed; but no one seemed to mind, so on we went into the darkened auditorium. In front of a raised stage, small supper tables were neatly laid with tea, cakes and satsumas, ready peeled and covered in clingfilm. People were already tucking in, mostly businessmen with their guests. It was a noisy, happy affair, the men becoming increasingly jolly and raucous as the opera progressed.

It was an extraordinary performance. Heavily made-up actors sang, danced and mimed between energetic mock swordfights, accompanied by piercing singing and grotesque facial expressions. Quite glorious. It was all as I had hoped and expected, but to see the faces of some of the Americans was entertainment in itself. Obviously unprepared, and never having experienced anything like it before, they thought they had joined a madhouse and looked forward to their escape. 'What the...?' exclaimed one. Marvellous!

Our final day, cold, clear, and blue again, offered a tour to Badaling and a climb of the Great Wall, followed by the Ming Tombs. As our coach left Beijing we came to a busy intersection, and I briefly happened to turn and look out of the window when, at that very moment, a lorry containing four seated Bactrian camels shot past and under the adjoining road. Large, brown, hairy heads facing into the wind, looking quite happy and eager. Rather hilarious in fact. I looked round, expecting the others to have seen this spectacle, but no one else had. It happened so quickly I didn't even have time to take a photo. No one believed me, but it truly was one of the funniest things I have ever seen.

Luckily Mum had enjoyed a good view of The Great Wall from the plane as we made our descent into Beijing a few days earlier; but unfortunately, when it came to this visit, her knees had finally given out, and were so painful she couldn't attempt the climb. So much for the Moxibustion! It was going to be impossible for her to be part of the group photo on a higher level of the wall, so I took my own photo of her, waving up from her bench below us. Poor Mum. Leaving her there to watch the world go by, I started the climb from Badaling with one of our group, June. Marching on, we left many Chinese behind, puffing and wheezing, holding on to the rail to pull themselves up. They were all small and slim, but probably suffering from too many cigarettes. The day being clear, views now were tremendous and we pressed on as far as we could go in the time. Leaving a camel with his owner offering photo opportunities behind us, we pressed on until the entrance area far below resembled a toy fort. It was an exhilarating experience and we wished we could have explored further, but time was against us and our coach was due to leave for the short drive to our final destination, the Ming Tombs. At the entrance to the Ming Tombs, a small red dragon train awaited those who needed a lift. Mum gratefully boarded, and the little carriages slowly filled up. In the gardens, the long, leafy and now quite autumnal road was lined at regular intervals with statues. It was a beautiful day, and I appreciated a quiet walk and the pleasant opportunity to admire the surroundings, recalling all the lovely times we had enjoyed on this unusual and really rather special holiday.

Dating from the 1400s, the Ming Dynasty Tombs are a series of thirteen mausoleums holding the lavish wealth of Ming Emperors. Only two were open, and one, a museum, displayed fantastic crowns, jewels and bronze objects of Zhu Di and his empress Xushi. Gorgeous silk garments had been reproduced from originals, and made at the very Suzhou factories we had visited at the beginning of our holiday. How long ago that now seemed.

On leaving the Ming Tombs, I noticed a few random stalls at the entrance and stopped in my tracks. I had found them at last, and there they were: door panels untidily stacked in little heaps. Most were unpainted, possibly modern and fairly crude reproductions, but lying amongst them was one in faded red lacquer with some gilding still showing. One small figure had damage to its face, but it was obviously an original panel and just what I had hoped to find. I asked Edward to help me purchase it, which, of course, he did, and was even quite impressed. Almost at the last minute, but I had found it. The panel was wrapped in crumpled brown paper and I lovingly carried my treasure back to the coach.

That night it was our 'Farewell' dinner, a Peking Duck banquet in a nearby restaurant. All too soon we were having to say goodbye to our American friends, who were leaving very early the next morning. It was so strange; after three weeks, almost as a family, we had become very close, and now it was all over. Exchanging addresses, and with hugs all round, we left the restaurant unusually quiet and returned to the hotel to finish packing.

June and I decided to get up in good time the next morning to wave off the first coachload for their early flight back to the USA. Amongst them were Rae and Kevin from Calgary, Canada, who had become really good friends. We promised to meet up again, remembering how Mum and Rae had suffered together, and laughed as we recalled the 'Moxibustion' incident.

Soon it was our turn to leave. Bidding our guide Edward a fond farewell, we prepared to board the flight home to the UK. Edward had been a gentle and courteous companion who took great care of us. How lucky we had been to have him. Lilian agreed and reminisced with us, especially recalling our dash in and out of the pits of Xi'an. So many memories. This was going to be a hard act to follow.

Back home, it was head-down for the Christmas Bazaar. Something which had started off as a small event, selling cards and a few Fairtrade gifts to the neighbours, had now burgeoned into a huge and very popular open day. I was beginning to realise it had to be run with almost military precision, but I had the support of many good friends and neighbours. I felt quite thrilled when Motivation chose one of my designs, 'Robin', to include in their Christmas selection. It was a best-seller and soon sold out nationally for them. For the next ten years or so I was to donate different designs for this most worthy of charities.

The stalls, stands and displays were set up, tea and coffee on the go, and we were off. What a day. As well as Fairtrade gifts from Tearfund and Motivation's cards, we now had a bring and buy table, piles of kindly donated new books, and a luxury raffle with generous gifts from local traders.

'Linda's Grand Christmas Bazaar' had now become a popular annual event, and one which would always affect any future holiday arrangements at that time of year. My new motto became, 'Think carefully about what you start. You may never be able to stop.'

TEN COUNTRIES (2002)

The Baltic

WITH THE NEW YEAR travel brochures arrived, and one interesting trip took our fancy. Noble Caledonia, who had taken us so successfully to Vietnam, were offering a Baltic cruise, visiting nine countries in one trip. The Estonian capital Tallinn was on the itinerary, and this country had always interested me since my old friend and fellow physio student, Aulie Tae, was Estonian. We booked up for the coming June.

St Petersburg was included, and although Mum had visited Russia way back in 1987, she was keen to see how it had changed; and I, having never been, wanted to see Russian art at close quarters. This would also be an opportunity to find some icons and view them 'in situ'.

We met our group at Heathrow and boarded a flight to Hamburg. Once there, we were taken by coach to our boat, *MS Bordeaux*, in Lübeck, a beautiful town originally in East Germany and the home of famous marzipan. One of our party, Ilse, had been a refugee from Lübeck during the Second World War, and for her it was a bittersweet reunion.

With the charming Ilse and three delightful ladies from Scotland, we became an inseparable group. Carol and Ursula, obstetric nurses from Aberdeen, were travelling with Carol's cousin Marilyn from the nearby Cruden Bay. We clicked immediately. What fun we were all going to have over the next two weeks.

On leaving Lübeck, our first port of call was Sassnitz on Rügen Island. Also originally part of Eastern Germany, this popular resort had a strange and interesting history. Enjoying a walk through dense woodland, overlooking the famous towering white cliffs, we came across a sinister lone wooden tower. Semi-derelict, it had obviously been a military sentry post.

Wooded dunes led to beautiful sandy beaches, and behind one was a huge structure. A truly monumental, three kilometre-long, building snaked across the landscape in what had been planned as the Nazi resort of Prora. 'Strength through Joy' was the mantra of the time for the Aryan population, who were encouraged to holiday there. Poster paintings showed groups of joyful, fair-haired holidaymakers running through the dunes to the beach. Prora was never completed, and the huge structure is a bleak reminder of that era.

On then to the pretty seaside spa town of Binz where we were warned not to get lost. Being quite random in arrangement, the streets of Binz have no grid pattern. The sun was shining, the sea sparkled, and the atmosphere was delightful. We felt quite confident. We all relaxed; some went to the bank to change currency, some to the market stalls on the Promenade, and others ambled along the sea front breathing in the pleasant air.

Mum and I wandered happily around but, before leaving the safety of the Promenade, we made sure we noted a large restaurant with many parasols as a marker to help find our way back easily. However, on returning to the spot where we thought the restaurant was, it had disappeared. No parasols were to be seen, and the landscape had quite changed. We were totally lost. Initially staying quite calm, we moved on, hoping to find the sea front, but found ourselves in a small modern housing estate. 'Don't worry,' I assured Mum, 'I'll ask the way.' Finding a lady working in her garden, I attempted to explain our situation, but panic set in as I realised she couldn't understand a word of what I was saying. She was so kind and anxious for us, but could do nothing to help us find our coach. In fact, nobody could. English was not understood in Binz. We walked on a little quicker, hearts beginning to pound, when after about twenty minutes, and to our great relief, we spied another couple from the boat. They too were lost, but 'safety in numbers', I thought, and we all felt better. At last, we came across our coach and climbed onboard only a few minutes late. 'Phew.' Settling down for our return to the boat, we just looked at each other and said nothing.

Our next port of call was Gdańsk in Poland. As we sailed past huge cranes in the shipyards, we remembered Solidarity, Lech Walesa, and the workers' heroic struggle of 1980 which eventually brought down communism in Poland and Russia. It was quite moving.

After a rather bold organ recital in a highly decorated church, we were taken for a city tour. Unfortunately the heavens then opened, and our walk was a dark, damp experience. Unusually, I had come down with a bad cold and felt a little rough, but not wanting to miss anything I joined the tour group. We only had this one day in Poland.

A university professor, 'Jack', was our guide that day and, as I was soon to find out, no lover of modern art. Whenever I wanted to stop at some newish sculpture in the street and ask a question or two, he would purse his lips, wave his hands, raise his large black umbrella skywards, and move swiftly on.

We walked into a picturesque street and Jack waved his arms from side to side, pointing out the stalls of beautifully embroidered goods. A lady vendor eagerly stepped forward, but Jack, with no intention whatsoever of stopping, walked briskly by, the group closely following. The poor disappointed lady shrunk back behind her stall. I couldn't bear it, so stopped to buy some small items. My group was speeding away, and not wanting to get lost in a strange city, I couldn't afford to linger. However, I made the purchase, the woman was grateful, and I felt better. My cold was no better though. Waiting outside a church, I suddenly had a 'catch' in my sore throat and, gasping for breath, made the most awful noises as I struggled for breath. I hid behind a corner and frantically sucked a sweet until the choking and accompanying tears subsided.

I have to say, despite his impatience with anything modern, Jack was a most instructive guide, and after his relentlessly brisk walk we ended our tour in a pretty street lined with lavish shops specialising in amber jewellery. Poland and Lithuania are the places to find superb amber, which, in its rough state, is washed up on beaches. Marilyn and I found ourselves in one of these smart establishments, where I bought a small amber heart; then suddenly, Marilyn, Jack and I were on our own. The rest of our group was nowhere to be seen. Perhaps they were in an adjoining boutique. It is the custom for shopkeepers to offer their customers refreshment, usually a drink of coffee and use of 'facilities', but here in this glittering shop Jack leant over to us and whispered 'you must have some Goldwasser!' The lady proprietor produced a bottle and four glasses. We toasted each other and took a large sip of the clear, gold-flecked spirit. Ooh, so powerful, yet fantastic. It nearly blew my head off, and miraculously took my cold with it. I was cured!

Rejoicing in our new-found vigour, we returned to the boat for the next country: Lithuania.

We berthed in the fascinating Lithuanian port of Klaipėda. Dating from 1252, it had been almost destroyed by the end of World War II, and as we stood in a large, infamous square, looking up at the balcony from where Hitler had made a speech, it suddenly seemed rather familiar. I remembered having seen photographs of that very event. It was such a quiet place, and with no banks open we couldn't change money into the local currency. Strolling round the almost deserted town, we visited such interesting shops selling exquisite lace and embroidery. However, with only a very few euros to hand, my only purchases were fairly rustic – a wooden spatula for myself, and a few carved spoons to give as gifts. The assistants would not accept either credit cards or dollars and, in fact, seemed rather uninterested in selling anything at all. It seemed the Lithuanians were still somewhat 'Soviet' in mind-set. I found I had just enough left for a postcard in the deceptively titled 'Tourist Information' building. We were to find quite different attitudes in neighbouring Latvia and Estonia.

On this beautiful day with the brightest of blue skies, we were whisked, by coach, away from Klaipėda, through dense forests to the Curonian Spit. This is a 97 kilometre sandy nature reserve, half Lithuanian and half Russian, with those beaches where amber is frequently to be found. Overlooking a lagoon, we walked around the dunes to a high point where, singing its little heart out on a tall and rather stark stone monument, was a yellowhammer. I had never seen one before. It was a delightful sound which, together with the quiet rustling of the fir trees and gentle lap of water on the beach below, made a memorable dream-like moment.

In the local resort town of Nida we were taken to a museum dedicated to the German writer and Nobel prize winner Thomas Mann, followed by a welcome visit to a rather lovely gallery. Displaying the most attractive glassware, silver and amber jewellery, this gallery was willing to take credit cards! The pieces here were quite beautiful and most inexpensive, but not having much time left it was difficult to browse. Here we had the money, but no time. As we were leaving, I noticed a perfect amber ring in a showcase by the door. It was very simple, but so attractive. I made a hurried purchase, but had to run after the group as they reached the coach for our return to the boat. It was parked in a forest lay-by where a few stallholders sold wood carvings; mainly of elks, it seemed. On our way back to the port we passed Witches Hill, a forested, elk-inhabited area with strange wooden sculptures; folk totems, we were told. Altogether a quite different experience, and reminiscent of fairy tales from long forgotten childhood books.

Latvia is sandwiched between Lithuania and Estonia, and possibly suffers because of it. There is one great tourist attraction, however: its vibrant metropolis, Riga. Our next day trip was to this true architectural gem.

Riga is a fascinating mix of Latvian, German and Russian culture, especially New Riga where the monumental German Art Nouveaux 'Jugendstil'-style buildings are to be found, the most famous being the work of architect Mikhail Eisenstein. We were transfixed by his ornate buildings, with their stylised, statuesque faces so typical of that era. The pioneering, black-and-white film, 'Battleship Potemkin', made by Sergei Eisenstein, son of that very architect, had always fascinated me. A dream of mine had always been to visit Odessa one day and see the very steps where the film has a famous, heart-stopping scene. A pram, together with a baby inside, topples down the steps during a panic caused by frenzied crowds.

The World Heritage-listed Old Town is quite delightful, with picturesque buildings in a mainly pedestrian area. I was very taken with a modern statue of a hen standing on a cat, standing on a dog, standing on a donkey, supposedly representing the Bremen Town Musicians peering through the iron curtain.

We were allowed to explore on our own, and despite being a damp day, our little group (the Scottish girls, Ilse, Mum and I) walked together around the area, finishing with coffee in a welcoming café.

We had a whole day at sea between Latvia and Russia. It was a welcome break, with time to relax and enjoy the company of our little group. Next stop: St Petersburg, where our stay would be for three whole days!

As we sailed through the Gulf of Finland into St Petersburg, we had glimpses of magnificent buildings and palaces. Berthed within sight of the golden dome of St Isaac's Cathedral, we could hardly wait to disembark; but it was always going to be a complicated process. We were instructed to show our passports each time we left the boat. These would be retained by the very serious-looking, extremely wide-hatted, security police and only given back to us on our return to the boat. No smiling was permitted.

The next few days were a fantastic whirl of palaces, gardens and great art, beginning with the Peter and Paul Fortress. Sitting in the ornate cathedral, we could see the tombs of Peter the Great, founder of the city, and also those of the last Tsar and his tragic family, whose remains had only recently been returned. Quite unexpectedly, a group of brown-robed men suddenly rose up in front of us. Out of their mouths came the most heavenly deep sounds of Russian religious songs. It was a perfect welcome to Mother Russia.

Walking through the grounds of the Fortress, we learnt of Peter the Great – a strange looking man, so tall, almost reaching seven feet, yet with a very small head. What an impressive intellect that tiny cranium contained. A great reformer with many 'western' ideas, poor Peter, with his facial tic and possible 'petit mal', eventually became rather a tyrant, and was not universally loved. Wikipedia offers an interesting insight to his legacy, believed to be written after the death of Peter the Great, by the Russian historian P Kovalevsky:

'We could enthuse forever about the greatness of Peter's actions and still not depict in all its fullness, brilliance and worth everything that he accomplished... But in creating, he destroyed. He caused pain to all in whom he came into contact. He disturbed the safety, peace, prosperity, interests, strength, well-being, rights and dignity of everyone he touched... Is it possible to love such a statesman? In no way. Such men are hated.' *(Source: www.cs.mc gill.ca/~rwest/wikispeedia/wpcd/wp/p/Peter_I_of_Russia.htm)*

On a glittering waterfront we marvelled at the huge Alexander Column, commemorating the 1812 victory over Napoleon. It was an impressive structure, with statues at its base and several nauti-cal sculptures protruding from its red column. This appeared to be the favoured place for wedding photographs. Despite the chill an assortment of white-gowned brides posed with their shy grooms around the base of the column, happy families looking on.

A performance of the ballet 'Giselle' was an optional choice that evening. Not quite top quality, as plenty of thumps were to be heard, but nevertheless it was a pleasant evening and notable for its gorgeous setting in the 200-year-old Hermitage Theatre. After the performance I bought a delightful small Russian doll in the foyer.

Next day we enjoyed a remarkable tour of Peterhof, the Russ-ian 'Versailles' and summer residence of the royal family, with its impressive gold statues and cascade of fountains stretching down to the Gulf. Ah, here it was, the very place I had seen in the distance from the boat as we arrived. The palace had been seriously damaged in World War II, but now mostly restored to its former glory.

The Hermitage Museum was scheduled for that afternoon. Founded by Catherine the Great, it is home to a heady mix of artistic excellence, with masterpieces from all corners of the world. In fact, it really seemed that the whole world and his wife was actually there thronging the galleries, which were positively overflowing with sumptuous old masters. Viewing these treasures was indeed very difficult, but I enjoyed whatever I could glimpse through the crowd, mostly looking forward to the modern section which would be our last stop. When we arrived at the modern gal-leries they were almost empty, offering unrivalled opportunities to view each masterpiece, though sadly we were rushed through. Our time was up! I managed a quick look at the scintillating 'Dancers' by Matisse before being ushered out.

In the evening we were treated to a Russian Folk Concert at Anichkov Palace. With typically exuberant cultural singing and dancing, it was a lovely occasion and, for me, much more enjoyable than the ballet. During the interval we were treated to vodka, caviar and champagne! I am quite partial to vodka, and would never say no to caviar.

It was an early rise again the next morning, and after the usual disembarkation rigmarole we boarded our coach for Tsarskoye Selo (formerly known as the Pushkin Palace). Ilse and I sat together at the front of the coach, and twenty-five interesting kilometres later we arrived at the gates of the palace, long before opening hour. After our early start many in the party needed the loo, but of course we couldn't get into the grounds to find one. This eventually turned out to be most fortunate for me, as our lady guide decided we should look in the carpenter's cottage. Feeling a little sheepish, in we all went, snaking through highly aromatic workshops, past bemused woodcarvers to form an orderly queue outside the one and only convenience.

Some, not too happy at the wait, quietly complained, but looking around I realised we were in an absolute treasure trove. Amidst wood shavings, paint pots and associated paraphernalia, men bent intently over exquisite carvings. Original wooden statues, carvings and cherubic putti, all badly destroyed in the war, were being lovingly and exactly reproduced. It was an amazing place, and one carpenter especially took my eye. His perfect reproduction of a large putti was quite remarkable. I gesticulated my desire to photograph him and his work. He happily agreed, and in Russian tried to explain the exact process. I didn't really understand him, but he was so keen to explain that I listened intently, and I noticed a tattoo of an anchor on the back of his hand. He had obviously been a sailor and, of course, like many others aboard their ships, had spent long hours carving. I shook hands with my kind and patient new friend. This was a most privileged encounter, and it filled me with ideas for a portrait when I returned home. The quite respectable loo was obviously an early edition, the flush pull having long been replaced by a plastic doll, but what a relief.

The interior of Pushkin was astounding. Fabulous rooms, one lined with priceless amber. and a gloriously gold-mirrored ballroom. What lavish luxury the royal family had enjoyed, but it completely cut them off from the multitude of peoples across their vast realm. The afternoon offered a choice: a boat ride on the River Neva through the city, aptly known as the Venice of the East, with onboard refreshments of vodka and caviar; or a trip to the Russian Museum. As attractive as the vodka and caviar sounded, for me there was no contest whatsoever, it had to be the Russian Museum. I always love to explore indigenous art in each country I am lucky enough to visit. As wonderful as the Hermitage is, and it is truly world class, you can see Rembrandts anywhere, but where can you find national art from earliest times to the present day? It offered an unmissable opportunity.

The appeal of a leisurely canal trip, with fortification from luxury titbits, wooed the majority, so, after lunch, just a small band of art lovers left for the Russian Museum. But what a treat was in store for us. Within sight of the multicoloured, onion-domed Church of our Saviour on Spilt Blood, is the Mikhailovsky Palace, home to the Russian Museum. This splendid building was built by the architect Rossi for Grand Duke Mikhail Pavlovich, youngest son of Emperor Paul I.

This glorious art museum was in fact one of the high points of my trip, if not my life. With fabulous icons dating from the thirteenth century, incredible garments, gold goblets, ceramics, statues and wonderful paintings, we progressed steadily in beautiful galleries and through the centuries to reach the present day. Unlike our visit to the Hermitage, there were very few visitors, so we had the space and time to take it all in.

To me, the most fascinating works after the icons were sensational portraits and paintings of the nineteenth and twentieth century. One large work stood out: a group of traditional Cossacks from Zaporozhye were compiling an obviously provocative and insulting letter to a local adversary. They were relishing the moment, guffawing and gesticulating as their chosen scribe scratched away. The painting is a fantastic composition; the nearest Cossack, his shiny bald head giving the impression of actually leaning out of the picture towards us, takes centre stage. Reproductions just cannot do it justice. It has to be seen.

Making our leisurely way, we progressed through the galleries, eventually reaching luminous nineteenth-century northern landscapes, avant-garde portraits of the early twentieth century, more militaristic works of the mid-twentieth century, and, finally, the present day. I was thrilled to find a truly lovely work of female nudes by Zinaida Serebriakova, 'In the Bath House', an oil painting and as exquisite as the pastel portraits of hers I had found in Paris at the 'Maroc' exhibition.

After an exceptionally rewarding visit, I purchased a well-illustrated book on the museum and wondered if I could find a similar publication of portraits. With time fast running out, I asked our guide if she could locate one for me in the gallery shop. 'What century?' she asked. Not expecting to have to be so specific, I blurted out 'Twentieth century?'

After intense conversation between the guide and an assistant, a massive book was produced: 'Portraiture in the XXth century'. It was that or nothing, as we had to go – and straight away. I made a quick purchase, the book was bagged up, and we walked hastily to our coach. This tome weighed a ton, but having a quick look through it on the coach I realised I had had a treasure. It was perfect and so beautiful I could have cried. My only concern being the remarks Mum would make when she saw its size and felt the weight. It is a purchase I have never regretted, and have since spent many hours poring over its delectable and inspirational contents. As with my Picasso and Braque catalogue from MoMA, it doesn't leave the house.

That evening *MS Bordeaux* set sail for Finland's capital city, Helsinki. As we slipped out of St Petersburg, the last rays of the sun, glinting on the golden dome of St Isaac's Cathedral, painted the whole sky a shimmering crimson before sinking into the sea.

The skyline of Helsinki is dominated by two cathedrals, the magnificent white Lutheran Tuomiokirkko and the red bricked Orthodox Uspenski. Approaching our berth near gleaming white ferries bound for Tallinn and Stockholm, the buzz of this friendly city was quite obvious. Making the most of their short summer, the Finns were enjoying outdoor living to the full. Market stalls filled the harbourside and overflowed with the sweetest local strawberries. These were shovelled into large containers and we ate them 'on the hoof'. At lunchtime, businessmen and women from all over the city descend on the aromatic fish stalls and food halls. Banners proclaiming 'Fish from Lapland' directed us to huge platters of roast salmon, sautéed potatoes and fish soup. We tucked in with the rest of the city, everyone looking very happy, not least large seagulls perched nearby, all keeping a wary eye open for dropped morsels. With loud squawking and a great flapping of wings, they descended upon the titbits, adding to the happy waterfront cacophony.

We loved Helsinki. A photograph shows us – the Scottish girls, Ilse, Mum and me – happily munching away under a blue sky.

We were taken on a sightseeing tour. This included the strange Temppeliauki, a church hewn from rock, followed by a visit to a park housing a huge abstract monument to Finland's great composer Sibelius, an enormous structure resembling a mass of organ pipes which 'sound' in the breeze. I remember my father loving the sweeping symphony 'Finlandia' which, movingly, we listened to in the coach as we made our way around the city. It was altogether an intelligent taste of a delightful and interesting country.

The next day we arrived in Tallinn, capital of Estonia, and berthed in view of this impressive walled city with its many huge domes, all a short and inviting walk away.

After breakfast we were taken on a city tour by a very tall law student. He was refreshingly open and cheerful, and we soon realised we were in quite a different place to neighbouring Riga and Klaipėda. Pointing out a large and stark hotel, reminiscent of earlier Russian dominance, he told us that after independence every room was found to have been bugged.

'KGB,' he remarked. 'Kindness, Goodness, and Beauty!'

'Can we use our dollars or euros here?' we asked. He quickly replied, 'We'll take any money here, as long as it is legal.' What an entertaining young man. We could see him going far.

The huge Alexander Nevsky Cathedral was on our route, and we marvelled at its richly ornate, orthodox interior. The many icons rekindled my interest, and a desire to find one for myself. From a high vantage point we looked down on the mediaeval walls with their many towers, each with a name, such as 'Fat Margaret' for the largest. With its cobbled streets, bustling markets and shops, Tallinn was a great place to spend the day.

After the tour we could wander around on our own, and so we made a beeline for the markets and apothecary. This establishment, dating from the 15th century, is believed to be the oldest in Europe, and we were recommended to find it. In the Old Town Square we spied the ancient drug store, and in we went. It was a dark panelled shop with huge old bottles and, on looking around, what do I find behind the main shop area? An antique shop specialising in icons from the 16th to 20th centuries. By then, time was running out, and *MS Bordeaux* was leaving at teatime. Mum and the girls were making their way back. I begged Carol, the most down to earth member of our group, to return to the apothecary with me. She wouldn't let me do anything silly. After a lot of deliberating, and icons all over the counter, I had to make a choice immediately, or risk missing the boat.

My eyes kept going to a small, beautifully painted wooden icon of the Madonna and Child.

'Last century Russian. £200,' I was told.

It was now or never. Card out, payment made, icon in bag, we ran as fast as we could back to the boat. The girls were on board looking out for us and we clambered up the gangway. The minute we reached the deck, the gangway was taken away. I had my beautiful icon, and with relief all round we made our way towards tea. We all needed a large cup.

Steaming out of Tallinn, we looked back at the dumpling towers of this delightful city and toasted each other with a little vodka from Marilyn's secret stash. Criss-crossing the Baltic again, we were on our way to Sweden. Next stop, Stockholm.

Sailing into Stockholm during the summer months must be one of the loveliest sea journeys. Thousands of forested islands with pretty houses and windmills lead into the beautiful capital. The weather was warm, the sky a brilliant blue, and we were ready for another adventure.

A whole day was ours to explore. What a lovely city it is, with imposing state buildings, and delightful Gamla Stan, the Old Town, with its quaint shops and cafés. Sparkling waterways were never far from our path, and we enjoyed freedom, fresh air, and happy conversation. We stopped in the courtyard of the Royal Palace to join a throng of people watching the impressive changing of the guard. What a colourful performance, and in such a setting! Never straying too far from the boat and harbourside, we felt quite relaxed and ambled on to a central park where concerts were underway. An appealing glass-fronted café took our fancy, and deciding on an outdoor lunch, we absorbed the joyful and fragrant atmosphere.

After lunch we joined the city tour, a highlight being the attractive Vasa Museum in the dockyards area. The Vasa, a highly carved and over-ornate wooden ship, obviously the pride of the fleet back in 1628, was now on display in all her reconditioned glory. Even to my untrained eye, she looked very thin indeed for her height. The shipbuilders had gone to town with lavish decoration, but unfortunately neglecting the required beam. With not enough width, she was unstable. On her maiden voyage she set sail with around one hundred crew members, an Admiral, and several women and children. The great and good of Stockholm waved and cheered her on her way as she proudly sailed away from the harbourside into deeper waters, whereupon, caught by a powerful gust of wind, she promptly keeled over and sank, drowning almost half of those on board, and all this in full view of the disbelieving crowds. She had travelled only thirteen hundred metres!

In 1991 the Vasa was finally lifted from the deep and, after extensive renovation and preservation, moved to this new museum, which is, fittingly, only a few hundred metres from the very spot she ended her voyage, and within site of the dockyards where she was built.

We walked in and out of the various 'mock up' quarters and, despite its tragic history, the museum gave us a valuable and fascinating insight into the life and times of the poor Vasa. We bought the book and returned to our ship for our, hopefully, safer onward journey.

Still in Sweden, our next stop was to be Visby and Central Gotland. A fine mediaeval heritage site which has been occupied for 5,000 years, it was something we were so looking forward to. However, as our passage progressed, the weather worsened. Soon, staff appeared on deck tying down tables and chairs, an ominous sight, as *MS Bordeaux* began to heave a little. Next came the announcement that travel sickness pills would be dispensed, and sadly the weather would prevent us from berthing in Visby. What a disappointment. But that was that. Nobody argues with Captain, and as I remember from our early boating days, the sea is master. We all settled down for a bumpy ride to our next destination, the Danish island of Bornholm.

We had till lunchtime the next day to relax and, in the morning, with the weather slowly improving, we wrapped up well and sat on deck to read and snooze. At one point, with no land in sight, we came across a huge wind farm, the arms spinning rapidly and obviously earning their keep. It looked like a futuristic forest in the middle of the sea.

By lunchtime the next day, the weather had definitely improved, and we arrived in the delightful town of Rønne which looked rather similar to Lübeck, but smaller and more picturesque.

Our guide was a very pleasant, informative lady, although dressed in a rather careless way. We noticed her work-stained hands and dark fingernails, but didn't like to ask what she did. Probably an overworked gardener or farmer's wife who, not expecting us, had rushed out to meet the boat.

Driving by wheat fields and forests on our tour of this small island, half-timbered buildings and unique round churches dotted the chocolate box landscape. We stopped by one of these unusual round buildings, the church of St Nicholas. Although renovated in the 20th century it dates from the 14th century, and inside we found wonderful wall paintings around its broad columns.

It was all so beautifully pastoral, and such a perfect, peaceful interlude. On we went, travelling past blue-flowered chive fields towards the coast where we stopped at a most imposing castle, Hammershus, said to be the largest and most beautiful ruin in Denmark. We clambered up a hill to explore its decaying ramparts, and from there enjoyed wide views of forests and the surrounding sea.

Our final stop was the famous smokehouses at Gudjhem. Being so well fed on the boat we certainly didn't feel at all hungry but, unable to resist, we wolfed down luscious plump herrings, straight from the smoking process.

In the village we found stylish and delicate ceramics for sale, and wandered admiringly around colourful half-timbered houses, their gardens lined with hollyhocks in full bloom. That sunny afternoon, our last day, was a fine ending to our trip. All too soon we were saying our goodbyes and leaving for home.

The family was slowly growing. Grandchild number two, a strapping and handsome Charlie, arrived in July. A really beautiful little boy for Rob, and a welcome brother for Chloe.

Back in Clifton my precious icon was put on display, and as the summer passed I started to plan the next Christmas Bazaar. This event was getting to be more of a major exercise and, organising the staff rota, I asked a friend, Diane, if she would man the Tear-fund Stall for me. Thankfully she agreed, and we got talking about holidays. I was still full of our Baltic trip, which prompted Diane to say how she wished she could take a holiday away from her demanding job at the Royal Infirmary. Out of our conversation came the thought of visiting a Christmas market abroad.

Prague

Scanning appropriate brochures, we found a very inexpensive, fully escorted four-day trip to Prague and, best of all, it was leaving from Bristol Airport. Four nights for £219! Such an opportunity could not be missed, and we booked up pretty quickly.

At the end of October the Christmas Bazaar was in full swing, teeming with people and the usual happy 'buzz'. Stylized 'Christmas Poinsettias' was my design for the Motivation card that year.

As Di and I were telling a group of friends about our planned visit to Prague, a nearby voice piped up, 'We are going to Prague in November too!' I looked over to see a couple I had only recently met, an aunt and uncle of young neighbours whose wedding I had attended. They belonged to a local Probus Group, retired businessmen and women, who were booked on the very same trip to Prague! We arranged to meet at the airport.

That November I was invited to exhibit my paintings at the prestigious Bristol Guild of Applied Arts Christmas Open Evening. This old-established store is a much-loved Bristol institution, and in charge of the art department at that time was Martin Williamson. Martin, an accomplished artist and budding actor, was to become a great friend and supporter of my work.

During the evening I saw someone eagerly looking through my prints of Bristol. He showed me a copy of the BBC website where my appearance at the Guild was mentioned. I had momentarily forgotten that a friend, Jenny, who worked at the BBC, had promised to let people know about the event. I hadn't realised she meant on the website! What a wonderful thing to have such exposure. So, this was Rob Bayly, a BBC producer and hot air balloon pilot, hoping to find his own balloon in one of my many prints. It wasn't there. Seeing a photograph of his balloon, I could understand why. It was beautiful, but a much too tricky design, so one I had avoided!

However, Rob was keen for me to produce a picture to include this very balloon, his pride and joy, and I soon embarked on the work. After some thought, I decided to place it as near to the Suspension Bridge as I could, making quite a feature of it, but following the strict rules and regulations. This became a large work, 'Dawn Rising', which I accompanied with a poem, my impression of a hot air balloon ride.

The painting was a success; Rob was thrilled, and asked me to arrange some large prints of the picture for him. Soon after, an invitation arrived from Rob to fly with him in his balloon at the next Bristol Balloon Fiesta. After decades of watching and hearing the balloons in the Bristol skies, I was going to experience it for myself. I was thrilled, but a little nervous as I recalled the occasion when a huge bear-shaped balloon ('Follow the Bear' from a TV advert) came down much too low and, despite the pilot firing up the burner, its massive feet padded noisily across my roof in Beaconsfield Road. We all cheered as he gradually managed to drift up and away.

December arrived, and our little Christmas Market group met at Bristol Airport. Di and I were immediately taken under the

Probus wing and included in a very happy holiday band. Arriving in Prague, we were greeted by an obviously seasoned guide who ushered us to the waiting coach. Ideally, for such a short stay, a central hotel would have been best, but who could complain for £219? As we drew up at a plain-fronted suburban hotel, our guide exclaimed, 'Ah... the dear old Juno.'

Prague was a winter wonderland. As we walked through the beautiful mediaeval Old Town, flecks of snow started to fall. Amidst decorated Christmas trees and coloured lights, we joined the crowds by the Old Town Hall where, on the hour, the Astronomical Clock comes to life. Wooden figures of the twelve apostles appear behind windows above the dial, and as the hour strikes, Death shakes his sickle, and Vanity nods. It is quite a spectacle, and always much appreciated by noisy gatherings.

In thin winter sunshine we walked across historic Charles Bridge with its unusual towers and thirty statues, navigating our way past the many traders lining its walls, then on to the old Jewish quarter with its jumbled, multi-layered graveyard. Packing it in to see as much as possible, we were driven up to Prague Castle and St Vitus Cathedral, both high on a hill overlooking the city. A tour of rather wonderful royal portraits in the castle was followed by a visit to the richly-ornate cathedral, and then the famous 17th century Golden Lane. This quaint area was absolutely full of tourists all wanting to cram into the tiny artisan shops. We homed in on a small café adjoining the castle to down a few glasses of hot spicy glühwein. The café was even smaller than we realised from outside but, managing to find a tiny table with two chairs, we settled down. Soon an army of German matrons marched in, looking for refreshment. We were still drinking as they stood right by our tables, arms folded, waiting for us to leave. How very peculiar, and quite intimidating. We felt like taking our time, but there was no point in being small-minded; and anyway, how could we enjoy a leisurely beverage being stared at so pointedly and at such close quarters. Smiling politely as we offered up our seats, we left with dignity.

'Ah, the dear old Juno!' These words rang in our ears each morning as we arrived for breakfast. Spread before us was a selection of sauerkraut of various hues, and something we thought was yoghurt but wasn't, and then the 'pièce de resistance', a large bowl of hard-boiled eggs. Each morning we wondered who would get the rogue egg. There was always one. Nothing surprised me after the cooked carrot omelette or slabette of fish, fried to within an inch of its life, which appeared at supper one evening. The Juno was clean and pleasant enough, but very basic, and being out of town there was nowhere else to go. Who could complain though for such a reasonable price?

Included in this bargain tour was a cruise on the River Vltava. We eagerly boarded our boat for lunch and yet more sightseeing on another bitterly cold, bright blue day. What a delightful experience it was now, though earlier in the year Prague had suffered from terrible flooding when the river rose to dangerous levels. Dark watermarks were still visible, even up to the first floor of many buildings.

Prague is as lovely from the water as on land. We sailed under bridges, passing buildings of note, especially the famous leaning Nationale – Nederlanden, affectionately known as 'Fred and Ginger' because of its resemblance to two dancers. All this whilst being entertained by traditional live accordion music. The atmosphere was very jolly, and feeling the intense cold we positively fell upon a large urn of steaming goulash, followed by some of the best patisseries I have had in a long time. After finishing with shots of the clove-infused, and very alcoholic spirit, Becherovka, I felt brave enough to venture out onto the numbingly freezing deck to take photos. I didn't stay long, and when I returned to the cabin my sunglasses densely and immediately fogged up with the welcoming warmth.

Our last afternoon arrived all too soon, and as we had free time until about 6pm we wondered where to go next. Most of our party decided to relax in a more up market riverside hotel, but Di and I ventured off on our own to experience as much as possible of this marvellous city before the flight home. After a walk around, and a nibble here and there, we found a gem. As darkness fell, our way was lit by hundreds of candles flickering in little glass jars placed on the steps of shops. Unexpectedly, we came across the Alphonse Mucha Museum. Mucha was famous for his decorative panels and posters of lithesome young ladies in the Art Nouveau style, and especially those he created of Sarah Bernhardt in fin-de-siècle Paris. His designs were in great demand at the turn of the century, and used in jewellery, stamps, and even bank notes. He was fiercely patriotic and spent many years on his 'Slav Epic', a series of paintings depicting the struggles of the Slav people. As well as working in oils, Mucha painted in pastel with such mastery, breadth and delicacy, and his pencil drawings displayed that day were exquisite. What a great experience for me, and to think we had come across this museum by chance. We had ended on a very high note indeed.

THE AMALFI COAST (2003)

URING OUR DECEMBER VISIT to Prague, Di and I planned a 'proper holiday' and discussed where we might go. I had enjoyed the luxury of many recent wonderful holidays, so I told Di to choose something. Recently widowed, and in serious need of a real rest, Di needed a good break, and preferably in the sun. It didn't take her too long to make a decision. The Amalfi Coast in late spring sounded rather heavenly, and we thought, 'Let's go for it!'

A few weeks after Christmas an email arrived. Di had found an escorted holiday with a travel firm called Crystal Italy. This looked like the perfect combination of location and price, with flights from Bristol airport. We booked up as soon as we could for the beginning of May.

Bustling sunny Naples welcomed us with clear blue skies, and there, waiting for us with a small minibus, was our tour guide, Constanze Cacace. We were the only people she collected and, best of all, just part of a group of only ten.

I loved the drive through dusty, jumbly, noisy Naples, with row upon row of colourful washing drying on countless lines above the streets. Making our way out of the city to our hotel, we were treated to the most scenic of coastal roads. The sea positively sparkled, as if filled with diamonds.

Arriving at the village of Sant'Agnello Di Sorrento further along the coast, and within sight of Mount Vesuvius, the minibus climbed a lemon-grove-lined hill to arrive at a beautiful and very modern hotel. This was the new and impressive 5* Grand Hotel La Pace. Could this be true? As we stepped out of the bus we were almost bowled over by the heady fragrance of lemon and orange blossom. The air was filled with it.

This heavenly introduction was only to be surpassed by our lovely room, complete with a terrace overlooking the hotel's large swimming pool, and with an imposing sight of Mount Vesuvius. 'Wow, and double Wow.' We had landed on our feet. Constanze advised us, 'Keep your eyes open for blue lizards. If you are lucky, you may see one.' She then left us to settle in, and would be back the next morning for our first excursion to Pompeii.

The hotel was bright, modern, and very comfortable, with a huge dining room and apparently very few guests. We entered on that first evening, both hoping to sit in a secluded corner, but were swiftly ushered to a table right in front of a group of expectant waiters. Perhaps they found us amusing to watch and kept us close by for their entertainment. We looked at each other and giggled with embarrassment, imagining that our every mouthful would be monitored. However, we swiftly selected a delicious meal and tucked in. Well, when in Naples...

Breakfast was utterly scrumptious, especially for a pair of chocoholics, with slabs of chocolate-marbled panettone covered very thickly in proper dark chocolate. Well-fortified for the day, we clambered aboard our minibus at the appointed time and introduced ourselves to the rest of our party, a pleasant group of fellow English. They may have been in our hotel, but the dining room was so large and sparsely populated we hadn't seen them.

The weather was really hot, ten degrees higher than normal, we were told, but who was complaining? Arriving at Pompeii, the sun beat down. We opened our umbrellas for some welcome shade as we began our tour through the ruins. It was easy to picture daily life before the catastrophic eruption of Vesuvius in AD 79. In my mind's eye I could see carts clattering and bumping through the ruts in the cobbled streets, and hear tradespeople calling out as soldiers tramped by. We immersed ourselves fully in this strangely emotional experience.

Especially poignant was a display of plaster casts. The tide of lava, totally enveloping people as they ran or tried to shelter, had hardened into their body shapes. What unimaginable terror. A mother with a child, bodies hunched and stretched in extreme positions. All so intimate and heart wrenching. Out again into the sunshine, it was a relief to visit the remains of shops, temples and squares, and even a brothel with its erotic paintings still plainly discernible.

Then there was Mount Vesuvius to climb! In reality it was only a half climb as we were driven part way up via the surprisingly rubbish-strewn lower slopes of the volcano. Offered walking sticks, we plodded up the gritty, ash covered pathway to the very rim of the volcano, from where we looked way down into its mysterious depths. Comforted by the knowledge of frequent scientific checks on its state of activity, I nevertheless felt rather brave and proud of my achievement. The hot and dusty climb was well worth the effort, and despite the haze we were rewarded with an epic, panoramic view over sprawling Naples and the surrounding countryside to the sparkling bay beyond.

With a full day of museums and churches, Naples was quite hard on the feet. The first church, Museo Cappella Sansevero, was rather creepy, being full of totally lifelike draped marbles of Christ and many others lying in death. The finely carved draping looked so real and ethereal. It was quite astonishing, and still seems to stick in my mind as much as anything else I saw that day. The National Archeological Museum also had superb statues, ancient mosaics and paintings, as well as more sad casts of people in their very death throes as they were surrounded by the ash of Vesuvius.

The most heart-breaking was of a mother with her babe in her arms. The next day promised to be a happier one.

In the early morning we joined a ferry from Sorrento to Capri. Constanze wanted us to enjoy this glorious island in the few peaceful hours before hordes of day trippers arrived. Of course, *we* weren't day trippers!

The ferry was quite full despite the hour, and in front of me sat the most beautiful young man. Very dark haired with an aquiline nose, he could have been the model for an ancient Roman statue. Leaning on the seat in front, he sat with his head on his arms looking wistfully out of the nearby window. I so wanted to photograph him, but felt self-conscious and, of course, the moment passed. He leaned back and started talking to his family. A lesson learnt. Never miss an opportunity!

Capri has such a lovely atmosphere, and we happily breathed in the fresh, warm and fragrant air as we climbed up towards Villa San Michele in Anacapri. We stopped at an inviting Limoncello shop and factory to have a delicious taste or two. Momentarily I was taken back to Rome and the Gorrys' hospitality.

Overlooking the Bay of Naples and Mount Vesuvius, San Michele was a revelation and rather a curiosity. Originally an ancient villa belonging to the Emperor Tiberius, it was restored and preserved by the Swedish physician and writer Axel Munthe, who lived there from 1896 to 1910. Munthe wrote the book 'The Story of San Michele', which is quite an extraordinary read. Was there anything the man couldn't do? He was rather full of himself and his many talents, and I was left wondering what to believe. What is true is that he lived in this most wonderful place and welcomed many eminent guests, including Queen Victoria of Sweden, who came for the health benefits.

Walking in the garden, through a colonnade above the bright sparkling sea, we were enveloped in fragrance and surrounded by darting yellow butterflies. We could have been in a gorgeous Alma-Tadema painting. Finally, we enjoyed a ride in a small open boat around the coastline, and into echoing grottos with their aquamarine waters and bright red coral.

Back on the quay we found the funicular railway and happily sang 'Funiculì, Funiculà...' as we waited for the ferry back to Sorrento. What a lovely day!

Massive bread lemons, as big as a human head, are sold in Sorrento, and I have never seen the like. I bought one to take home for Mum, and luckily had the foresight to photograph it, still glowing and fresh, bathed in the marvellous light of Amalfi. I balanced the hefty lemon on our balcony, within sight of Vesuvius, planning to use this image as an aid for a painting before handing it over. 'Nice, but not as tasty as small lemons,' was Mum's considered opinion.

Ceramics are widely sold in Almalfi, and I managed to find an attractive bunch of very life-like cherries. There were also small plaques depicting cats, with the warning 'Attenti el Gatto'. 'That b..... cat has "catitude,"' said James of pretty Fifi. Visitors needed to know that her beauty was deceiving before being carried away and stroking her, only to receive a sharp nip. It took me ages to find a plaque with a grey cat, but I did, so Fifi would be able to continue to hold her fluffy head high.

Herculaneum had been a rather upmarket seaside resort, with elegant patrician residences and vineyard-clad hills. Unlike Pompeii, the town was not covered in lava and ash from the eruption of 79 AD, but engulfed, up to ten metres high, in boiling mud. Consequently, Herculaneum has been well preserved over the centuries, and excavations are still on-going. The site had a much more tranquil air and we spent a pleasant afternoon, despite the obvious tragedy which brought about its ruin.

Towards the end of our week we decided to walk down the cobbled streets to have a last look at the glittering sea. Such sparkle. Then, trudging up the hill on our way back, we passed a man picking lemons from his walled garden high above us. We smiled up at him as he greeted us.

'Buongiorno!'

He said something else, and then, smiling, threw lemons down for us. Laughing in the sunlight, we dashed around picking up the fruit, trying to catch them before they reached the cobbles. We felt very young and happy.

With arms full of lemons, we started off again for the hotel; and then, glancing down onto the cobbles, I saw something shiny. Looking like coloured silver paper, there was a blue lizard, sadly squashed, but it proved they did exist.

Daily we marvelled at the tremendous value and content of this superb tour. Still to come was a visit to Casertavecchia, an ancient hill town, and a full day on the famous Amalfi Drive.

The whole Amalfi coast is a jewel. From the bustle and excitement of Naples to the beauty of Capri, it is an area with ancient history so rich it must surely be one of the very best places to visit. This despite, of course, the brooding yet somehow strangely reassuring presence of the volcano.

We returned to Bristol refreshed and uplifted, but having to leave Naples on a Friday is surely the worst day to travel. The whole world and his wife appeared to be in the scrum of Naples Airport, and at one point, nearing our time for boarding the plane, poor Di got lost. Breathless and rather shocked, she found me in the queue – just in time.

June was a good month. The day after my birthday, Mary and James produced their first child, a darling little girl, Grace. She looked like a sweet tiny bird in its nest, and James was just bursting with pride, and tears, of course, whilst Mary was her usual composed self.

THE BALLOON FESTIVAL (2003)

A UGUST, AND THE INTERNATIONAL Balloon Festival was approaching. Rob Bayly contacted me for the promised flight in his famous balloon. It would be a first for me. When the day came, at 6am and feeling rather nervous, I arrived at Ashton Court only to find all flying was off because of poor visibility. Undaunted, I enjoyed the day with other balloonists, taking in the atmosphere from the other side of the barrier for a change. I was less nervous by the evening when flights were definitely on, and we took off successfully. Luckily, my poem, written last year to accompany Rob's picture, proved fairly exact, and the trip was a balmy treat. Hot hazy sun bathed us as we flew silently over the Suspension Bridge and the city. Other balloons bobbed around and, at one time, the huge head of a Scottish Piper loomed right in front of us. A surreal but fabulous experience.

I was in awe of Rob's piloting skills as we came in to land. Expecting a bumpy greeting from the field in Long Ashton, the basket settled down as if on cotton wool, and then Rob said, 'I think we'll go a bit further over there.' With a tug on the rope we were off again, only to land a few yards away in similar comfort but on slightly flatter terrain. None of the upheaval and tossing out I was expecting.

DAWN RISING

Dawn rising,
bridge approaching,
glorious silence
in the early morning mist.

Dream riding,
spirits lifting,
sky forever
as the river winds below.

Sky winging,
heavenly moments,
a bird's eye view
whilst the city slides away.

Day drifting,
distant dogs barking,
basket muttering
to the wires shift and strain.

Time for landing,
breath holding,
tension rising
as the field comes into view.

Now descending,
ground approaching,
jolt and tipping,
knuckles whitening

...safe homecoming.

I photographed the balloon deflating and being packed up as Rob's team and family arrived in their Land Rover to take us back to the festival grounds for supper. There I was presented with my Flight Certificate celebrating my 'ascension'. It was a perfect end to a perfect day.

One balmy Sunday evening, John and Lizzie asked me to come with them to Cumberland Basin as 'official photographer'. Part of a school project, young Timothy had been invited by Captain Bigwood, the Bridgemaster, to visit the important swing bridge.

The tide was in, and the Suspension Bridge was looking majestic against a clear blue sky. Our excitement mounted as we were invited up the steps into the elevated control building to meet Captain Bigwood, the most informative and generous of men. As he pointed out all the equipment, knobs and switches for Tim's benefit, miraculously, a small yacht appeared around the bend of the River Avon and approached the swing bridge. The rule is, at high tide, the bridge must close to traffic and swing open, even for one little boat.

'Would you like to open the Bridge?' Captain Bigwood asked Tim. He couldn't believe his luck as he pressed the buttons to start the process. Sirens sounded, lights changed to red, and the traffic was brought to a halt. The huge bridge swung open to allow the yacht, from Swansea we were told, to sail serenely through and moor in the lock. Such excitement! Top marks for Tim's project I should think!

COLONIAL FRIENDS (2003)

I N LATE SUMMER OUR Canadian friends we met in China, Kevin and his mother Rae, ended their European cruise in Southampton. John and I drove down to collect them and bring them back to enjoy the West of England, before travelling on to London and eventually home to Canada.

Thank goodness John decided to take his old Volvo estate. I had forgotten how much luggage our colonial cousins need on their cruises. There was indeed a mountain of it, and it all just about fitted in. The route back to Bristol goes west out of Southampton and meanders through main roads canopied by trees and thatched hamlets. 'Mary Poppins Land!' exclaimed a delighted Kevin.

They were so thrilled to see us. We planned to make their stay as interesting as possible, on that very first day calling in to Salisbury Cathedral, then Stonehenge, before eventually arriving in Norton St Philip near Bath where, handsomely situated, on the curving main road, is the old pub, The George. This also is the site of the Battle of Sedgemoor and Pitchfork Rebellion from the time of James II. The historic scene was completed by distant baying of hounds from the local Hunt. It couldn't have been a more traditional introduction to the Mother Country and old-world England.

Their visit turned out to be a real joy, and such fun for us all. Our first outing the next day was to nearby Berkeley and, I was rather ashamed to admit, a first for me!

Beautiful Berkeley Castle, owned by the same family for 600 years, exudes history at every turn. It so happens that Kevin's favourite poet, Shakespeare, was commissioned to write 'A Midsummer Night's Dream' for a family wedding, and the play is occasionally performed in the formal gardens. Sadly not that day though! In lovely late summer weather, this was a fitting introduction to the West of England.

Dear Sandy and Mollie. As soon as they knew the Gaults were to visit, they drew up a suggested itinerary. This included a City Walk around Bristol, led by the knowledgeable Sandy, and a day out to Stratford-upon-Avon. This was turning out to be a full week, and one that well suited our visitors. I was struck by how 'themed' Stratford had become since my last visit back in the 1950s, but Kevin revelled in the atmosphere, wanting to see as many Shakespearean sites as possible. Unfortunately, we were too late for Anne Hathaway's cottage, arriving there just as it closed. Poor Kevin could only walk around the outside of the house and peer through its darkened windows.

However, all was well, as we arrived home to Mum's delicious stew and dumplings.

After multiple open-top bus rides in Bath and Cardiff, we ended the week with a jubilant supper, and the next day a farewell luncheon, during which our actor friend and neighbour Derek Weeks recited a poem he had written especially for them. A most happy and laughter-filled send off for Kevin and Rae, who insisted we visit them in Calgary at Stampede time the following year. We most definitely agreed. 'Yeehaa!'

ANDALUCIA (2003)

T HE TRAVEL FIRM PAGE and Moy sent a small leaflet advertising some attractive short holidays. Rather extravagantly, Mum and I couldn't resist an escorted visit to Andalucia. The passionate, historic heart of Spain beckoned, and on 10th October, with preparations for the Christmas Bazaar all completed, off we went.

We became part of a quietly friendly, cultured group, and gradually got to know each other as we drove away from Malaga airport deep into Spanish countryside. Three hours later, and constantly amazed by the sheer number of olive groves seemingly stretching as far as the eye could see and blanketing the Andalusian hills, we arrived in Córdoba.

Córdoba, the very heartbeat of Andalucia, remains foremost in my memory. Under the hot sun this beautiful city positively radiated atmosphere, with its flower-bedecked alleys, quaint streets and cool courtyards, where dark-skinned men passionately played their guitars.

Escaping the heat, we visited the 10th Century Grand Mosque, the Mezquita. With a veritable forest of jasper, marble and granite Moorish columns, over 800 in all, contributing to fantastic light effects in its interior, this Islamic Mosque had also been a Christian Cathedral in 1236, and is altogether an incredible sight. I loved Córdoba.

The next day we set off for our second destination, Granada. Rising imposingly above the city, the sight of the fabled Alhambra palace does not even begin to hint at the glories within. This sumptuous palace of the Moorish Kings is indeed a wonder, with gorgeously tiled interiors, frescoes, marble columns and lush gardens, limpid pools, and sparkling fountains.

En route to our next destination, Cádiz, we stopped in Seville for a flying visit. There was just enough time to tour the city and marvel at its sights from the confined comfort of our coach. We did manage a quick stop, in bright and beautiful sunshine, at its great Gothic cathedral, the Moorish Giralda Tower, and the fountains outside the Alcázar Palace. Finishing with an ice cream by the river bank, and a brief cruise on the exotically named Guadalquivir river, we were soon back on the coach again, off to the coast and Cádiz.

The Port of Cádiz is rather lovely with its flower-filled squares, cobbled lanes, and excellent shopping. We stayed outside the city at the Hotel Bahia Sur, in the village of San Fernando, for three whole luxurious days. Bahia was an apartment style hotel, and we were allocated a large multi-roomed flat with its own front door, which opened out onto a concourse with lift access to a huge supermarket. Mum was very excited,

Our first day: Jerez, and the prospect of sherry tasting in a local cellar. A pleasant interlude in a smart, small business, with stables housing rather handsome horses. The sherry was delicious, so I bought a couple of bottles to take home for Christmas. Our next planned outing to the delightful and ancient town of Ronda was one I was so looking forward to; but, absolute horror, I developed one of my mega migraines, and was forced to stay behind. Off Mum went to Ronda with the rest of the group, as I languished in the apartment for the day.

A tour of Cádiz plus boat ride was planned for the following day, but another group staying at Bahia were visiting Ronda. Our thoughtful tour leader had arranged for me to go with them if I felt well enough by the next morning. According to the leader, it would still be possible for me to visit Cádiz on my own for a few hours on our final day. I was assured that local trains were very regular and, anyway, we would not be leaving until noon. I could make my mind up the next morning, as at that moment I was still feeling weak and unable to do anything which involved much effort or thought.

However, when the next morning arrived I had definitely improved enough and decided I could just about make it. A quiet rest in the coach to Ronda could be just the thing. I wouldn't know anyone either so, best of all, no talking. I reminded Mum to take her water bottle to Cádiz, and left her having breakfast with our group.

The quiet drive to Ronda was wonderful. The party was very small so I made the most of the space on board, and by the time we reached our coffee stop I felt much better. These coffee stops were fun. Always the same: glass mugs of strong milky coffee in atmospheric roadside café bars, surrounded by olive groves.

Ronda turned out to be a very interesting trip. It is indeed a beautiful clifftop town, straddling a deep gorge where red-beaked choughs continually call and circle. The Bullring was heavily atmospheric, and a visit to its small colourful museum was most enlightening. I came to realise how bull fighting is not just a sport, even though a cruel one to many, including me, but has this deep spiritual element indelibly etched in the Spanish psyche. I couldn't possibly watch a bullfight though.

Then a strange thing happened. A very serious local guide took us on a tour around the town and, being interested in the elaborate but quite modern art work in the churches, I asked why there was no old work to be seen. The reply was intense and angry.

'You do not know what you are asking!'

Obviously I should have known more about local history, but didn't, hence the question, and I was very firmly put in my place. The group looked at me with sympathy, and afterwards a young girl travelling with her Spanish mother promised to tell me more later. Sadly, time ran out, so I was never enlightened, but it was obviously all to do with the Civil War. I planned to look it up when I got home.

We returned quite late to the hotel, and I made my way quickly to our apartment. Mum would be waiting to hear about my day. I rang the bell, but no answer. Perhaps she was having supper. I went to the dining room, but there was no sign of her, so back I went to the apartment. After ringing the bell many times, I was just about to go for a spare key when the door opened and a frail looking mother appeared. She was obviously very poorly and quickly returned to her bed. I felt her head. It was hot, and it dawned on me that she, never ever drinking much, was very dehydrated.

'How much water did you drink today, Mum?'

'I had my bottle with me,' she replied weakly.

'Yes, I can see the bottle,' I said, which I noticed was almost full, 'but how much did you actually drink?'

No reply.

Luckily there was some Coca Cola in the fridge, so I made her sip it and the transformation was almost immediate – to my great relief she wasn't suffering from food poisoning, or worse. To be honest I felt rather cross, and she was very apologetic. Since then, she regularly sips more water, winter and summer.

I left her recovering and went off for supper, where I found the Cádiz party who were by then wondering where Connie was. They had noticed how little she was drinking on such a hot day and kept reminding her. They always got the same reply: 'I have my bottle.'

The next morning I was assured by our leader that I had time to see Cádiz and still be back in time for the coach taking us back to Malaga airport for our return home.

It was rather pleasant waiting in the sunshine at the little local station, and as promised, along came the train, exactly on time, and off we trundled, past salt pans and abundant birdlife to the city of Cádiz. The morning was warm and brushed by gentle sea breezes as Cádiz appeared white and jewel-like in the autumn sun. My walk through a fascinating maze of side streets to a park and flower market was quite a joy. I felt rejuvenated and free.

Suddenly, as I was looking at my map and thinking about the time, I was approached by an elderly gentleman with his granddaughter in a pushchair. He couldn't speak English, and my Spanish was pretty basic, but it was obvious he was to be my unofficial guide. Such a delightful and modest man, he proudly pointed out all the places of interest and made my excursion very special. He eventually showed me where the station was, and back I went, bang on time, reaching San Fernando by 11.30 am. Mum was relieved to see me as she had been rather dubious about this last minute arrangement. We spent our final half hour having a short walk near the hotel, passing a music school where a lesson of castanets could be heard in full foot-tapping flow. What a finale!

As our coach approached Gibraltar, the landscape became decidedly scruffy. How different to our initial pull up into the grey-green, olive tree hills at the start of our tour. Suddenly we appeared to be in a hot-mock England, with large department stores, Mothercare, Toys R Us, Barclays Bank... leading us to endless walls of white apartment blocks, all facing the coast.

Behind this huge development, machines were tearing into the mountains. To me it seemed like the rape of the land. Would this assault reach the sultry beating heart of true Andalucia, and where would it all end? Yet this must be what people wanted, and developers were not disappointing them. After revelling in the delights of rolling hills and gorgeously historic cities, encompassing a passionate people and their music, I tried, unsuccessfully, to obliterate this brief scene from my mind.

John met us at Bristol but had forgotten where he had left his car in the airport's extensive car park. Mum and I were flimsily dressed for warm Spanish sun, and not a chilly English autumn and we shivered as John spent about twenty minutes searching. It was dark, and every so often John could be seen in a pool of light running one way, and then a minute or two later, in another pool of light, running in the opposite direction. Eventually the car was found and we gratefully piled in, asking for the heater to be on – full blast, please!

THE CONCORDE, BRISTOL (2003)

2003 WAS AN EVENTFUL year internationally, and the one when Concorde finally came home to rest. On a damp blustery morning I joined a rather muted crowd of thousands dotted over the Bristol Downs, awaiting her homecoming. In collaboration with French Aerospace in Toulouse, Concorde had been designed and built by Rolls Royce in the northern suburb of Filton, and this was a source of great pride for the good folks of Bristol. And here we were, in thoughtful groups, waiting for the moment when she would pass over the city for the very last time. Cloud cover was thick, and we wondered if we would even be able to glimpse our own beautiful 'bird of the skies'. Children jumped up and down, playing on the wet grass as we all chatted rather quietly.

Suddenly, as if by magic, the clouds parted, and for a brief few minutes the sun shone weakly through. In the distance we heard a noise, and looking to the south, we strained to see if it was Concorde on her way. It was, and in one of the most moving moments of my life, Concorde boomed into view, fittingly, over the majestic Suspension Bridge, to swoop low over our heads, making her way to Filton. That gorgeous shape, never again to pass over her city. As one, the huge crowd started to applaud. No cheers or yells, just a respectful acknowledgement by a quietly tearful audience. Even now, the memory of it is quite sad. The sun went in, and we all headed homeward.

November was a busy month, with an early event to enjoy, courtesy of Martin at the Bristol Guild. I was invited to display my latest work, and with it would come excellent media interest and generous publicity. The *Western Daily Press* gave me a half-page spread in colour, right next to an article on the Beatles. What an opportunity!

I also had the forthcoming Charity Christmas Bazaar on my mind. My offering for Motivation that year was 'Holy Night'. In the spring John had suggested I should paint a more religious subject, so 'Holy Night' came to be. It was quite vivid: the three wise men and their camels in the desert at night, with a large bright moon behind Bethlehem and the star shedding its light over the town. The cards arrived, but they were too pale. What had happened to the vivid scene? Nothing could be done now, but luckily Motivation's sales appeared brisk, and the event itself was another huge success for them and Tearfund. However, in future, I was going to monitor colour reproduction myself, and more closely. The Christmas Guild event had gone well, and I exhibited Rob Bayly's bridge picture amongst a mix of Bristol Scenes, as well as a new group of Arum Lily studies. Each year, as these robust and stately flowers emerged, I told myself I would not paint any more flower pictures, but they were so impressive I could never resist. My garden had earlier enjoyed a makeover from our Irish friend, the stonemason, Paddy, and the lilies now occupied three stone roundels, keeping them under control. One day I happened to be admiring them – how could you not? – and as I watched snails underneath the large leaves, it suddenly struck me that this was a fabulous perspective. I spent the next few weeks dashing out to the garden and lying on my back to get the best view for three 'High Flyers' portraits. In each one, the lilies were reaching up to the sky; the first depicting our visiting swifts, and the second, seagulls that constantly fly over from the River

Avon, to the Harbourside, via the Zoo for penguin and seal feeding times. The third showed the slow, upward progress of snails. The 'high flyers' could have been either the plants or the wildlife; it would be for the viewer to decide. I loved painting this group, but I am sure my neighbours, watching me running in and out and then lying on the patio, would think I had gone quite mad!

MUNICH (2003)

THE PREVIOUS MONTHS HAD been hard work, but Christmas was coming and I could ease off. Once more, Di and I had been invited by the Hambrook Probus to join them for their Christmas Markets trip, this time to Munich. At the beginning of December we met up at Bristol Airport again, with the knowledge of a better hotel this time. None of your 'dear old Juno'.

We arrived at the smart Kings Hotel in Dachauer Straße and excitedly discussed our plans for the next few days. I was slightly unnerved by the name of the street, which indeed related to Dachau, the terrible Nazi death camp. A visit could be arranged, but not for me on this occasion. It was a strange feeling, and one which constantly hovered in my consciousness during our stay. It was history, but still...

Christmas in Munich must surely fulfil anyone's dream: the air crisp with occasional flecks of snow, beautiful buildings all decorated and illuminated, traditional brass bands, and a huge sparkling Christmas tree dominating the main square. Here, in the market, painted wooden booths were selling typically festive goods, such as wooden toys, puddings, and sweets. There were long queues at one of the stalls selling mammoth dumplings that settled heavily in pools of steaming custard. Plain or jam-filled, with or without spices? I went the whole hog, asking for jam-filled and spices! Well, it was Munich!

Father Christmas greeted the children as bells tinkled on horse-drawn carriages, the animals' breath steaming in the cold air. With all this colour and atmosphere, apart from the happy children, the good bürgers of Munich seemed rather sullen and severe. In fact, the only time I witnessed unbridled jollity was in the Bierhaus. Happy diners delved into massive plates filled with what looked like half a hog's leg, a whole duck, sausages and dumplings... per person. Everyone was overjoyed. Not being a great meat eater I was somewhat defeated, but Di, heroically munching, did full justice to her platter. I told the waiter I was more than happy just to have the dumplings, so when the tray arrived I took my portion of two cannon balls plus gravy. I was just managing to finish them, feeling extremely full, as the waiter arrived with even more dumplings which the chef had prepared just for me! Oh dear. I smiled and thanked him gratefully but could only manage a mouthful or two. 'Dumplings, anyone?'

'People watching' in a Bierhaus is an entertainment in itself. Bavarians know how to enjoy their food and drink, and *could* it be the only place they look truly happy? One expects to be served by buxom wenches in traditional dress, laughing coquettishly as they cheerfully slap steins of beer onto rough wooden tables. Sadly, not that night; no heaving cleavage or ruddy cheek was to be seen. The chief waitress, although giving a nod to tradition in her very tight traditional dress, was definitely not in her prime, and not too happy. She puffed her way around the hall, heaving herself up wooden steps, beer spilling out of the steins before plonking them down, rather carelessly, I thought, in front of her gleeful customers.

An optional visit to Augsburg turned out to be a spellbinding winter experience. At the main station we hopped on board the waiting train to make our way through a snow-filled landscape. Another Christmas market with dumplings, of course, but the main highlight was an evening Advent carol service at the Rathaus. As the event progressed windows opened and, in each, a child dressed in white as an angel was caught in spotlight. It was beautiful, and we looked up, enraptured, sipping our steaming glühwein.

On our free day I decided to visit the Lenbachhaus. Originally a private house but now an important art gallery, it is certainly worth a look, so I asked if anyone else would like to come with me. I was joined by several of the ladies, as the men were off to the Mercedes-Benz factory. We were in for a treat.

It was quite a walk to the Lenbachhaus, but eventually we found the rather beautiful, Italianate villa built by Franz Von Lenbach himself. Known as the 'Prince of Painters', Lenbach used this building not only as his family residence and studio, but also to house his paintings and those of the Blauer Reiter group. It is now an important international gallery with a most impressive collection, having been acquired and further enlarged by the city of Munich after Lenbach's death.

I have always admired the work of Franz Marc and August Macke, and to see these, and with others in a similar vein, was a wonderful experience. Klee, Delaunay, Kandinsky... all fabulous.

With Christmas coming and work easing up, I had time to ponder Mollie and Sandy's invitation to join them on a trip to Ukraine the following spring – a cruise on the River Dnepr from Kiev to the Crimea on the Black Sea. My dream to visit the fabled Potemkin Steps in Odessa might now come true. This, as well as the promise of a totally different cultural experience, was much too enticing for me to refuse. Plans were made, and we were booked in for a fortnight the following May.

LONDON EXHIBITIONS AND THE
UKRAINE (2004)

F OR SOME YEARS I had been vaguely aware of a large white van parked outside the RWA. Eventually it dawned on me. It belonged to Art Moves of Chelsea, who transport artworks to various London exhibitions, so I wondered whether I should try my luck. The Friends of the RWA magazine always listed various open exhibitions throughout the UK, and this year my eye had been taken by The Pastel Society exhibiting in March, and The Society of Women Artists in June, both in The Mall Galleries.

I was rather fond of my 'The Bread Lemon – Amalfi'. It had turned out exactly as I wanted, so on the strength of that I filled out the official application forms to the Pastel Society and submitted the work. Lo and behold, my picture was selected! What a thrill to have work recognised by the Society. I planned to be in London for the private view and proceeded to tell a few London friends in case they were free. Amazingly, they all turned up!

At the private view, my dear friend Lilian Neuberger from our China holiday had beaten us to it. I had arranged to meet cousin Bill from County Durham for lunch at the nearby National Gallery, and by the time we reached the Mall Galleries Lilian was at the entrance, excitedly beckoning, 'I have found where it is!' Bill took a beautiful photograph of us by the picture.

The Society of Women Artists was accepting submissions for their Open Exhibition in June, and so riding a 'high' I tried again, and this time submitted the larger 'Waterlilies and Sky'. I had enjoyed this work, which combined a selection of water lilies and sky reflections found quite unexpectedly in a Henleaze garden. I had been taking tea with Jenny Brooks, a most accomplished miniature artist, and sitting in her sunny garden I had been transfixed by a well-established pond. Luckily I had my camera with me and took many photographs of the lilies, but it was only when I started working on the composition I realised how striking the root forms and sky reflections were, and eventually became quite absorbed by this mass of intricate shapes. The SWA results arrived, and I could see from the colour of the returned form in the envelope window that my picture had been accepted. I could hardly believe it.

But first, in May, it was time for our fortnight in the Ukraine with Mollie and Sandy Brown. We met our leader, Richard, and a party of fellow travellers at Heathrow and settled back, relaxed in readiness for this new adventure. Later, in Kiev airport, awaiting our luggage from the conveyor belt, we soon realised we had a problem. Mine arrived safely, but where was the Browns' luggage? Poor Mollie and Sandy patiently and expectantly waited, but with no sign at all of their suitcase. It was a sad sight. Richard eventually asked me to leave them and go ahead to join the rest of our party onboard the waiting coach which would transport us to the River Dnepr and our boat, *MS General Lavrinenkov*. A short while later, with my case emptied and all contents neatly stowed away, we were joined by Mollie, Sandy and Richard, but *sans* suitcase. This was to arrive four days later, at a convenient mooring, when its transport eventually caught up with the boat.

But, for now, we were moored for the day in historic Kiev (pronounced 'Keev' by the locals), the ancient capital of the Ukraine.

Our city tour was a feast for the eyes. Kiev, being one of the oldest cities in Eastern Europe, is charming, exotic, and also modern, with a fascinating history going back 1,500 years. Our guide introduced us to the tales of King Vladimir and his son Yaroslav the Wise (Sandy's new name for the duration of the holiday), the magnificent Byzantine Cathedral of St Sophia, and the mediaeval Golden Gate. We were listening to our guide when I could just detect some melodic string music. Walking in its direction, I found an impressively moustached gentleman in national dress playing what I thought was a rather oversized balalaika. I listened, mesmerised. He looked up at me, smiled, banged the top of the instrument and said 'Bandura' in a loud voice. Obviously not to be mistaken for a balalaika! He continued playing for me as I photographed him in the short time I had before remembering the group. I thanked him and quickly and joined our little band before they disappeared. Why had no one else followed the wonderful sound? Perhaps he was the Pied Piper of Kiev, and I had had a lucky escape!

During the afternoon, I came to know Helen who was travelling with an elderly friend, and both from Melbourne. We hit it off immediately when we met in the tiny shop of St Sophia Cathedral, choosing our painted eggs, and were great companions for the rest of the tour. We walked past gilded and painted domes in varying sizes, all for sale and just lying on the cobbled pavement, as we moved on to a Cave Monastery. Wearing the required head coverings and dressed appropriately, we entered a fascinating but eerie place, with mummified monks on display in glazed alcoves deep in its chilly depths. At one point, coming across a shrunken leathery hand peeping out of its shroud, Mollie and I laughed in shock and were immediately reprimanded by a serious monk who, frowning, put his finger to his lips. Heads down as chastened children, we finished the tour in silence.

We came squinting into the daylight and passed a bank of twinkling candles with the opportunity to buy one and light it in memory of someone. I thought of Paul. Paul Bloomfield, a family friend who with his wife Liz had been a great supporter of my work, tragically died at the age of 49, and not long before we left for this trip. I was having to miss his funeral service in St Peter's, Henleaze, and this was a fitting opportunity to remember him and his family. I lit the slim candle and, placing it with the others, prayed and thought of Paul, and how there wasn't one thing that wasn't lovely about him. A delightful and kind man.

Returning to the boat, we were assigned our dining tickets for the duration of our stay in the Kiev Restaurant. This we shared with some other nationalities, mainly French, it seemed, as the whole of the upper, and hopefully not better, Odessa Restaurant was taken by a party of Germans. Strangely, we never seemed to mix with them.

That evening, after our welcome cocktails with Captain Vladimir Bilenko, we dined in the Kiev room and were entertained by pianist Alexander and the ship's band, 'Seventh Day', as we set sail for our next port of call on the mighty Dnepr, Dnepropetrovsk.

Our first day aboard started early for those of us energetic enough to join Dasha on deck for pre-breakfast gymnastics, where I quickly learnt to count to ten in Ukrainian. The Dnepr is such a wide river, with sandy stretches and small villages, but mostly deeply edged by banks of tall rushes, obviously hiding millions of birds. Quite unseen by us, their chirruping was a loud and intense cacophony accompanying our progress. I loved it and had never experienced anything quite like it before, other than one early morning many years previously, when I was awoken at home by a quite deafening dawn chorus of birds. How I miss it now as our species decline.

Dnepropetrovsk was our first stop. Such an exotic name to our western ears, and quite a challenge to pronounce it correctly. An important industrial town, Dnepropetrovsk had been founded on the site of an old Cossack settlement, and is the home of an excellent local history museum. The museum was virtually empty, and we spent a happy couple of hours being escorted around impressive displays of historic implements, photographs and art. This was followed by a walk along the open waterfront, passing various Soviet-style concrete installations, all with an emphasis on military might, then back to the boat for lunch and another *'sail away'* to our next destination.

It is amazing how quickly time passes when doing not very much but watching passing scenery, eating and drinking rather well and, for those who wanted to increase their knowledge, various lectures. Today was 'Ukrainian History', an interesting account of the nation's complex struggle. We had arrived at the time of the 'Orange Revolution', and although the young people of Ukraine were in optimistic mood, those over fifty were very resigned to the Russian-style, old Eastern European way of life, and just shrugged their shoulders. 'Nothing will change,' said Lilya, an older guide.

On our third day, after gymnastics and breakfast, we had ex-tremely valuable talks by Lilya. The first was a brief foray into the Ukrainian language, followed by her version of borscht which she regularly prepared for her husband. This traditional, but very time-consuming, labour of love was quite a revelation, and made some of us feel rather lazy. How often would we spend several hours precisely slicing and dicing vegetables – mainly beetroot, of course – to offer our beloveds a warming nutritious soup? I don't think Lilya used a tin opener – that is, if she even owned one.

Lilya was a lovely hardworking woman, earning money as a guide to put her son through university. This, she told us, was the considerable sum of $500 per year, 'and how could he afford that?'

I felt so ashamed later when Lilya approached me to say in a very sympathetic tone, 'I hear British pensioners are having a bad time nowadays with not enough money.' I couldn't believe my ears. How could anyone say that after hearing her description of Ukrainian life? No doubt one of those 'poor pensioners' who complained to this good woman earlier in the day may have brought more than $500 with them as spending money.

After lunch we arrived at Novaya Kakhovka, with a walking tour through the city to the concert hall where children from the local dance school were to entertain us. Sadly, it bucketed down with rain, so we quickly made our soggy way to the hall. It was one of Mollie's favourite moments, with the talented young people in colourful costumes putting heart and soul into their energetic display. I later painted a portrait of one of the fresh faced, flower bedecked dancers.

By the next day I was slipping easily into the morning routine. 'Early risers' coffee', followed by gymnastics – 'Odin, Dva, Tri, Choteri, P'yat, Shist, Sim, Visim, Dyev'yat, Dyesyat' - and then breakfast. This was to be the day we would arrive in Odessa and, praise be, Mollie and Sandy would be reunited with their suitcase.

Odessa, known as the 'Pearl of the Black Sea' and gateway to the Ukraine, is of course home of the famous Potemkin Steps. We were very excited at the prospect of a city tour and, as we waited, leaning on the rails, overlooking the harbourside, we couldn't help but notice several rather well-dressed women on the quayside obviously waiting to sell things. As we disembarked and waited for everyone to join us, Mollie and I crossed over to look at the colourful items the women were selling. Some of these dear ladies happened to be teachers, boosting their meagre incomes with lovely handmade aprons depicting Ukrainian maidens with long golden plaits made of wool. We, of course, bought one each.

It was a beautiful day, showing Odessa at its sparkling best. Imposing buildings and glittering domed churches, wide tree-lined boulevards, a beach and spa, as well as, of course, the famous Steps. We noticed how clean the city was. Numerous rather elderly women, scarves tied tightly about their heads, were bent double as they earnestly brushed the streets and pavements.

The 192 steps of the Potemkin Stairway, wide and unusual as they are, were initially rather disappointing. Instead of sweeping down to the sea, they now descend to embrace a new busy main road. I dutifully walked the steps, appreciating the optical illusion afforded by ten landings between the steps, and of course had my photo taken at the bottom. From there only the landings are visible, and from the top only the steps. This was, after all, my main reason for coming here. In their defence, the stairway descends majestically, ever widening, from the magnificent Primorski Boulevard towards the harbour. However, to reach the harbourside, keeping close together, we rather nervously proceeded to cross the fast-moving highway at the base of the steps.

There were various optional extra excursions on this day. Some of our party decided on Chernobyl, others, a winery, but I had booked a visit to the art gallery. There, to my amazement, I found paintings by Zinaida Serabriakova! What luck. Our day ended with a visit to the theatre and fine performances of the traditional ballet Carmen, followed by a modern ballet, Shopeniana. A perfect finish to a lovely day.

Next morning, and still moored in Odessa, we enjoyed a fascinating small tour to Bessarabia in the wine-growing Moldavian countryside. It was another beautiful sunny day for us with not a cloud in the sky as we arrived at the peaceful garden village of Schabo . It felt quite remote, and the friendly villagers were definitely rural in their dress and pace of life. Women in headscarves tended bountiful gardens, and there seemed to be flowers and fruit everywhere.

The houses were small, and on the dusty earth streets children of all ages happily gathered together. Large and very prominent in the village was the white domed church which we all wanted to see, but first we were hoping there might be a loo somewhere in the vicinity. We found one in the church grounds, a slightly ramshackle privy housing a primitive but clean 'squattie'. A queue formed, and after each visit a smiling little boy ran in with a bucket to flush away the evidence!

It was a charming village and so productive one could understand why the Ukraine had been called the breadbasket of Russia. We were told that children starved on the streets of Moscow after Ukraine gained its independence.

We climbed into our coach, waved goodbye to the villagers, and sped off to the coast for the mediaeval Akkerman Fortress of Belgorod-Dnestrovsky.

This solidly-built defence structure occupies an ancient site overlooking the Dnestrovsky estuary and is said to date back 2,500 years. We walked along its walls, viewing the citadel, various towers, a dungeon, and the remains of a Turkish Mosque, hence the name 'Ak-Kerman'. After three centuries Turkish dominance ended as recently as 1944, the year of my birth.

Such an interesting and quiet place now, despite its bloodthirsty history, with goats grazing calmly and a few stallholders selling basic souvenirs in the shade of some trees.

After a great morning we looked forward to lunch on board and our 'Sail Away' on to the naval city of Sevastopol, and it had to be the best time ever to arrive. Bright spring sunshine and blue skies were a perfect backdrop for the annual May Day military processions, and we were there to witness it in all its pride and ceremony.

In the past, the May Day procession had been a mighty show of strength, with tanks, rockets, and military paraphernalia taking centre stage beside the troops. Now, however, it seemed to have more of a holiday air. The navy was moored in the port and sailors in their best dress uniforms paraded proudly, whilst aging veterans of former conflicts, heavily bedecked with medals, stood to attention. Some looked too frail to carry the weight of their very many rows of decorations.

We were supposed to walk in a group around the town and were advised not to stray in the throng of people but, disorientated in the bustle, two of us were suddenly on our own. However hard we looked, our shore party was nowhere to be seen. We gave up quite quickly and decided to treat ourselves to coffee on the balcony of a restaurant perfectly overlooking the harbour. There we sat in the sun, happily sipping away, watching the crowds of sailors and fishermen from our excellent vantage point, until our group returned. Lilya led the way, holding aloft the placard bearing the name *MV Lavrinenkov*. We called down to them and waved. 'Oh, there they are!' they cried, looking rather envious.

A bright morning heralded another fascinating day at the seaside town of Yalta and the historic White Palace, by way of 'Swallows Nest'. This was a real curiosity, resembling a fairy tale gothic castle, clinging precariously to the rocks about 40 metres above sea level in the bijou health resort of Mischor. Local vendors manned rough wooden stalls and sold beautiful unpolished amber necklaces, beeswax candles, and some sort of thin colourful sausage. The amber necklaces were a must. I declined the sausages.

Overlooking the sea in well-manicured grounds, the White Palace had been a gorgeous holiday residence for the last Russian Tsar and an historic venue for the Yalta Conference in 1945. It was quite something, looking at black and white photographs and walking around the panelled room which had been the actual meeting place for Stalin, Roosevelt and Churchill at the end of the Second World War. In other rooms, photos of the last Tsar and his family filled the walls, making for thoughtful viewing.

In the grounds there were the usual stalls where I found exquisite scarves and stoles for sale. Pictures of goats adorned the stalls, so I presume they were made of some sort of cashmere. I came across a trivet of fragrant cedarwood, which I bought and still use.

We had rather a nice lunch in the Oreanda Hotel in Yalta before Mollie, Sandy, Helen and I set off for a walk along the sea front. Obviously 'quite the thing' in Yalta, along the broad Promenade were dozens of theatrical tableaux where holidaymakers could dress up and be photographed. Bewigged, hatted and crinolined ladies giggled behind their fans as they sat in ornate velvet chairs and arranged themselves in a correct stately pose. It was bizarre, but rather fun.

We walked on, admiring the work of street artists and breathing in the salty air, before returning to the boat for an 'Italian Supper', followed by a short walk to the local concert hall. Here we enjoyed a riotous programme of musical delights and energetic Russian-style dancing from the Black Sea Fleet Band and Dance Company. A young wizard on the balalaika and a portly baritone, not in the first flush of youth but nevertheless impressive in his ample naval uniform, both stole the show.

The following morning we were off to Bakhchisarai, the former Crimean Tartar capital with its typical Turkish buildings, harem and mosques. In the Khan's Palace we came across the marble Fountain of Tears immortalised by the Russian poet Pushkin. It is said that thanks to this poem the palace was not destroyed in 1944 after Stalin's instructions that the Crimean Tartars should be deported. A delightful Tartar lady with beautiful, dark, almond eyes was our guide that morning, as we were transported by scenes fit for the fairy tale '1001 Nights'.

Back to the boat for lunch, and with still no sign of the Germans, then off to 'Panorama' to see 'The Defence of Sevastopol' in the Crimean War of 1855. We toiled up a steep hill towards Panorama and gazed at the one remaining tree from that time. On reaching the top we were confronted by a large, circular, and ornate building housing an amazing panorama. In its dark interior, we quietly took in lifelike scenes depicting the assault on Malakhov Hill by British and French allies, and its heroic defence by Russian soldiers who ultimately won the day. We were rather awestruck. It was so realistic, showing in sound and tableaux the full horrors of that conflict.

Finally, we walked around the charming and wealthy-looking port of Balaklava. With its boat moorings and well-kept seaside houses, it could have been an English coastal resort, except for the still ominous presence of a large cave-like opening across the water. Secreted here had been an enormous subterranean plant for servicing Russian atomic submarines. On the way back to the boat it became rather foggy, and it was in these conditions we came across the Valley of the Six Hundred, site of the infamous Charge of the Light Brigade. Although now a fertile wine growing area it had a strange atmosphere and, as we plodded around in the mist and mud, we felt sombre and sad. We didn't linger.

Sailing took up most of the next morning, and we passed seemingly endless wide steppes and wheat fields, vineyards and gardens until we arrived at Kherson. Here small boats transported us through canals to Fisherman's Village. It was so green, so rural and so idyllic, with people fishing on the river bank. We met the villagers and were invited into their homes where, sitting around large wooden tables, we were offered cherries and drinks. After this refreshing break, we walked towards the river where a local man was selling his really beautiful, typically Ukrainian oil paintings, and for just a very few dollars. There were so many, and it was difficult to choose one, however, time was getting short. I found a small study of a Samovar, most sensitively worked, and paid the seven dollars asked. It now hangs in my kitchen and is constantly admired. I photographed the artist, a gentle, smiling young man.

Early risers coffee and gymnastics with Dasha prepared us for the long day ahead and our visit to Zaporozhye, historic city of the Cossacks. It would prove to be a most fruitful and inspirational day. A massive hydro-electric power station and dam spanned the wide river, and after our city tour we were taken to see it. Surely this would have been forbidden just a few years earlier? I felt rather excited by the prospect. At the gates we were met by a charming elderly gentleman, a retired engineer who, despite not speaking English, was a proud and delightful escort around these gargantuan works.

I asked if he would allow me to take his photograph and so, outside in the sunshine, standing smartly to attention in his best shiny suit, Engineer Ivan Petriovich was a willing subject. The portrait I eventually produced, and of which I am very proud, shows him inside his beloved hydro-electric hall.

After lunch on the boat, still no sight of the Germans, we set off for the island of Khortytsa and a Cossack horse-riding display. On arrival at the wooden-staked compound we waited, wondering what we had to do next, when suddenly and without warning, a voice boomed out...

'Dobra Den!' (Good day)

I jumped and turned to see a large, bald, heavily moustached Cossack Chief astride his horse, looking very fierce but obviously welcoming us to his lair. We hurried in.

Sitting on wooden benches, we were entertained to a show of incredible horsemanship, whip cracking, swordplay, and general intimidation. These men, worthy descendants of the feared Cossacks, were masters in their own territory, and we all felt we wouldn't have wanted to cross them back in the 17th century. It was quite thrilling. A young Cossack, with typical half-shaved head, sat smiling in the shade. A few chickens and a cockerel were running around, scraping in the dust. Could I take his picture? He nodded and gave a cheeky grin. This image, together with the cockerel, would become a favourite pastel portrait.

Driving back through the city, we passed a substantial concert hall dedicated to the composer Glinka, and with a statue of the great man seated in front of the main entrance. It brought back happy memories of listening to his evocative Russlan and Lyudmila Suite on Dad's old LP's.

On our return to the boat, we found local villagers selling trinkets. Blankets were laid out on the river bank with various ornaments which, on close inspection, were obviously their household and personal items they were desperate to sell. Amongst them were some delightful porcelain figures. What a different world to ours, and such poverty, yet only a few hours away from home. Now wrapped in old paper, I had found a charming and delicate small figure of a Russian Bear playing his balalaika. I decided I would give it to little Charlie, who would soon be two years old. Helen bought a porcelain bird and a sweet figure of a girl holding a basket of flowers.

As the boat pulled away, a rather lovely thing happened. Seemingly from nowhere, an elderly man suddenly appeared. Bedecked in red trousers and jaunty hat, he played his violin for us in a most exaggerated manner. Reminding me of 'Fiddler on the Roof', this dear fellow serenaded us, and was soon joined by another man with a plastic shopping bag. They waved us goodbye!

Our holiday was soon coming to an end. It had exceeded my expectations, which happened to be high in the first place. We had a whole day just cruising, with activities on offer such as a quiz in the bar at 10.30 am, or a visit to the engine room, then lectures on 'Orthodoxy and Icons' and 'Ukraine Today'. I thought I would try my hand at the quiz, which was to be on the Ukraine and general knowledge, then attend both lectures. I came in joint first in the quiz, which I wouldn't have done if Sandy, 'Yaroslav the Wise', hadn't decided to visit the engine room. The prize was a glass of champagne. How nice, I thought. I would enjoy that tonight. However, the champagne had to be taken there and then. Not being a great imbiber, I sipped at the champagne and eventually had to wander back to lunch still holding a half-filled glass. The many fellow passengers I passed at 11 am would definitely get the wrong idea.

It was our last full day, and by 9.30am we had arrived back in Kiev. After a brisk and final exercise session with Dasha, we had breakfast then joined the bus for a morning visit to the open air museum of Pirogovo. Here, traditional wooden cottages and churches from all over the Ukraine had been relocated to make a large village. With the interiors authentically reproduced and 'inhabitants' in traditional dress, we really caught the flavour of old Ukraine. It seemed romantic, but in reality it must have been a very hard way of life.

That afternoon Helen and I decided to be adventurous and go off to find the main Museum and Art Gallery, first using the ornate funicular railway to get us up from the river to the city. Being spring time, many flower sellers sat in the sunshine surrounded by buckets of lilies of the valley. It was a lovely sight. On reaching an underground station we found, to our consternation, all signs and notices in the Cyrillic alphabet. Map in hand, we had a few moments' discussion about which direction we should travel, and following our instincts off we went. Luckily we chose the right platform, and duly arrived at the correct station.

On arrival we were excited to find a large leafy park full of concrete benches and people in deep concentration playing dominoes, chess and draughts. We joined the locals to watch for quite a while before crossing over to what looked like, and fortunately turned out to be, the National Museum. It was a dark place, but full of treasures. Very few others were there, so we enjoyed a peaceful and delightful few hours, and with some surprises. In one gallery, locked away in a large glass cabinet, we found porcelain with makers' marks very similar to the pieces Helen and I had bought on the river bank. It was rather sad to think we had acquired such lovely things so easily, but at the time those villagers looked relieved.

Before returning to Melbourne, Helen was to visit more of Europe, and it was during a Rhine Cruise that many of her souvenirs were stolen, including some of her porcelain treasures from the Zaporozhye river bank, and the traditional decorated egg from St Sophia's Cathedral.

The day, and indeed our holiday, ended with a magnificent concert in the richly ornate St Andrew's church, a fitting finale, before taking our leave of *MV Lavrinenkov* the following morning. Helen and I said goodbye at Kiev airport with promises to keep in touch.

As this book goes to print, a cruel and senseless war is being per-petrated against this lovely country and its peoples. It is with great sadness I remember my happy sun-filled days in the Ukraine.

Back home, and the private view of the Society of Women Artists Open Exhibition was due. It was all slotting in rather well. This Society combines its Open Exhibition with the Society of Miniature Artists which was most appropriate in the circum-stances. It was in the garden of my friend, the miniature artist, where I found the pond and waterlilies, the very picture chosen to be exhibited. On this occasion I decided to stay in London for the weekend and offer my services to steward for a morning. At the private view I was joined by Eirene Crook, my old neighbour from Beaconsfield Road who I hadn't seen for some years. It was so good to catch up, and a great occasion for us as the Patron, Princess Michael of Kent, soon arrived, and was genuinely inter-ested and charming. She made a warm speech, and it was obvious she felt quite at home with this artistic group. I noticed she spent a long time looking at every work hanging there, and appeared quite a different person to the 'Princess Pushy' I had read about that very morning in the newspaper.

Now eighteen years old, poor old Fifi the cat was beginning to show her age and, although eating well and appearing happy, starting to look a bit scraggy. The year before she had had a funny 'turn', after which her personality had changed. Although always loving with me, and occasionally with my brother, she was suspicious of most visitors who, taken in with her sweet good looks, would be bitten if they got too close. Blood could be spilt. At that time the vet recommended she should be put to sleep, as it is notoriously difficult to diagnose pain in cats. I just couldn't agree then, as her quality of life seemed fine to me.

During my Ukrainian trip I had sent Fifi to the usual excellent cattery, the only one always happy to take her and where there was one person she trusted, although this girl had to wear a gauntlet!

On booking her in, the owner asked if I would like to pay another one pound to cover veterinary insurance. Thank goodness I did. Telephoning the cattery on my return, I was told that Fifi had stopped eating, the vet had been called and she had been put on a drip! They had liaised with my vet, who wanted me to bring her in as soon as possible for a check. All this for just one pound.

Fifi was brought home in the usual cage, and as soon as she arrived and the cage opened, she jumped out and starting purring. 'She hasn't done that before,' said the girl. Poor Fifi had pined. Our Canadian trip to visit Mum's friends in Vancouver, and then the Gaults in Calgary, was imminent, and I wondered how Fifi would cope with another stay in the cattery.

We visited the vet, who this time said, and very kindly, she should definitely be put to sleep, as she wouldn't survive another upheaval at her age and in her state of health. I just couldn't agree there and then, so the vet said to come back in three weeks.

'Make it four,' I said, knowing that was as close to the Canada trip as possible.

Fifi seemed fine for three weeks, but then I noticed she was sleeping a lot more, and although still following me around the house, would take her time negotiating the stairs, and she didn't want to go outside.

I realised the time had come, but not wanting to put her through the ordeal of being transported to the vet in the hated cat box, I asked the vet to call. I was expecting some resistance, but she agreed straightaway and would come that very afternoon. It all seemed too soon, but the vet arrived with her nurse and I was touched by their sensitive behaviour. Acting with such kindness and respect for Fifi, it could have been a human being they were dealing with.

The deed was done, and much too quickly. I started to sob, which I hadn't expected. Fifi was carefully wrapped up and carried out with such dignity I think that act made me sadder than ever. I was never a great cat lover, but I cried all afternoon, and years later tears easily come to my eyes when I think of how she trusted and loved me. The boys haven't helped, accusing me of murdering the cat! Fifi had been Rob's pet originally but, as with the goldfish, Dryden and Ellis, and St John the Staffordshire Bull Terrier, they were all eventually left with me.

CANADA AND ALASKA (2004)

OUR TRIP TO CANADA promised to be quite an adventure. As we passed Bakers Dolphin travel shop in Clifton Village earlier in the year we decided to pop in, just on the off chance, to see what was on offer. Soon taken with a delightful young girl, who obviously loved arranging all the details, we looked no further. The final itinerary became a full and extremely interesting one. Starting with a stay in Vancouver, followed by a seven-day Alaskan cruise which returned to Vancouver in time for the Rocky Mountaineer train through the Rockies to Calgary, our final destination. There we were to stay with our friends from China, Kevin and Rae, who had booked several visits to the famous annual Stampede.

2004 was a memorable year in many ways, and especially for me, as the dreaded 60 was looming large. My birthday in June was the reason I decided to leave the country for the month! It was then I understood exactly how poor Dad had felt back in 1983. He never recovered from getting older; sixty happened to other people, and it seemed to be the one thing in life he couldn't do anything about! Well, I suppose he did win in the end as he never reached real old age.

One teatime in June, Mum and I were comfortably transported by Air Canada from Heathrow to Vancouver. Just two hours later on the clock (in British Summertime!) we settled into the Pacific Palisades Hotel for five whole days. This gave us time to see the sights and meet up with Auntie Joyce's and Mum's old friends who hailed from Northumberland. Some years earlier, the two sisters had visited Vancouver and had always been rather boring about its delights, but I was soon to find out for myself what a truly marvellous city it is.

Many years before, Teddy and Jean Latimer had emigrated from Whitley Bay to Vancouver. On one of their previous visits, Mum and Joyce had presented them with my pastel painting of the lighthouse on St Mary's Island. Teddy had immediately put it in pride of place in their living room. Sadly, by now, Jean had died but Teddy and his daughter Karen with her family were looking forward to meeting up. Also, Fraser and Gill, back in Northumberland, were keen for us to make contact with their friends, Rosie and Trevor Baruth, who lived in the fashionable Steveston area. I was beginning to wonder how I was going to fit it all in to the five days before the Alaskan cruise.

Phone calls were made and, shortly after, Rosie picked us up from the hotel, and on a gorgeously warm afternoon she generously drove us around Vancouver on a great city tour. What a fabulous city. We finished up in Stanley Park amidst the famous totem poles where we all took turns having our photographs taken. We said goodbye and promised to meet again after our Alaskan Cruise.

Karen telephoned me at the hotel that evening to say they were in the middle of moving house, but would be home after our cruise. This gave us more time to see the sights, so we booked a few trips with a local bus company.

Our first excursion was across the water to Vancouver Island. It was a long ferry voyage, but on our arrival it was a delight to find such a charming, old fashioned town. We had time to visit the glorious Butchart Gardens, where we found roses in abundant perfumed masses. I have never seen anything quite like it. The fragrance and colour were almost overwhelming. I had my photo taken under a rose arbour; it was the best birthday treat I could have had.

Back in town we made an obligatory visit to Rogers, a rather superior chocolatier and restaurant, and after a cuppa bought plenty of dark chocolate to keep us going. We had just enough time for a short walk around some rather classy shops before the ferry back to Vancouver, when suddenly I came across Artina's, the most beautiful silversmith I have ever seen. I found myself inside the shop looking at large displays of indigenous silver jewellery, realising soon enough the prices were rather out of my league. I wasn't giving up, and eventually found a pair of exquisite silver earrings with a typical First Nations Eagle emblem, simply but perfectly engraved. My purchase was carefully wrapped in tissue and placed, together with the maker's details, in a large white box. Evidently the artist, a Donald Lyle Lancaster of mixed parentage, with a Pentecostal Minister father and Kwakiutl mother, works with simple traditional hand tools and had become a recognised talent of contemporary West Coast art. What an amazing find, and as a birthday present to myself I wore them straightaway. Back on the ferry we got talking to a resident of Vancouver who, I am pleased to say, admired my earrings.

The following morning we visited Vancouver Aquarium. In the dramatic blue depths under and around the huge beluga whale tank two young children pressed their hands against the glass and peered in, transfixed by these pure white, rather comical looking creatures. This was definitely going to be a subject for me when I got home.

Our afternoon was spent in the trendy Granville Island area, with its quirky shops, street entertainment and a covered food market. It must have been the height of the blueberry season, for rows of wooden stalls positively overflowed with huge, luscious and extremely cheap fruit. We bought a goodly amount and tucked in over the next few days. Mum decided to explore a few shops when we returned to the hotel, and I found I still had time, if I got a move on, to walk to the main art gallery before it closed. It was holding a Warhol exhibition, and I hadn't seen original Warhols since our visit to MoMA in New York back in 1989.

We had booked ourselves onto a trip to Grouse Mountain for the next afternoon and so, wanting to explore as much local culture as possible, I took a bus to the University of British Columbia's Museum of Anthropology. I wished I'd had the whole day to spend there, as it was the most wonderful and unforgettable experience. The rather understated low building, reached down a slope and almost hidden by trees, was nearly impossible to find. However, what unexpected riches await those who persevere. The light and spacious building houses large quantities of art and cultural artefacts from the Pacific North West First Nation peoples. I joined a tour led by a knowledgeable and gentle local lady who was obviously extremely sympathetic to the First Nations, their culture and history. The hour or so flew by as she guided us through various halls with artwork, massive totem poles, and finally a terrific wood carving by the artist Bill Reid. Resting on a large plinth and illuminated by a circular skylight, a colossal raven perches on top of a clam shell which is splitting open to release the first humans. Titled 'The Raven and the First Men', it dominates its own darkened gallery and is a majestic, emotive, and tremendously powerful work.

For that experience alone it was worth the journey, but there was so much to see and learn I was in danger of being late for Grouse Mountain. I decided to stay as long as possible, forget the bus and get a taxi back. Having an extra half hour or so, I enjoyed a sit down in the café and then looked around the small museum shop. My eye was immediately taken by some handmade blankets. The only cot-size one had a design depicting a grandmother and a 'welcome' copied from a First Nation wall painting in Vancouver Airport. I bought it immediately, despite the cost, as we had recently heard David and Katie were expecting their first baby. It would be the perfect gift.

I made it back to the hotel, but only just in time to meet the Grouse Mountain party, and off we went, visiting the Capilano Bridge on the way.

One of Mum's famous experiences had been on the Capilano Bridge, that narrow, swinging stretch of wood and rope spanning the Capilano River. It was here, on her previous visit, she met her neighbour from Tickenham right in the middle of the bridge. She regularly finds someone she knows in foreign parts! I had always accused her of 'romancing', as Grandma Taylor called it, but by then I realised it was all true. I duly lurched across the bridge and, although I didn't meet anyone I knew, I received my certificate to prove I had completed the feat.

On Grouse Mountain we caught a cable car to where, munching on something sweet and delicious called a 'beaver's tail,' we watched the Lumberjack Show. All very touristy, but huge fun.

In a large, open, wooden building incorporating a totem pole, some First Nation Canadians were demonstrating carving and weaving. The women had such sweet faces, and the man was so pleasant, I decided to have a chat. These were Haida people, and the man, sensing my obviously genuine interest in their culture, gave me a map of Canada with all the tribal areas marked. I was thrilled with it. Thanking him, we turned away to look for our group, and when we turned back, the blinds had been pulled down; the building had closed. I couldn't believe my luck – one enriching experience after another. A few minutes later and we would have missed them.

The next morning, we were off to Alaska. We had never experienced a 'proper' cruise before, and here was the perfect opportunity. I had always wanted to go to Alaska, but Mum was definitely underwhelmed when I first broached the subject. However, she eventually agreed. Our excellent small boat cruising to Vietnam and the Baltic were more along the lines of expeditions with intellectual lectures, and very little emphasis on 'entertainment'. However, the *Norwegian Sun* was the 'Full Monty', offering a bewildering range of on-board entertainments, shops, several restaurants, and a huge selection of on-shore activities at each port of call. Everyone was catered for, from the wheelchair-bound to the serious mountaineer.

As soon as our taxi arrived at the berth, we were whisked through the most slick and efficient processing one could imagine. Suitcases were labelled and taken away, and before we knew it we were having photos taken for our ship's passport. Seasoned cruisers, used to the process, made sure they were posing to best advantage, whilst we, rather startled by the speed of it all, blinked woodenly and wide-eyed into the lens. I made a mental note to remember this another time, especially after viewing the hideous image later in the voyage. 'No, thank you, we would not be buying it as a souvenir.'

Fairly far down in the bowels of the *Norwegian Sun*, we settled into our small but quite comfortable stateroom with, luckily, a very large porthole window. I would have preferred something a little more upmarket, but Mum was adamant.

'Ee, our Linda. This is perfectly alright. If you can afford it, go and see if you can get something else.' Needless to say, I stayed put, and it was fortuitous. Our cabin was quiet, and I would get plenty of exercise by climbing all the stairways instead of using the lift.

Queuing to book our trips from the hundreds on offer was an interesting although time-consuming experience. For future reference, book up before you go! Popular excursions were already full, but we eventually came to a happy compromise, and with mostly easy excursions for Mum to manage.

'This is ridiculous.' It was all too comfortable. 'We must have one adventurous outing. We may never get back here again!' I persuaded Mum to have another look at the tours, and especially a Float Plane trip to Taku Glacier Lodge, one hour away from

Juneau. The clincher for Mum was the salmon feast on reaching our destination! There was just a small grumble and intake of breath at the price, but she agreed. Bookings over, we could now relax and get on with our voyage. There was so much to see and do, with keep fit classes, Pilates, Yoga, nightly cabaret entertainments and films, shopping in a small mall, loads of restaurants, and of course, my favourite, the fabulous changing landscape and light. The sunsets quite took my breath away.

Our first port was the historic small city of Ketchikan, a colourful, bustling community, rich in the culture of native Tlingit, Tsimshian and Haida people. In all our ports, bald eagles were as numerous as seagulls are back home, and away from the waterfront ravens continually cawed from the deep forests beyond. It was magical.

We were whisked off to Saxman Village, so named after a school teacher who, back in the late 19th century, was lost searching out new locations for the tribes of Tongass and Cape Fox. Here, massive totem poles from all over the region made fascinating viewing. They had been brought from their initial sites, restored as much as possible, and then relocated in Saxman Village. Here also we were able to watch local artists carving new poles. It is such an intricate and complicated craft which I was soon to appreciate when, back at home, I worked on my totem pastel painting.

Led into a dark, traditional longhouse and seated on benches, we were treated to a performance of dances from the gifted Tlingit people. I was struck by their intensity and pride, especially that of a young boy who looked so proud and optimistic. These gentle people had just moved out of the way and without any protest when the Americans constructed the Alaskan Highway in the 20th century. Hopefully the future is looking better now for the young people.

Our day ended with a walk around the town, especially enjoying the stilted boardwalk of colourful Creek Street. Originally a red light district, the premises are now a maze of galleries and craft boutiques where I purchased some very traditional Alaskan carved dolls for Grace and Chloe

Next stop, Juneau. We awoke the next morning to a continual buzz from the sound of float planes taking off and landing every minute or so. This was the easiest way to move around the region, and the planes were as frequent as taxis. We could have watched this activity all day, especially with the now common site of bald eagles catching fish in their huge talons. I couldn't take my eyes off these powerful birds as they quickly flew down to the water and then rose up, clutching large wriggling fish in their claws. However, we had to make a move as this was the day of our big adventure.

It was a rather misty morning, and the surrounding forests loomed mysteriously out of the haze as we waited on the slipway for our plane. We were guided to a very small four-seater. I hoped I wasn't going to be airsick, as the flight to the remote Taku lodge would take about an hour. To take my mind off it, I went over the safety instructions we had been given in the event of a Bear incident!

Make plenty of noise when entering secluded areas.

Respect their space!

Stay calm and don't run (this could be difficult in the heat of the moment!).

If attacked, roll over into a ball, hands behind head, and protect vital organs.

I am sure this would work with a nosy black bear, but possibly not with an aggressive grizzly. I would do my best to keep us out of trouble.

Helped by the young pilot, Mum, gamely stretching her plump little legs to climb in, reached the back seat and settled down as to the manor born. I was next, followed by another couple who sat in front of us. We put on our headphones to hear the commentary and cut out the engine noise, then looked eagerly out of our windows as we took off. I had no need to worry about feeling sick; it was as smooth a ride as I had ever had, and swooping over rivers, glaciers, waterfalls and snow-capped mountains, we looked in awe at this majestic wilderness until, almost too soon, we were landing on the water and taxiing over to a boardwalk. Engine now off, the couple in front climbed out, to be followed by Mum, then me. Unfortunately, Mum couldn't get out. She was stuck in her seat and, trying very hard to lever herself out, was overcome by giggles and then became absolutely helpless. Of course, I couldn't get out until she did. After a fruitless effort, we had to resort to brute force. The poor young pilot, no doubt with a time issue, one leg on the side of the plane for extra leverage, pulled Mum's arms as I pushed hard from behind. Eventually she shot out like a cork from a bottle, still laughing but extremely pink and embarrassed. Our plane quickly left us to the truly splendid backdrop of a huge glacier, and we made our way to lunch at the Lodge as nonchalantly as possible.

Our stay at Taku Lodge was quite wonderful. The salmon bake was something to behold. Huge pieces of local salmon, the biggest I've ever seen, barbequed in front of us, and accompanied by an array of wholesome salads and homemade warm bread. We tucked in inside the Lodge, watched over by moose heads and the paraphernalia of winter life in the mountains. We drank water from the glacier, and were then shown a large chunk of glacier ice so pure it was transparent.

The Lodge is used as a scientific station and covered with forty feet of snow each winter, but I had seen swallows nesting in its eves and, watching them intently, I just happened to catch some small things flitting by. It happened so fast I couldn't quite see what they were, but thinking them to be some sort of speedy butterfly, I kept looking. To my amazement, these tiny objects were hummingbirds! Alaska is most certainly a country of incredible beauty and contrasts.

After lunch, Mum stayed close to the Lodge as I went on a small walk around the area. Well-wrapped in jacket and scarves, and making plenty of noise, of course, I admired the unusual large soft mounds of moose moss on the spruce firs, and I looked for wildlife. There were plenty of 'No See'ums', the tiny midge-like creatures who continually bite without being seen, but luckily no bears that day. The impressive 'Hole in the Wall' Glacier was quite something. As I approached, the temperature immediately plunged. I inhaled the cool fresh air and, of course, had a photo taken.

Soon a plane arrived, and I suppose the greatest indignity. It was a roomier eight-seater sent to bring us back to Juneau. Mum was unfazed, especially as she saw black bears hauling themselves in and out of rivers on our return journey. For her, it was very special. Thank goodness I had persuaded her to go.

There was only time for a quick shop in Juneau – some earrings for the girls – before we were on board again, heading to Skagway and the Yukon.

Because of the distance we were travelling, we had a couple of cruising days which I filled with Pilates, Yoga, brisk walks around the deck, landscape and people watching, and, luxuriously, a visit to the beauty salon for manicure and pedicure. There was plenty of time for people watching, and I have to say we have never seen so many very large bodies and strange shapes. Mum was beginning to feel quite sylph-like. We shared a table with a lovely normal-sized couple from New York, but what a shock when later seeing them with their rotund son. He was such a nice-looking young man but not very tall, so his normal small head looked out of place on his huge, kaftan covered body. He ordered Diet Coke and proceeded to put sweetener in it! I felt rather sad for him.

Eating on board could start from the moment you got up until your head hit the pillow at night. We decided to be as strict as possible, but it was so difficult with food continually on offer, and it all looked so delicious.

Before arriving at Skagway we cruised into Glacier Bay. As we approached, the temperature noticeably cooled as chunks of incredibly blue glacier ice silently floated by. Everyone rushed to the decks to get the best view, and soon the premium vantage points on all decks were taken. I had a brain wave and dashed down to our cabin, and there, framed exactly as in a photo, in front of our large porthole window, was this monumental glacier in all its majestic frozen glory. It was breathtaking. I think I had the best view.

On reaching the frontier town of Skagway, we were soon to find ourselves in Gold Rush country. Originally known by the Tlingit name of Skaqua – the windy place – it had been an old Indian trading post serving early prospectors to the Yukon. We decided to join a gold panning group at the Klondike Gold Dredge. After finding a few specks in our sieved pans, we enjoyed listening to tales of the many trials of early prospectors from an entertaining 'Pistol Pete'. We spent a happy hour there before boarding the narrow-gauge White Pass train to travel into the Yukon.

The aptly named White Pass was whiter than we would have liked that day, with an almost virtual 'whiteout'. Persistent drizzle and clouds obscured what would have been most marvellous views of its waterfalls, bridges, glaciers and gorges. At least we were able to enjoy a pioneering atmosphere, with tales of dastardly doings by the outlaw Soapy Smith and his gang who terrorised the area in the late 1890s. Soapy Smith eventually had his come-uppance, killed in a shootout by the town hero Frank Reid. As the heavy mist gradually lifted, we could see Gold Rush Cemetery, the last resting place of many a stampeder and outlaw, including Soapy, but sadly also Frank Reid, who died of wounds from the shooting. The Wild Wild West indeed.

Being a slightly smaller vessel than most, the *Norwegian Sun* was able to berth in the delightful inlet town of Wrangell. It was a typically misty and drizzly morning, so well-prepared in our pac-a-macs and armed with brollies, we all disembarked.

At the quayside we were met by a smiling, bearded young man. He introduced himself as Jeff Marbles, our guide for the morn-

CANADA AND ALASKA (2004)   113

ing, and led us to an old and rather cumbersome looking bus parked nearby. Walking to it, we passed stalls selling delicious local shrimps and tables displaying heaps of raw garnets, some still nestling in the very rock they were chipped from. Found on the surface at nearby Garnet Ledge, a deed dictates that the garnets can only be mined by the children of Wrangell, using just hand tools, and sold for their benefit and the Boy Scouts of America. Despite rather persistent rain, the children manning the stalls welcomed us with eager, friendly smiles. I was very keen to take some garnets home for gifts, as they would make perfect small paperweights. On every side we were greeted by smiling, welcoming faces. Even the local policeman stopped to talk, and posed for a photo before resuming his leisurely pace along the street, chatting happily with locals as he passed. Wrangell seemed a peaceful, old-fashioned sort of place.

We clambered into the old bus and Jeff started up a very noisy engine. The heavy vehicle obviously took quite an effort to manoeuvre, but Jeff, cheerfully straining away on the large steering wheel as we moved off, gave us a running commentary on the area at the same time. And what a remarkable area it was turning out to be.

We passed several churches, all duly pointed out, until we got to the Assembly of God that had Jeff's special attention. He was the Pastor! The Roller Skating Rink and Fire Station adjoined the church on one side and a senior centre nearby. We were definitely getting the impression of a friendly, united little community.

Our first stop was the picturesque Petroglyph Beach, a State Historic site with ancient and mysterious carvings lying on the seashore. By now the rain had stopped, and in the first watery sunlight of the day a small gravel road led us to wooden steps, the only way down to this unspoilt beach. With gorgeous mountainous scenery as a backdrop, we found curious rock art just lying around amongst pebbles and driftwood. No one seems to know the age of these artefacts, although possibly the work of early Stikine Tlingits from about 1,000 years ago. However, there appear to be signs of habitation as far back as 8,000 years, so possibly even older. As the stones are found lying very exposed on the shore, it is thought they were created to be seen by passing canoes.

Some carvings had been removed to the safety of the local museum, but there were still many just lying there in their beautiful natural surroundings. Most are quite recognisable, such as an especially fine whale design, and nearby, a porpoise, the sun, and even a turkey.

Chief Shakes Island was next as we lumbered on in our bus, Jeff still straining at the wheel, towards another of Wrangell's historic landmarks. Chief Shakes tribal house, with its poles and intricate carvings, is said to be a faithful replica of the original Frog Clan meeting place. Traditional potlatches, the tribal meetings, are still held there, continually renewing the fascinating native culture of that area. How sad if it were ever to be lost.

After visiting Chief Shakes's grave, impressively marked by two killer whale totems, we made our way to our very last stop, the newly opened museum on the waterfront. With a typically grand backdrop of mountains and sea, the banner over the entrance welcomed us: 'Helping Others is an Alaskan Tradition'. We made our way inside and were, indeed, warmly greeted by the staff.

The museum houses even more totems and native artefacts whilst depicting the history of the area in chronological order. All is embraced, from early indigenous culture through to the fur trade, gold rush, mining, military activity, logging and fishing, to bring us up to the present day. It was an informative and delightful finale. From the small museum shop I bought the illustrated book 'Petroglyphs of Alaska'.

Bidding a fond farewell to Jeff, Wrangell, and indeed Alaska, we climbed back on board the *Norwegian Sun* to prepare for our return to Vancouver, my small purchases of garnets, nestling in stone, safely packed away.

Back in Vancouver, we had just a few days left to do everything we wanted before boarding the Rocky Mountaineer for Calgary and the Gaults.

Rosie came to the hotel again, this time taking us to her home in Steveston to meet her husband Trevor and 'the boys', their much-loved dogs. I was asked to photograph them and then paint a double portrait when I got home.

After a seafood lunch at the waterfront, and seeing whale watch boats leaving the harbour, Trevor insisted I book myself a trip. There happened to be just one slot available. My one chance, so I thought I'd better secure it.

Our small party boarded the craft and off we set on our adventure, me keeping a bag of ginger close by and seasick bands on my wrist. The weather was lovely, but as we left Steveston harbour the motion was so violent I clutched the seat tightly and stared straight ahead grimly, wondering whatever I was doing there and how would I last the next five hours in these conditions.

Miraculously, after about 20 minutes everything became calm, the sea was smooth, and letting go of the seat I allowed my head to move and looked around. We were off to the Gulf Islands, and all was well.

Orca sightings can't be guaranteed, but after a short while we came across a pod of these beautiful animals. What is it about whales that stirs the heart so? It was an emotional moment as the family group passed around us, then under the boat. The biologist on board had lowered a hydrophone, an underwater microphone, so we could hear their whistling and singing as they kept contact with each other. It was a lovely experience. We watched the pod for about an hour before they swam off and we returned to Steveston harbour. Along the breakwater bald eagles and cormorants perched on wooden stakes as sentries on our return. Five hours richly spent.

As we approached the pontoon, Karen was there to meet me. Off we went to a peaceful waterside restaurant where, with Mum and the rest of Karen's family, we enjoyed a typically delicious seafood supper. The following day, Karen's husband Jim was leaving for Japan and we were departing for Calgary, Alberta, aboard the Rocky Mountaineer.

Waiting to board the train at Vancouver Pacific Central Station, we purchased a wooden box with the Rocky Mountaineer carved on its lid. It contained a wooden penknife – just the thing, we thought, for my brother John. We packed it away and promptly forgot all about it.

'All Abo-aaard!'

The whistle blew as we set off, and with uniformed porters lined up and waving, we chugged out of Vancouver on the Kicking Horse route for the Rockies and Calgary. It was to take two whole days, with an overnight stop at Kamloops.

As we settled into our seats in the Red Leaf carriage, I rather hankered for the 360 degree views and silver dining service of the upper deck Gold Leaf. However, as we progressed we became a happy band of travellers, sharing the open platform at the rear of the carriage for photography and making the most of our windows. Mum was very happy indeed as the food was excellent and, it seemed, continuous. In fact, by the second day I was beginning to dread the arrival of yet another platter of some delicacy or other. I wasn't moving around enough to do justice to it all.

We left the fertile fields of the Fraser River Valley, and as majestic peaks of the coastal mountains rose ahead of us we entered Fraser Canyon. Following the Thompson River we made for Kamloops, passing landmarks with descriptive names such as Hells Gate, Scuzzy Creek, Avalanche Alley, and Jaws of Death Gorge. We were in raw pioneer country.

The turbulent Jaws of Death Gorge is a favourite of white water rafters, and it was my luck to be on the platform as we passed this spot. A boat full of helmeted rafters 'hallooed' up to us and waved excitedly. Sadly I missed the osprey nest, but I gather the privileged Gold Leaf passengers were on its level and eyeball to eyeball with a sitting bird! Not to be outdone, I spotted a family of black bears clambering on a nearby slope above the track, and what turned out to be a handsome hoary marmot sitting regally on a ledge just a few feet from the train.

I have never ever seen so many trees. The land and mountains were blanketed in them and huge logs continually floated down rivers. Frequently, through gaps in the trees, we would glimpse bull-nosed lorries transporting great lengths of timber at high and noisy speeds along the trackside roads.

I had thought of Kamloops as a one-horse town, but arriving there we found it to be huge, but virtually all one-storey, spreading out over an area as large as New York. Thankfully we were staying overnight in a basic but comfortable hotel, after experiencing some real homespun hospitality and a lively show at the local town hall.

In old-fashioned pioneer dress, the good folks of Kamloops provided a truly magnificent and delicious homely feast for us. Obviously the highlight of their week, they put their hearts and souls into looking after us. Our dinner was followed by an extremely good show about the local stagecoach and not too successful bank robber, Billy Miner. With lots of shooting, singing and dancing, it depicted the flawed exploits of the soft-spoken bandit Billy, who is said to have coined the phrase 'Hands Up'. Settling near Kamloops in the early 1900s, his botched train robbery was the subject of the show. Expecting a big haul, they held up the wrong train and obtained only the equivalent of £15.50.

The following morning, bleary-eyed, we made an early start back to the train for the final leg to Calgary. Our ever-cheerful attendant was ready with hot drinks as off we set again.

We were now passing through quite different terrain. Sparkling lakes and rivers rejoicing in romantic wild west names: Shuswap, Salmon Arm and Eagle Creek greeted us en route to Revelstoke and the Columbia River. Chugging through Beavermouth, Kicking Horse Pass, and eventually Calgary, we were in real cowboy country. The last animal I happened to glimpse was a wary wolf, half hidden in bushes, about a hundred yards from the track. It was quite a thrilling moment, as we had passed the spot so quickly. I was fortunate to see it.

As we entered Calgary station, the whole carriage noticed a man in a smart business suit running alongside. It was Kevin, making sure he was on the spot to welcome us to his hometown. How good it was to see him again, and to be actually off the train after two long days. Knowing how thoughtful and kind Kevin is, we eagerly anticipated another series of exciting adventures, although I had no idea then how important for my work this visit would be.

Kevin whisked us off in his new super-luxury car, (the old one 'blew up' on the freeway, he announced) to the leafy suburb of Bonavista, where Rae and sweet little Ginger the dog were waiting to greet us. The front garden of their home had a most impressive and absolutely huge fir tree laden with cones. It was a magnificent sight, and Rae's pride and joy.

My hopes of missing my 60th birthday were dashed as a grand joint barbecue party had been organised for Kevin and me. Kevin's birthday being a few days before mine, it was a good excuse for a double celebration, and his family all gathered at Lake Bonavista Drive. It was such good fun, with the crowning central piece being a huge ice cream cake, decorated with hot air balloons, from Dairy Queen. Dear Kevin had remembered Mum mentioning how she always bought an ice cream cake for my birthday. I didn't bother to mention it had been the 1950s and about one quarter the size of Dairy Queen's offering.

Taking some time off work for special days out, our first planned trip was to be a scenic drive to upcountry Edmonton, home of the largest shopping mall in the world, and then on to the Rockies. However, plans are often subject to alteration. A close friend of Rae's had recently died, and so we attended a funeral in Edmonton first, giving the Mall a miss. As it turned out, a freak rain storm had flooded the Mall and it was shut that very day.

Right outside the funeral chapel in Edmonton, a hare jumped around on the lawn. In we went and sat discreetly at the back. The deceased's family must have wondered whoever those two English ladies were sitting at the back of the church, quietly paying their respects at Mother's funeral.

After doing our duty, we set off on a marathon trip to the Mountains. Kevin was keen to show off his smart new car. Making our way across to Jasper, then down the Icefields Parkway, we gazed in absolute amazement at the soaring beauty and splendour of the peaks around us, with a clear blue sky, snow-capped mountain, huge lakes and, seemingly, never-ending swathes of fir trees surrounding us for hours. It was all quite stunning, and anything we had seen from the Rocky Mountaineer train trip was put well in the shade. The magnificence of the Rockies is almost beyond description.

En route we stopped for a break at lovely Lake Moraine, where the water sparkled a glorious turquoise under snow-capped mountains. On reaching Banff and Sulphur Mountain, we took the gondola cable car up to the viewing area. Carefully avoiding mountain sheep and golden banded ground squirrels, we gazed at the veritable sweep of panoramic views surrounding us.

On reaching Lake Louise, Kevin refused to get out of the car but parked to let me walk over to the lake. I could see his point. The traffic and crowds of tourists made it an uncomfortable experience after the peace and tranquillity of Lake Moraine. However, I had to see it, and it is of course a fabulous lake, with the famous hotel and its mountain backdrop towering over it amidst a multitude of fir trees.

At Bow Falls, the day was beginning to take its toll on Mum and Rae, so Kevin and I left them near the car and made our way up to the waterfall. When we came back, the weary pair were walking towards the car, arms linked, singing, 'Show me the way to go home, I'm tired and I want to go to bed...' A First Nations family, trying not to smile too much, passed discreetly by.

We stopped to watch magnificent elks feeding by the roadside and, as the night drew in, we made our long way home. It was about two in the morning when we arrived back at Lake Bonavista Drive. We, or rather Kevin, had driven over six hundred kilometres, keeping ourselves awake by singing loudly most of the way home. Kevin's rendering of Good King Wenceslas was especially memorable, with emphasis on the 'Brrring me FLESH and brrring me wine, brrring me pine logs hither!'

With immaculate timing, Kevin had planned an intriguing visit to the world famous Tyrrell, a Dinosaur Museum, in the mysterious and barren Badlands. Exceptionally impressive, the Tyrrell is always shown with pride to visiting foreign dignitaries, and you could see why. It is a dinosaur paradise. The terrain here forms a strange, almost menacing landscape. Huge rock formations bulge in such a desolate manner, yet it was here we were later transfixed by a deeply moving performance of the Canadian Badlands Choral Passion Play, held in the amphitheatre at Drumheller.

This outside event took over three hours, and during it we must have had every sort of weather. The organisers, knowing how conditions can change hourly, were well prepared. Waterproof ponchos were purchased for one dollar, then Mum was comfortably transported to her seat in a buggy. We were transfixed by an amazingly moving and realistic performance, but were amused at the same time by ground squirrels squeaking and scampering from burrow to burrow.

The final scene took us by surprise. We suddenly became aware of angelic figures appearing, arms outstretched, high on the bleak hills above us. The sincerity and beauty of the whole performance reduced Mum to tears, and especially at the end when the participants came over to greet us. I wondered how long it would take the ground squirrels to recover, though. During the Crucifixion scenes, which were accompanied by loud drum rolls of thunder and lightning, the little animals took their chance and scurried, nervously squeaking, in and out of their holes in the ground. As we returned home, we were all rather thoughtful and quiet for a change.

Being Stampede time, many of the big business firms in Calgary hold family parties. Wearing cowboy hats, Kevin and I took Brent and Jessica, his niece and nephew, to his firm's party, the likes of which I have never experienced before. It took the form of a mini-stampede, with entertainments for the children and abundant food and drink on a 'help yourself anytime' basis. It was all great fun on a super, hot day. Towards evening, the children were lassoed and tamed as we prepared to make our weary way home.

The arrangements continued to be impeccable. The following day, after an early start, we made our way south to reach Fort Macleod, the museum of the North West Mounted Police. The site had been in active service from 1884 until 1920 when it moved to its permanent headquarters in nearby Lethbridge. Here at the old Fort, and seated amongst the original timber buildings, we were treated to impressive displays of horsemanship, including the famous Musical Ride. The few onlookers couldn't fail to be impressed by the precision of the horses and their riders, all in extreme heat and wearing full red dress. Walking around the wooden museum, we enjoyed a very intimate insight into the daily life of the original police force.

Next stop was Head-Smashed-In Buffalo Jump. On the vast hot plains of Alberta we watched a Naming Ceremony, followed by celebratory dances in full native dress. It was the high spot of my visit, and the richest source of material for my work. I couldn't believe so few people were there, but we, the lucky few, witnessed an incredible spectacle that day, although thankfully seated under awnings to shade us from the scorching sun.

A white man, a university professor, was being honoured for his work with the Blackfoot nation. He and his family sat on the ground as an elder proceeded to make a very long speech indeed in the Blackfoot language. Every so often I could recognise a word or two, the most memorable being 'Bill Clinton'! By his side the old man had a large pile of blankets, obviously a traditional and obligatory gift from the new member of the tribe. After the speech, the newly-admitted man, adorned in full-feathered headpiece, ceremonially paraded together with his family and other tribal members. All were in full dress; one as a bison, in a genuine skin and head, making an impressive spectacle.

This ceremony was followed by a series of the most beautiful Blackfoot dances, some extremely energetic, whilst others were very deliberate, but all performed in the open under a burning sun. The traditional War Dance, Men's Fancy Dance, and The Old Style Chicken Dance, performed by young men, and all quite distinctive in their own way, really inspired me. The War Dance was rather terrifying with its menacing beat, whilst the modern Fancy Dance was all frantic swirls and ribbons, and then the Old Style Chicken Dance was a realistic rendition of a strutting, pecking bird. A Blackfoot Princess moved in a stately fashion in the Women's Traditional Dance, and then a serious young woman, with 365 bells attached to her dress, performed the ancient healing Jingle Dress dance, believed originally to be from the Ojibwe. The final dance was a beautiful and graceful rendition of the Women's Fancy Dance. Although there were others that afternoon, these were the ones I wanted to eventually represent, and which seemed to be a good cross section of male and female dances, ancient and modern.

The proceedings ended with a mass dance, and we were all invited to participate. I was a little hesitant, whilst Kevin and Rae stayed firmly put, but Mum surprised us all by being one of the first up to join the long line of First Nation performers. She entered into the spirit of it all completely! As we danced, the aroma of barbecued buffalo steaks wafted our way. Finishing with a taste of Saskatoon berry soup, we stayed on to listen to a talk about the historic importance of wolves to the tribe, and a short film about traditional buffalo hunting.

Traditionally, young boys would be sent out to find newborn wolf cubs before their eyes had even opened and bring them back to the camp, so the very first thing the cubs would see would be the people. They then became hunting and guard dogs, as well as babysitters, looking after the young children in case they wandered from the camp. They were even harnessed to stretchers and used to transport belongings and babies.

Before saying goodbye to our hosts, we visited their little shop to purchase some gorgeous beadwork, and then made our way home. Down on the hot plains, a group of tepees stood bright white against the blue sky.

That night, back in Calgary, we experienced a major storm. The local television had already advised people to take cover in a basement area if necessary. It all seemed rather exciting at the time!

As the evening progressed, the sky turned a weird yellowish colour, then darkened as the storm approached. I felt like Dorothy holding her little dog Toto in the Wizard of Oz. 'We aren't in Clifton now, Ginger.'

At one point we heard the strangest sound, as if a huge ship was heaving and groaning in a heavy sea. 'Whatever was that?' we all said, wide-eyed.

Eventually, and quite abruptly, the storm subsided and we cautiously peeped out of the front door. To our horror, we saw Rae's beautiful fir tree wrenched out of the ground like a corkscrew and lying strewn across the road, cones everywhere. This must have been the weird noise we had heard. As I looked closely, I noticed something glinting under the blanket of branches.

'I think there is a car underneath.' And so there was. The next-door neighbours' rather smart four-by-four was almost completely enveloped by the tree. 'I hope there isn't anyone in it.'

'Oh dear!' exclaimed Kevin. He was an attorney, and had visions of a big claim.

As the sky brightened and things calmed down, folks from all over the neighbourhood arrived to see the catastrophe. It was quite a local talking point. Luckily the neighbours weren't that concerned about their vehicle, which luckily was unscathed. They had a much bigger and messier problem. The violent rainstorm had flooded their basement living area, and would take a long time to put right.

The next morning dawned bright and clear as a city works lorry, together with a large crane, arrived. Hard hats donned, the lumberjacks sawed away at the tree and cleared it away with speedy efficiency.

It was then time for Ginger's morning walk, so off we went to inspect the area. It became apparent that a tornado had sped down the road, uprooted the fir tree as if a cork from a bottle, then turned at a right angle, carrying on along the road opposite. Fir cones were strewn right along that road, whilst to our left, the other roads and sidewalks were clean as a whistle. What a phenomenon!

Rae and Mum enjoyed a quiet day at home, and with Kevin at work I made my way to the Glenbow Museum in town. Featuring the history of the West and its cultural heritage, the Glenbow was exhibiting paintings of Charlie Russell and Frederic Remington. Dating from around the 1880s, their paintings are a truly evocative expression of the Old West.

The most famous of the two, Charlie Russell, had worked as a cattle wrangler, becoming known as 'Kid Russell the Cowboy Artist'. His work powerfully illustrates the interaction between indigenous peoples, Mounties, cowboys and animals. Remington became very attached to the Blackfoot Nation and had said, 'They are a fine outfit, those Blackfeet'. He was especially fond of painting different types of frontier people.

I could have spent all day just looking at these wonderful works, but time was limited and I had noticed that there was a talk by 'Charlie Russell' scheduled for that morning. I had about half an hour to sit in as an actor, donned in cowboy gear, gave a most realistic representation of Russell's life. I had to leave before it had finished, and only just made it in time to the Mall where Kevin was waiting to take me to see his office, followed by lunch, way up in the Calgary Tower.

From the Tower's circular restaurant there is a panoramic view of the city, and we could look over to the Stampede site and Saddledome where we would spend the next two days.

After lunch, a spot of retail therapy was on the itinerary, Kevin seriously needing to update his old fashioned, slightly 'ten gallon', cowboy hat. A visit to the traditional cowboy store, Riley and McCormick, was absolutely essential before the Stampede. You can't miss this store, with a full-size model of a horse standing outside. Watching people going by, I realised that many Calgary folk dress in cowboy boots, shirt and hat all year round. The difference being that at Stampede time, it is all brand new! I noted the crease marks.

After a lot of trying on, we eventually found suitable well-fitting hats; then, wearing them, of course, went off to celebrate with coffee in the lush and relaxing oasis of nearby Devon Gardens, a tranquil covered water garden in the centre of town.

Our last two days in Calgary were spent at the Stampede. Kevin's firm, a large oil concern, was a joint sponsor of the event that year, and so he had managed to acquire excellent tickets for the four of us. We arrived, suitably attired, and joined the crowds making their way in. Nearly everyone was wearing a cowboy hat of one type or another, and we weren't even allowed into the arena until we had yelled a very loud 'YeeHaa!' In fact we had to do it twice, as our first attempt wasn't convincing enough.

The amazing thing about the Stampede is its totally happy family atmosphere. The huge alcohol-free campus had no jarring notes to spoil the holiday fun. Aromatic food, a funfair, fresh fruit drink outlets and incredible raffle stalls were the order of the day. Daily prizes weren't just a basket of fruit, weekend at a spa or cuddly toy. Here you could win a house, the latest car, a trailer or state of the art motorbike, and every night the prize-winners were announced on local TV.

The evening finals of the Chuckwagon Races were the main feature of our first visit, and this event has to be one of the most thrilling to watch. Traditionally the chuckwagons were home to the pioneering cowboys when on the range, and it is so easy to imagine their evenings by the camp fire, leisurely strumming guitars and talking amongst themselves, with the cattle lowing nearby. However, this tranquillity ended when they headed into town. With a 'hootering and a hollering', the men would make for the nearest saloon as fast as their wagons would take them. Last one in paid for the first round!

Modern chuckwagons are much lighter and safer than their heavier, well-laden predecessors, but the enthusiasm and excitement is surely as great, especially with fifty thousand dollars to be won! Each wagon has four fine horses, and their terrific speed and energy is quite something to watch as they race around the track.

After nine heats, with speed and penalties taken into consideration, the overall winner was announced. He stood on the podium amidst a spectacular show of fireworks, alongside a brand-new white pickup truck, obviously in addition to his cash prize. He deserved it!

The evening ended with the spectacular Calgary Stampede Grandstand Show on a huge stage. This was truly dazzling entertainment. 'The Spirit of the West' featured a hoedown, rock 'n' roll, First Nations tableau, and finished with a heartfelt rendering of 'O Canada'. What a night.

The much-anticipated Grand Finals day was next, and another gloriously sunny morning! With hats at a jaunty angle and a loud 'YeeHaa', we took our seats near to the front of the arena. Finals

Day is very special. Mounted Police wearing their traditional red dress uniforms mingled with cowgirls and cowboys as they proudly sauntered around in their best bib and tucker. As I settled down with a delicious liquorice ice cream, the programme began.

You need to be young and very fit to participate in this day's events. After each round, many cowboys limped or were carried off by the Rodeo Clowns. These clowns are an essential part of the spectacle. They literally clown around during some events, whilst others use their bodies and wits to shield fallen cowboys from angry bulls or stallions.

We watched in awe as the day's exciting programme unfolded. After the Grand Entry came the Championship rounds: Saddle Bronco Championship, followed by Tie Down Roping of Calves, Bareback Championship, Steer Wrestling, and the most incredible of all, Bull Riding. In between each round, the clowns entertained us after the usual prizegiving and fireworks.

Late in the day we made our weary way home, but by now we were thinking of our return journey to the UK. It was all coming to an end, and much too soon. We had to make a major effort to pack our suitcases. I say 'suitcases' as we had to buy another in Sears department store to accommodate our increasing number of souvenirs and gifts.

In true Plains fashion, a rapid change of weather delayed our departure. As we reached the airport, a severe flash storm closed everything down for an hour or so. Rae and Kevin stayed to have a cup of coffee with us, and then we had to say goodbye to our generous, good friends.

The shop at Calgary airport is especially interesting with its fine range of First Nation souvenirs. I was first through the security area, waiting for Mum and enjoying a leisurely look, when a tall serious man, wearing blue disposable gloves, approached me.

'This isn't the time for shopping, Ma'am.' I looked round to see poor Mum, red-faced and flustered, unpacking her holdall as several security staff looked on. How strange, I thought...until we found the by now long-forgotten penknife from the Rocky Mountaineer. Oh dear. Seeing us seriously shocked, they took pity on us as and kindly offered to let me go back to check in the holdall. I had to run all the way there and back as, due to the storm, time was getting short. However, when all was correctly dealt with, we boarded the plane, relieved and very light-handed, thinking about the Gaults and if we would all meet up again.

At home, my mind was immediately on a new project. The next few months I kept my head down, and produced a series of paintings inspired by this wonderful visit to Alaska and Canada.

In November I was invited once more to show my work at the Bristol Guild of Applied Art. I hadn't realised what a following the North American Indian has in this country, and because of extensive press exposure by the Guild's PR people, I was extremely busy. It was very encouraging.

On a family level, we were coming into an exciting period. Each of my son's wives produced a son within weeks of each other. Jack arrived at the end of November, with Christopher and Dickie following in January. How lovely for them all to be so close. Suddenly, there were six grandchildren!

Trying to think up something different for Motivation's Christmas Card selection that year, I came up with 'Christmas Candles'. Colourful and festive, it seemed to sell well for them.

CANADA AGAIN (2005)

W ITH THE NEWLY ARRIVED babies it was such a happy time for all of us, but the year was eventually to be a sad one. My darling Auntie Joyce, Mum's younger sister, died that April. Her life, though, had been a miracle. Born in 1923 with a hole in her heart, she was always very ill, but not enough was known about the condition then and so it wasn't diagnosed. After her second child, Avenell, she became dangerously ill. Very soon after, she had her lifesaving and, at that time in the 1950s, pioneering operation to repair the damage. The change in her was indeed miraculous. I watched as she actually ran up the slope from the beach to the Promenade in Whitley Bay, and this was the same young woman who had been unable even to walk down the slope without holding me tightly.

Her final two years had become very difficult, and she finally succumbed after a brave 80 years. I still can't believe she isn't there at the end of the phone. 'Howay the Lads', we used to say when we rang each other up.

Avenell, who had recently emigrated to Australia with her husband and son, travelled back and forth many times during her mother's final illness, but was unable to make the funeral. She had, after all, been with her mother when she was needed most. Mum and I promised to go over to Australia the following spring.

Some years previously I had befriended the Toths, a Canadian family from Edmonton who were staying next door during the summer holidays. Ellen, a specialist in diabetes, was attending a course at Southmead Hospital. Her nine-year-old daughter, Jennifer, a budding and enthusiastic artist, came round to me for a few pastel lessons. We kept in touch over the years, and when I was in Calgary with the Gaults, Ellen Toth had hoped I could visit, but there wasn't enough time. However, this year, an invitation arrived for me to spend a few weeks with the Toths in the summer. I accepted immediately.

'Do bring your pastels. We would love you to paint our house and the view!'

In July, pastels duly packed, I flew to Calgary once more, this time to be collected by Ellen and her husband Charles, who were returning from a trip to their beloved Mountains. We were so excited to meet up again. I squeezed into the well-packed vehicle and we chatted away as we motored north. Stopping briefly in Red Deer for coffee and muffins, we eventually arrived in Edmonton during the early evening.

The Toths lived on the very outskirts of town on old Indian land. The views from the backyard were typically wild Canadian, but sadly soon to be lost through housing developments, hence the request to paint it. I quickly set to, with daughter Jennifer's easel assembled in the middle of the quiet road, prepared to paint the house.

The sun beat down, and despite my large sunhat and cool shirt, my colour quickly turned from its usual pale pink to blotchy lobster, and I soon realised this endeavour would have to be finished at home. Anyway, there I would be cool and undisturbed which, I was beginning to realise, is an almost essential prerequisite to my work. So, sketching as much as possible as the day cooled slightly, I took several photographs and packed up.

My next few weeks were spent in this festival city during a lovely hot summer. Edmonton sure knows how to party! It seemed as if there was something happening on every corner of town, and I soon learnt to find my way around when Ellen was working.

I was keen to visit a famous museum, but had trouble finding it. Ellen dropped me off on the way to work, and I arrived at what I thought was the correct place, but signs pointed to a museum with a different name. Beginning to panic slightly, I thought I was well and truly lost, until I realised it was indeed the very place I was looking for. The name had changed. Queen Elizabeth II had recently visited and, in her honour, it was not now the Provincial Museum of Alberta, which I had been vainly looking for, but The Royal Alberta Museum. As I was soon to discover, it is a spectacular showcase of local human and natural history.

I was particularly moved by one exhibit, a large meteorite displayed on a wide plinth. This had been the property of a First Nation Tribe, who believed they would always be safe so long as they had the protection of this heavenly body. However, missionaries came along and eventually confiscated it. It appears the tribe soon disintegrated through this interference. How very sad they couldn't be left alone and just keep it. What harm could this lump of rock do?

Edmonton was celebrating 'Klondike Days', and I was there for the Grand Parade. Ellen's husband Charles, originally from Hungary and affectionately known as Karcsi, took me along for the impressive celebrations. We planted ourselves on the sidewalk, enjoying a front row position on one of the main roads in the centre of town. The Parade went on for hours and was an astounding spectacle of floats, processions of First Nation people, brass bands, clowns, cowboys, and mega trucks with the biggest wheels I have ever seen in my life. Flags were waved and we all cheered until the last float passed by. Such a happy, family friendly, celebration, which seemed especially Canadian. Soft drink cans filled the rubbish bins and the pavements were so clean.

Karcsi's nephew Reni was soon due to arrive from Hungary, so we set off to do some shopping in a huge supermarket nearby. Wheeling a massive trolley, Karcsi proceeded to buy an industrial sized box of healthy cereal which he thought would suit me (it did and was scrumptious), a sack of dog food for old Paw, and a bed for Reni!

Reni arrived, and Karcsi and I took him to Hawrelak Park where another global event was being held. We went our different ways and arranged to meet up later. The park was heaving with people from all over the world. Performances from First Nation peoples, as well as African, South American, European and the Far East were held on stages between rows of catering and display tents. It was a fascinating melee and, for me, another source of marvellous ideas for portraits.

Walking into a tent selling leather and beaded jewellery, I was confronted by a fearsome-looking Native Canadian. Very dark skinned, with long hair, buckskin jacket and wearing sunglasses, he made a rather terrifying sight. I tried not to stare, but I knew he would make the most terrific portrait. Camera to the ready, I plucked up courage and approached. This was a public place after all.

'May I take your photograph for a portrait? I am an artist and love to paint people.'

He turned his face towards me. 'Yes, of course. Do you want me to look dangerous?'.

We both laughed. 'No, but please would you take your glasses off?'

He introduced himself as Aaron Lee, and the photo was taken. I bought one of his leather and beaded pieces, and we said good-bye. He was absolutely charming.

A First Nation Dance group was starting to perform on a nearby stage and, as I made my way over, another fascinating individual caught my eye. A short elderly man, sporting a multi-coloured jacket, pigtails and feathered hat was talking to a crop-haired young man. I waited until they had finished their conversation, and as I went over the old man started to sway in time to the beat of the dance group, moving from one foot to another, stamping on the ground. He looked as if he had 'attitude', so I approached warily and asked the usual question.

There was a moment's pause, it seemed much longer, and then he said, 'Mmm. Yep.' This was the Blackfoot Elder, Francis Bad Eagle. He suited this name, I thought, but wondered later if he was actually called Francis Black Eagle! He was a generous model, and remains Francis Bad Eagle for his portrait. When I asked, in my ignorance, whether he was from the Blackfeet Tribe, he very sternly replied 'BlackFOOT!'

The young man was still nearby, but didn't seem to me to be such an interesting subject. Not wanting him to feel ignored, I asked his name and whether I could take his photo as well. This was Alan, and he agreed. Photos taken, I thanked them both and went over to watch the tribal dancing. Very soon, Alan was sitting by my side and obviously wanted to talk. He told me he was a Métis Mohawk searching for his roots, and Francis Bad Eagle was helping him. He was such a delightful young man. I often think of him and eventually really enjoyed producing his likeness. Thank goodness I took his photograph that day. The portrait is a poignant reminder of Alan's struggle with his past, and possibly his future.

I already knew that the word Métis meant 'half caste' or 'cross breed' from old Western films and history. These people were the offspring and descendants of French and Scottish fur traders with Native Canadians.

A few days later, I came across the 'The Raven's Eye' near the main Edmonton Art Gallery. Its owner was Kimberley Bird, herself Métis, and from her wide range of First Nation Art I bought a leather beaded choker, only to find it had been made by Aaron!

In a glass counter cabinet lay a tiny pair of elk skin moccasins – obviously for a new born baby. Kimberley took them out for me. As I gently turned them over, I detected a faint smell of woodsmoke. 'Home smoked' said Kimberley. Goodness, what a find. These darling bootees are now on display in my antique glass cabinet along with other special treasures.

Nearby, under the glass counter, was an exquisitely carved wooden hummingbird. This was made by another Métis artist, a James Martin who had carved a delicate feather on the reverse alongside his signature. Kimberley surprised me by saying he was homeless and carried his carvings around in a black bin bag. The work was so fine and reminded me of the hummingbirds we had seen in Alaska, so I made another purchase. On a later visit to the gallery, Kimberley told me that the poor chap's bin bag had been stolen soon after, and he had lost all his work. At least the hummingbird is safe.

Dear Karcsi, he just loved getting away to the mountains. Bank Holiday weekend was coming up, so he desperately tried to find some accommodation for us. It was rather late in the day, and he spent hours on the phone and computer. Everywhere in the Rockies appeared to be booked up. Were we too late?

At last, success! He had found something suitable in Hinton, offering limited bed and breakfast accommodation, but it would have to do. The following weekend, in bright sunshine, and with nephew Reni and the old dog Paw in tow, we crossed the prairies towards the Rockies. We made a happy band, with country music playing on the car radio, speeding along on our mini holiday. Stopping for lunch at the remote Lake Obed picnic site, we were entertained by eagles calling to each other across the water. It was moving, and so peaceful.

Hinton was really hard to find, and eventually, arriving in the dark at around 11pm, the anxious owners were beginning to think we were not coming after all. The owners, a Canadian with his Mexican wife, had themed their homestead as a Mexican hacienda. It seemed quite surreal, but was comfortable and very clean.

Unfortunately there was only one bedroom, so Reni and I took up residence either end of a large sitting room / diner, but as we entered we thought we were sharing it with another. Leaning on a sideboard, as if asleep, head on hands and covered by his very large hat, was a small dozing man. Momentarily nonplussed, we approached, then realised this was a mannequin, with the biggest sombrero I have ever seen! We became rather fond of him during our stay.

My bed was one end of the room, with nephew at the other and a screen between us for privacy. It all worked well, and the next morning we tucked into a breakfast of delicious strawberries and blueberries, followed by a stack of hot pancakes with maple syrup.

We enjoyed memorable excursions from our Hacienda that weekend. One was a rugged trek up Whistler Mountain at Jasper, where our reward was sweeping, panoramic views, but it was so windy we could hardly stand upright.

Another fabulous trip was to gorgeous Lake Maligne, with a view to making a Trail Hike. On reaching this incredibly beautiful lake, we were told the longer Pearl Trail had just been shut since two aggressive grizzlies had menaced an earlier party.

Setting off on the shorter Opal Trail, Ellen said, 'We'll send Paw ahead of us so any hungry bear would get her first, then Reni can follow with the bear bell.' I didn't argue, and kept very close to our party. We completed the walk without any confrontations, although the poor old dog ran into a fast-flowing stream. Weakening, she was completely unable to get herself out, and it took a huge effort to pull her back onto the steep bank. Dear old Paw, unconcerned, resuming her role as bear bait, trotted on quite happily and, puffing away, we followed.

Our walk being shorter than planned gave us time for a boat ride along the lake to the mysterious and lovely Spirit Island. It was a peaceful place where you could just imagine native canoes sliding in and out of the still waters.

On our way back to our Hacienda, we visited the Miette Hot Springs near Jasper. These are the hottest natural mineral springs in the Rockies, and there we bathed lazily, high up amidst snow-topped mountains and fir trees with eagles circling above us. It was a magical few hours, and we ended the day with a pizza supper in a log cabin restaurant.

The next morning our Mexican hostess produced another filling breakfast, and well stocked up, we left for home, via Athabasca and the Sunwapta Falls to the Columbia Icefields Parkway. On arriving at the Icefields, a snowmobile took us as far as we could go, and there, on the pristine crackly glacier, we were able to explore and drink crystal clear meltwater flowing down from one of the many rivulets. Walking on solid ice and breathing in the crisp pure air under a blue sky was a chilly, slippery, and thrilling experience.

In a township on our way back to Edmonton, we stopped at Smithy's Diner for supper. To me, this was a typically North American experience. The long, fairly empty main street with low buildings either side led us to the diner where a sign creaked in the evening breeze.

I couldn't resist fish and chips - with gravy on the side!

On one of my days in town I caught a bus to an area with many indigenous art galleries. Hoping to find the Bear Claw Gallery, and asking for directions, I came across a First Nation lady called Meadow Soloway. Meadow was immediately helpful, offering to show me where to get off the bus as she lived very near the Gallery. She told me she worked for a transgender charity in Edmonton and asked what I did. On hearing I was an artist, she took a small passport-sized photo out of her purse and asked if I would paint a picture of her partner, Carson Otter, a good-looking young native Canadian, and send it to her. This little photo, not much to work on, looked well-worn and precious, so I said I would do my best and took her address. She then introduced me to two First Nation women sitting in front of us, and we all chatted until it was time to get off.

The gallery was close to the bus stop and Meadow escorted me in. She was a quite tall, striking lady, and when she told me the two we had been talking to on the bus were men and not women, I began to think about her, but said nothing. I eventually said goodbye to kind Meadow and carried on looking around this wonderful gallery. I found some small stones painted with animals and birds, all of spiritual significance to the First Nation Peoples, and chose some for friends and family back home. The one with Raven I kept for myself. Raven, the clever trickster.

That evening, telling Ellen and Karcsi about yet another fascinating encounter, Ellen offered to make sure Meadow received the picture and I should send it to her. Aboriginal people tend to 'up sticks' and move around so Ellen would make sure it reached its destination.

Ellen's home help offered to take me out for a day and suggested the nearby Ukrainian replica village, and then on to Elk Island. There is a large Ukrainian community in Canada, and after my recent trip to the very land itself it sounded rather wonderful. It was indeed a delightful place, with 'inhabitants' in costume playing out the roles of the original Ukrainian settlers. It certainly appeared to be a very true representation of Ukrainian life in the 19th century. The food was authentic, and we tucked into a hearty lunch before making for the extensive nature reserve, Elk Island. Staying safely in our four-by-four for most of the afternoon, we were soon accompanied by a massive bison. It came through the forest and hoofed alongside us with steam rising from its dense brown coat.

We eventually came to a lake where, in the distance, we could see a large flock of rare Trumpeter swans, and deciding to risk actually getting out of the vehicle, we reached a lookout. Standing on a wooden platform, I scanned the still water through fixed binoculars to see a wading moose with its calf alongside. It was a beautiful moment.

Working as a doctor with the Aboriginal people, Ellen was desperate to find a good Pow Wow for me to visit before I went home. After a fair amount of research, the undaunted Ellen found one, to be held soon, at a place called Enoch, and on the assigned day we set off. Enoch proved elusive, and after going round in circles and getting lost we eventually came across a First Nations family, also apparently lost. They had stopped their four-by-four and were making anxious calls on their mobile phones. We teamed up and eventually found a rough track which thankfully led to the Pow Wow.

We parked and made for the main meeting place when I came across Alana, the Dance Troupe leader I had seen in Hawrelak Park. She was putting on her traditional outfit. I said 'hello' and, introducing herself, Alana said I could photograph her as long as I was quick, as she was preparing for the dancing.

Ellen pointed out various places we could not enter. These were private meeting places for the men only. As we walked up to the arena, a voice called out 'Doctor!' and a distinguished elderly lady greeted us. She was covered in furs and exquisite beadwork from head to toe, and was obviously someone of importance in the community. This was the delightful Mary, a Stoney Sioux. 'One of my patients,' said Ellen.

The main site was quite a spectacle. Tepees were placed at intervals, and the whole area was a throng of First Nations Peoples, as well as Native Americans from south of the border. Amongst the thousands of indigenous people that afternoon I counted only about four white faces. What a privilege.

The sound of pounding music led us in the direction of the huge main tent. We entered and took a seat on one of the tiered benches. Around the edge of the main arena groups of musicians, in turn, energetically performed traditional drumming. This was a serious competition, with each group attempting to outdo the rest with their intense efforts. Men, women and children in full traditional dress paraded around the arena. Young people were being presented to their Chiefs and, in celebration, beautiful dancing was performed. I can hardly believe, even now, that I actually witnessed this tremendously moving and important event.

For a few hours during the afternoon, I walked around and met many delightful people. Everyone I asked, bar one, gave me permission to photograph them. The one who refused was a very young and rather beautiful Sioux boy. "No' he said, his little face looking quite stern. His parents were really disappointed and tried to persuade him, but he was quite adamant, so I photographed his very cute baby sister instead.

The traditional homelands of the Cree and Stoney people are found in this area, and coming across a young boy in full Cree dress, I asked his name. His voice was so very quiet and gentle I could hardly hear him, and had to ask many times, but eventually caught his name as Tegan.

Some teenage Stoney girls passed by, the most striking being Regina. I photographed her distinguished profile and, giggling with her friends, she loved the result.

Then there was the magnificent spectacle of Dennis and his son, another Tegan, fully dressed in their Sioux outfits. This day offered me riches I could never have imagined, and I felt humbled to be allowed to be part of it, and to be able to record these kind and beautiful people. My Saturday mornings at the Vandyke cinema had been well worthwhile.

Ellen and I ended our day buying trinkets, including two dream-catchers of feather and deerskin and some silver earrings from a Navajo lady. Dreamcatchers should hang in a bedroom window, to catch the good dreams to keep and allow the bad to pass through and away.

It was soon time to return to the UK and I was very sad to go, as I felt so at home with the Toths and really loved Edmonton. Leaving Edmonton, I had to change planes at Calgary, and in the queue there my head started to throb sickeningly. It was to be a full-blown migraine, and I spent the whole flight lying down, luckily near the loo, with the kind Air Canada hostess doing what she could. As we approached Heathrow in the early morning, it began to subside.

Katie was bringing Mum to meet me, and we were being driven to Biggleswade for a few days before going home. However, there was a hitch. My luggage, booked through from Edmonton, failed to arrive. I waited and waited, until the last person, plus luggage, from my flight had disappeared, and with no sign of my case the conveyor belt then stopped. For all I knew, it could be in Newfoundland, New York or New Guinea, and still feeling rather weak from the migraine, I couldn't work up too much concern. I was sure it would turn up sometime, and anyway, I had my camera on me so nothing valuable would be lost. Meanwhile I was given an official form to fill out, and had almost completed it when a noise made us turn round. The conveyor belt had suddenly juddered into life, and trundling along on it was a lone suitcase, mine, leaning on a large brown paper parcel!

On arrival at Sally and Peter's in Old Warden, it was announced that friends were about to turn up with their two Labradors for me to paint. I didn't know whether to feel grateful or disappointed. I was exhausted and not quite my perky self. However, the Sherriffs arrived plus two energetic dogs: Spudley, the older white female, and Harry, a jet-black young dog. I had my work cut out. Pure white and full black are not the easiest to capture.

Peter and his Labrador Max came with us as we ran round the adjoining field, taking photographs whenever possible. All three dogs were so excited it was difficult to keep control, but I eventually managed to take a few 'possibles', and mudcaked, with the light fading, we plodded back to The Firs for some welcome tea. It was good to meet these lovely dogs and get to know them, so the portraits I eventually produced would capture their spirit and personality rather than just a likeness.

These portraits were an interesting and valuable exercise. Spudley was such a pale creamy white there was a danger she would look transparent and disappear into the background if I didn't accentuate the darker contrasts in her thick fur. With Harry, he would have looked so very flat if I didn't introduce other colours into his glossy black coat. Luckily both portraits turned out well, and the Sherriffs were happy

As soon as I returned home, I completed two pastel paintings of the Toth house, front and rear views. My next task was to portray Carson Otter from the tiny passport image. Happily I managed it and, hoping it would please Meadow, I packed it up carefully, together with the precious tiny photo and the two house views, and dispatched them by airmail to Ellen.

The Toths loved both their views, but I had to wait a long time before hearing from Meadow. Poor Ellen, with her huge medical workload as well, had many weeks of detective work to locate Meadow, who indeed proved elusive, but at long last the connection was made and emails eventually arrived from them both.

From Ellen:

'Yes it is done!!!!!!!!!!!!

When she called this time, I did not tarry. I was at her place within 2 hours!'

And then sadly from Meadow:

linda hi its been a long long wait for this photo not that it matters, as things have changed over this period of time. and yes i am on my own again but that's okay. but i would still love to have his picture, as he is no longer in this world with us he past on (died in a car accident) so its been a very trying time for me this past year, and at least i would have that as a memory and reminder that he still exists in my life even if i have to continue on my own.

as always meadow soloway'

Soon followed by:

'well how are you? me I am doing just fine well I finally received the picture gosh that is a spitin image you done I love it and I know

his grandmother will appreciate it as I will be delivering it to her this weekend up in Calgary p.s... thank you so much.' (sic)

What a tragic end, and how strange to have met Meadow that day.

For much too short a time, Bristol hosted another museum and one of great importance. This was The British Empire and Commonwealth Museum, located in the old engine works at Temple Meads Station Approach. Such wonderful exhibitions, all beautifully curated, but sadly in the wrong location. The phrase 'location, location, location' was never more apt. Sadly, passing trade was virtually nil in this traffic-congested, fume-filled thoroughfare on one of Bristol's busiest roads. Passengers dragging their suitcases, shoppers making for Bath or commuters to London were hardly likely to linger, but for those few years the city could proudly boast a museum of international standard, and one especially meaningful to Bristol with its historic involvement in the Slave Trade era.

For eighteen months or so the museum presented a major Pow Wow Exhibition, and I was invited to show my six portraits of the Blackfoot dancers. These, the organisers hoped, would encourage visitors up to the main display area. I felt very honoured. This superb museum eventually left Bristol to make its home in London.

My Christmas Bazaar later that year was bustling as always. Motivation had included my new design 'Just Looking!' in their card selection. I used a rather frayed old robin tree decoration to hang opposite a red glass bauble so I would get the right reflection. I didn't want anyone saying 'It wouldn't look like that.'

SINGAPORE AND AUSTRALIA (2006)

I T WAS SPRING. OUR exotic journey to Australia had arrived, and we were in a jolly mood as we set off for Heathrow on a National Express bus. Arriving at our Terminal, I led the way, both passports in hand, pushing a trolley piled with luggage as Mum, together with her stick, brought up the rear.

'Just follow me,' I puffed. 'Singapore Air check-in is very near the entrance.'

I hauled the trolley into the Departure Hall and made for the nearby check-in desks and produced our passports. I was getting my breath back and turned round to smile at Mum, but she was nowhere to be seen. 'What the...?.'

Mother and stick had completely disappeared. Really, how could she possibly get lost in the few yards between the entrance and check-in? As the minutes ticked by, I began to feel a little embarrassed; then a wave of panic hit as concerned staff looked on, and others took my place in the queue. After about twenty minutes or so I was beginning to think we wouldn't even reach the plane, never mind Australia. Where had she gone? We then had the indignity of a message being read out over the airport intercom.

'Would Mrs Constance Fry please come immediately to the Singapore Airline Check-in Desk where her daughter is waiting for her.'

A few minutes later I caught sight of Mum, way in the distance, hurriedly hobbling our way. Pink-cheeked and breathless, she announced, 'I thought I was following you but it was somebody else!'

Where she had eventually ended up I had no idea, and neither had she. This was a good start. All now calm, we checked in and, in due course, comfortably seated, we took off for the Far East. A fourteen-hour flight offered the prospect of nice meals, three or four new feature films, and no stress. I sat back and relaxed to enjoy the latest Johnny Cash movie.

Arriving over Singapore we looked in amazement at the size of its vast busy harbour, where literally hundreds of ships bobbed in a glistening sea. Then, soon after landing, we were whisked away to the Pan Pacific Hotel.

'Would you like to book some trips?'

The driver handed us a small leaflet, and what choices it offered. Half dazed by the time change, on top of intensive heat and lack of sleep through watching too many films, I just about managed to make sense of it all.

It was early in the morning, about 6.30 am, so we decided on a city tour that afternoon. Being a little groggy and disorientated, we would try to keep awake as long as possible rather than snooze too early. Continuing to look at the leaflet in a strange spaced-out sort of way, we eventually managed some decisions. A city tour, Night Zoo visit with supper, then an island trip on a Chinese Imperial boat seemed attractive, and the most manageable. Aaah! We sighed, then sat back and took in the scenery as we were transported along roadways lined with exotic Travellers Palms, the emblem of Singapore, towards the Pan Pacific Hotel on Raffles Boulevard.

It was still too early to book in to the hotel, but the staff, looking at a wilting elderly Mother, most kindly and ceremoniously escorted us to our room. Although a large skyscraper building, the rooms are designed in triangular corner clusters, giving the feeling of small intimate areas. It was quiet, private, and just the thing. Our very spacious room overlooked a koi carp pool towards the famous harbour, and our escorts made quite a show of opening sliding glass doors to the balcony. We had obviously been upgraded.

Slightly refreshed, although still tired, we waited in the foyer for our city tour. Our driver duly arrived, and seeing Mum limping towards the taxi, decided China Town should be our first visit. The knee had never recovered from climbing Mount Huangshan to reach lunch back in 2001. So Dr Kwong Ong in his well-stocked emporium was consulted. This was a pharmacy like no other. Long-deceased snakes coiled in jars of liquid, whilst desiccated crocodiles hung around the door. We were slightly apprehensive as, eyes wide, we took it all in. Dr Kwong Ong soon calmed our fears and prescribed a lotion that, he assured us, should give immediate relief. Puzzled, we looked briefly at the box, covered as it was in Chinese writing, but taking the learned doctor's word for it's efficacy, purchased two bottles to 'see us through'.

I have to say, it was indeed miraculous, but our hotel room now had an overpowering smell of horse liniment; as did Mum, who happily walked around, without limping, enveloped in a cloud of the healing vapour. A city tour with a visit to the botanical gardens was enough for that day, and we returned to the Pan Pacific for early supper and a lovely long sleep. After the effort of pushing Mother in a wheelchair around the hilly and intensely humid botanical gardens, I was out like a light as my head hit the pillow!

Still jetlagged, a late and leisurely breakfast was taken at 10am the following day. To my delight, I found steaming urns of congee, the delicious rice porridge I became addicted to in China, and amongst other delicacies, Miso soup with tofu. This was definitely the place to be, and soon we found a large outdoor pool and stayed there, swimming or lounging in the shade, until 3pm. The temperature was soaring, and every half hour a beautiful girl arrived to spray us with cooling jasmine water. It was absolute heaven.

By 4 pm we felt able to visit busy Orchard Road, We were disappointed; it was hot and teeming with shoppers, like Oxford Street in extreme heat, but then came a sharp rain storm. We dashed for shelter into a nearby Tourist Information Office. A smiling assistant came towards us. 'Do borrow an umbrella to enjoy the monsoon'. We thanked her, and without letting on we had come in to actually escape the rain. The storm soon ceased, and we retreated to Raffles for tea. Oh, the luxury of it all.

The Pan Pacific is situated on Raffles Boulevard, as is Raffles Hotel, and best of all, the Singapore Art Gallery. It is a good fifteen minutes' walk from the hotel to the gallery and too much for mother in such humidity, so I went on my own. It was certainly worth it, and I enjoyed a long, cool visit.

Our voyage on the Imperial *MV Chengho* was scheduled for the next morning. With jetlag retreating we were up early and, well 'congeed', made our way down to the harbour where we boarded this highly decorated vessel. The weather was glorious, and we felt quite relaxed as we chatted to fellow passengers on our way to Kusu Island. Kusu, we were told, means 'Turtle'. As we approached the island, we couldn't believe our eyes. With palm fringed golden beaches and bright crimson hibiscus, it looked as if it had been taken from a glamorous tourist brochure, but with not a soul to be seen. It was so beautiful, a tropical paradise, and Mum was in raptures. There were no shops or other visitors, except our few fellow passengers from the *Chengho* and a middle-aged couple, guardians of the island's small temple. Our main companions that day were the hundreds of turtles living there.

On arrival back at the hotel the pool beckoned and, in total holiday mood, we booked a massage at the poolside spa. Mum took some persuading, but eventually agreed 'When in Singapore...'

I began to feel very sorry for Mum. We changed into nothing more than tiny modesty thongs and gauze hair nets, then were led into a double massage room. Awaiting us were two white-coated attendants, one male and one female. 'I hope I don't get the man!' whispered Mum, as with huffs and puffs she lay face down with her head in a hole on the massage table. She had the man! With my face firmly held in the head opening, all I could hear was a string of muffled 'oohs' and 'eehs!' We were oiled and pummelled to within an inch of our lives, and this was meant to be the gentle massage.

I was waiting for the complaints, but a pink and energised Mother with a spring in her step, all aches and pains gone, made her way to the poolside lounger for a celebratory fruit cocktail. So, what with Dr Kwong Ong's unguent and the luxuries of the Pan Pacific, we were in love with Singapore.

That evening, we decided to be adventurous and eat out in the nearby busy shopping mall. We spied an open-style restaurant spread over the walkway, but with a long snaking queue of Singaporeans. We took a closer look. This was a 'cook your own' establishment and very inexpensive, but it looked rather daunting. Not wanting to feel embarrassed by ignorance, I was going to try somewhere else. I returned to where Mum was holding our place towards the end of the lengthening queue when a tall man approached. This was the manager, who insisted on taking us out of the queue and to a prominent table where he explained how to negotiate and cook the many offerings. We now felt really embarrassed, being treated as honoured guests, with drinks on the house and a charming companion at table. Two boiling soup tureens were brought as we were escorted to counters laden with vast choices of raw fish, meat and vegetables. Our new friend piled our plates, and back we went to the table to start cooking. It was delicious, and such fun. With lots of smiling faces around, our elevation to teacher's pet hadn't worried anyone, and we spent a long happy evening with an extremely small bill at the end.

The Night Safari was a busy touristy affair, but interesting nonetheless. Sitting in our carriage, we were transported around the zoo in quiet darkness, with only the animal compounds illuminated. As they couldn't see us, we were able to watch them go about their usual nocturnal activities, but it felt rather sneaky when the odd wild cat would suddenly look up with ears pricked in our general direction.

Supper at the zoo was a big free-for-all, but ample and tasty, so Mum was happy and it was a good note to end on. Tomorrow we would be in Australia, and the beginning of a love affair with that familiar but exotic continent.

Singapore Airport has to be amongst the loveliest. Bright, clean, spacious, and full of orchids. Passing a flower stall just dripping with the blooms, I had an idea: 'Let's take some over for Avenell. They last for weeks.' We chose a pretty spray that was well wrapped for us and officially sealed for transit.

'It is ok to take them into Australia, isn't it?' I queried. 'Fine,' was the reply, 'as long as they are sealed and not unwrapped.'

We boarded the flight for Sydney and enjoyed our journey which, at just seven hours, seemed surprisingly short. Towards the end of the flight, we were given forms to fill out before landing. To be on the safe side, I entered our sealed bouquet of orchids as well as Mum's horse liniment under 'Anything to Declare/ plant material/ drugs etc', hoping none of it would be confiscated. Any liniment spillage might cause alarm, and its smell would fill the airport for days.

After landing we lined up for security clearance. Suddenly I noticed the sweetest little dog sitting right by my side, looking up at me.

'Ooh. Hello!' I said.

'We need to examine your hand luggage, Madam. Have you anything to declare?'

Oh, the embarrassment. A sniffer dog had homed in on me, and it wasn't Dr Kwong Ong's potion but the orchids that were opened and closely examined. Fortunately I had entered everything I could think of on the form, and all was well, but with heart beating a little more rapidly, we entered Arrivals to find Avenell looking anxiously for us. As soon as we were spotted, she rushed over and burst into tears as we hugged each other. We had arrived.

A two-hour drive north brought us to Connaught Road, near lovely Lake Macquarie and the town of Warners Bay. Avenell and Bryan's home was a typical modern Australian construction, large and mainly one-storey but with a spacious open plan interior. Unpacking, we were instantly enchanted by its situation on a wide leafy road backing onto the bush. Strikingly coloured birds flew over the balcony, lorikeets, king parrots, little rosellas, and each morning I was woken at around 5.15 by a hysterical cacophony from the local gang of kookaburras. It was all quite wonderful.

We soon got to know the area, finding favourite coffee houses in Warners Bay and good shopping a little further away in Charlestown. There was a bus stop right outside Avenell's house, but it wasn't for nearby Warners Bay. There is a virtually unwalkable mile or two to get there, and so we had to catch a bus to Charlestown, several miles in the opposite direction, and then catch the right bus back to the bay. So very time consuming, but we were on holiday and in permanent sunshine, so it was all leisurely and fun.

Nearby Newcastle was a fascinating place. I soon became familiar with its trendy cafés and the bohemian shopping area of Darby Street, which also has the excellent Newcastle Art Gallery close by. Although small, the gallery had an impressive selection of art, and the little shop area was beautifully stocked. I couldn't resist some Australian-made green resin hooped earrings. Studying the display with me was a young woman in a bright red t-shirt, with lettering emblazoned on its front. It read,

'All I'll say is a lot of art teachers have a lot to answer for', and underneath in smaller lettering *'Steve Peters, packing room, Art Gallery of New South Wales'.*

'I bought it at the Archibald Prize Exhibition in Sydney,' she told me, 'it is a superb show.' I was determined to go when we were next in Sydney in a few week's time, and hoped the t-shirts hadn't run out by the time we got there.

Luckily the bus stop outside the house on Connaught Road took me straight to Darby Street with no changing. The main city itself looked a little run down, but the surfing beaches are quite magnificent, and especially the famous, very picturesque Nobbys, a favourite of Avenell's. With little Rufus the border terrier in tow we enjoyed many walks along the sea front, and occasionally amongst the great rocks onto a concrete promontory towards the lighthouse.

Avenell delighted in driving us to many local beauty spots, including the nearby Hunter Valley area. Here we visited 'Audrey Wilkinson's', an old winery with a gorgeous aspect where we could sit in the sunshine and eat our picnic lunch, accompanied by wine purchased after prolonged tasting!

Nelson Bay was another family favourite, so off we went with a view to dolphin watching and seafood sampling. As it turned out, I did the dolphin watching on board an appropriate vessel for several hours over a lunchtime, whilst Mum and Avenell tucked into flatfish and chips. I never heard the end of its perfection and taste. I did see dolphins, but the fish shop was shut when I returned and I remained quite peckish as they kept telling me, in all innocence, how delicious it had been.

We were soon preparing to leave for a big adventure, but with a few more days to go Avenell squeezed in two more outings to keep us occupied when she was away at work.

The first was a pleasant coffee cruise around Lake Macquarie. Right on our doorstep, situated alongside the Pacific Ocean, this vast and picturesque area is said to be Australia's largest coastal saltwater lake, with beautiful bays, beaches, and ancient Aboriginal birthing caves. A calm, gentle cruise proved to be a very leisurely way to spend a few morning hours. Passing Warners Bay, we could pick out our favourite coffee shop behind the palm trees, and watch flocks of pelicans on the foreshore.

We were so close to the renowned Hunter Valley it was essential to have wine tours. The fact that neither Mum nor I enjoyed drinking that much wasn't the point. I wanted the experience, and Mum, as ever, was happy to tag along.

Most wine tours leave from Sydney, but Avenell found a small private firm and arranged to have us picked up in the local area. Not in Warners Bay, but in a convenient lay-by on the way to Avenell's work. Our return was to be slightly more complicated as we would have to be dropped off in Charlestown, but of course we knew we could easily bus home from there.

We waited, and after about ten minutes a minivan with the slogan 'Diabalo Tours' arrived to collect us. A small plump fellow, looking positively cherubic, got out of the driving seat and cheerfully welcomed us to his tour. This was our guide and driver, Graham. Clambering in, we found three other couples already seated, and saying our 'Hellos', set off. We were to have a marvellous day.

Sweeping hills welcomed us to the Hunter Valley, and with Graham pointing out various notable landmarks, our first stop after about an hour on the road was the modern Capercaillie Winery, with its own local arts and crafts gallery. Before starting the tour, Graham unloaded morning coffee from the side of the van. This was quite unexpected, but by then we were ready for sustenance. On the verandah, by the side of the entrance to the gallery, table and chairs were arranged, a tablecloth spread out, and homemade fruit cake passed around. It was so homely, and old-fashioned even! It was probably just as well we lined our stomachs. Serious wine tasting was about to begin.

We soon learnt that Hunter Valley conditions favour Semillon wine, although many other types were there for the sipping and, indeed, we sipped away knowingly, made serious comments, and then moved on to the next offering. We were already becoming experts.

Pokolbin was our second stop. Here we found another delicious winery, in a small complex including a cheese shop and chocolate boutique. Even the cheese and olive oil were to be sampled, and it was here I came across Dukkah for the first time. We dipped bread into olive oil, then into different types of Dukkah – a deliciously addictive seed and spice mix of North African origin - and I then came across a small bottle of mulberry vinegar which I couldn't resist, so bought it to take back to the UK.

One more winery to sample before lunchtime, and we drew up at Kevin Sobels. This delightfully located business, as with Audrey Wilkinson, had quite a history, and its family ownership stretches back over 150 years. With a cult following, the Sobels are known for their winery dogs as much as their hospitality – beautiful prize-winning St Bernards. As we left the very generous tasting session, I turned to see a pink cheeked Mum, arms limply hanging by her side.

'I just can't drink anymore.' she blustered.

Poor Mum had thought we were visiting a wine factory to see how it was made, not a series of prolonged tastings. Although she insisted to the contrary, she obviously hadn't done much spitting out, and there were two more wineries to go!

I wanted to take some wine back for my friends and neighbours, but as interesting and mostly very delicious as the wines had been, I hadn't as yet found the perfect one.

To be honest, I hadn't indulged in much spitting either, it seemed such a waste, but luckily next stop was lunch. In the nearby township of Cessnock, we drew up outside the rugby league supporters' club where an ample lunch was provided. A full sit-down affair in comfortably familiar rugby surroundings. Over a large plateful of fish and chips, Mum gradually composed herself.

Golden Grape was our next stop. Tastings here were especially generous, and I came across a most delectable concoction, Butterscotch Schnapps. I had visions of summer afternoons on my patio offering guests a taste of this golden nectar, and immediately bought a bottle. In hindsight, I should have bought several!

Our fifth and final stop was the much larger and very commercial McGuigan's. Whether it was just unfortunate that day or normal behaviour, the assistant, who served us with comparatively meagre helpings, and a large dose of snobbery, could have put me off buying, but I had to admit their new rosé was quite delicious. I decided to smile charmingly and buy a bottle for each of my dear friends back home.

Our tour had come to an end and, very well satisfied, we made our journey home. The light was fading as we passed through Kurri Kurri with its huge town murals and Graham, still full of information, explained that Kurri meant 'wet', so Kurri Kurri was 'very wet'. Driving between Brokenback Mountain and the Barringtons, night quickly fell and, before we knew it, we were dropped off at the bus stop in Charlestown. Our bus eventually arrived, and my bag of bottles clinked quite tunefully as we boarded and asked the driver if he would let us know when we arrived at Connaught. The journey would take at least forty minutes, so we relaxed back into our seats and chatted about our day.

I soon realised we had a problem. With very little street lighting it was absolutely pitch-black outside as we peered through the bus windows. Only house lights at intervals were visible. How were we to know exactly when to get off, and what if the driver forgot us? He hadn't, but unfortunately he wasn't quite sure of the exact stop. I had a feeling we might be in the right area, so the dear chap slowed down to look. With him, and all the rest of the passengers peering out, we looked for a recognisable street signpost. As we started down a hill, my instincts told me we were in the right area but had gone a little too far.

'I think we might be here now.' Thanking everyone for their help and concern, off we got.

The street was sort of recognisable, but not quite. It was a hot, dark evening, with night sounds of crickets and toads amplified around us. Mum's legs were tired, we were in foreign parts, and quite lost! There was nothing else to be done but ring someone's doorbell and ask for directions. Leaving my bag of bottles on the pavement, I climbed some steps to a nearby house and rang the doorbell. No answer here, so I tried again a bit further on.

'Keep me in sight, Mother, don't dawdle. I'll try again.' The houses were typically large, detached, and all in extensive plots, so it took a while, but eventually I found one with lights on.

What great relief as a young couple with babe in arms came to the door. Yes, we were in the right area but just too far down. They instructed us to go back up the hill and turn left at the top.

Off we plodded, a little more relaxed, but we seemed to go on and on, and it still didn't look right. 'Don't panic, Mother, I'll try asking at another house. It can't be far away.' I wondered then if the young couple thought we had a car and not just weary legs.

At the top of the hill, one house looked most welcoming... and floodlit. A downhill driveway led to the front door. Mum, leaning on her stick, waited at the top as I clinked down and rang the bell.

A young girl opened the door, and behind her I could see a dining room with the family having their supper.

'I am so sorry to disturb you, we are looking for Connaught Road but in the dark we got off the bus at the wrong stop. I know it isn't far, but could you point us in the right direction please?'

I picked up my bag of bottles. They clinked again. This was embarrassing. Would they think we were boozy 'down and outs'? I tried to look cheerful and non-threatening.

The young girl's father rose from the table and came to the door. 'No problem, I'll take you right there in my car. It's not far.'

'Oh, please don't let us disturb your meal. We can walk there if you point us in the right direction.'

He looked at me as automatic garage doors opened. 'I'm not asking, I'm telling you. It will be a pleasure,' he beamed.

With such relief, especially as poor Mum really was on her last legs and I was dying to spend a penny, we got into the car and off we went. The drive was indeed quite short, and the man so very charming that was typical of the kindness and generosity we found in Australia. There was only one small problem. I was dying to spend that penny! He was very interested in our day out and where we came from in England, so that by the time we arrived at Avenell's house it was a while before we actually got in.

Avenell had been extremely worried for us, and opened the door with an anxious look on her face.

'Where have you been? I wish I'd given you my mobile!'

'I'll explain in a minute.' I hauled the bag of bottles in and dashed to the loo.

Avenell later emailed cousin Diane in Yorkshire who had been wondering how we were getting on in Australia: 'Auntie Connie and Linda went to a big wine tasting tour today, and obviously enjoyed it too much as they got lost on the way home'. We will never live it down, although no one seemed impressed with my *almost* perfect sense of direction. We could have got off the bus anywhere in the darkness but at least we were in the vicinity. All Mum ever says is 'Ee, our Linda, it was so hot, wasn't it?' Our grand tour to Queensland and the Northern Territories was upon us. Avenell drove us down to Sydney Domestic Air terminal. 'See you in a couple of weeks!' she said, and off we flew to Cairns.

It was late in the evening when we arrived, and Cairns was hot and muggy. Our transport collected us and took us to our accommodation: Coral Sands Resort on Trinity Beach. It seemed quite a long drive in the dark, and when we arrived the reception was shut, but instructions had been left for us to retrieve our key from an outside safe. So far, so good, and clutching key no.8 we made our way through exotic foliage and over poolside walkways to a large and attractive two-bedroomed apartment. This looked very promising.

A well-fitted kitchen made us feel hungry, so we took a walk outside the main gates to find the small row of stores we had glimpsed from the taxi. Luckily they were still open, and a delicious aroma of fish and chips beckoned, so we stocked up for breakfast and queued for our supper. Back in the apartment we settled down to our meal, feeling very optimistic.

The following morning we made our way through idyllic gardens and, with the sound of the sea enticingly close by, found the reception to introduce ourselves. A friendly young receptionist welcomed us, and soon the owners, Rob and Sue Willemse, arrived. Rob and Sue were Scottish, and the most delightful people who went out of their way to help us. Little did we know then how much help we were eventually going to need!

Our two booked tours were confirmed, the first to the Barrier Reef that very morning, and soon we were picked up and on our way. Relaxing back into our seats, we were transported along a most beautiful coastline. The bush seemed to reach right down to the sand, where long, narrow sickle-shaped beaches, fringed by palm trees, confirmed our exotic location. We peered through the coach windows at wild wallabies as they congregated in the more open expanses, feeding amidst sugar cane plantations. The lush green miles of sugar cane came as quite a surprise, but this was just one of many surprises to come that day.

We arrived at Port Douglas, boarded a Quicksilver Vessel and made for the outer Agincourt Reef. Mum had been rather anxious about this excursion. but I assured her 'underwater diving for the over 80s is not a pre-requisite. Just relax and enjoy the cruise.' To be honest, I wasn't keen to do anything underwater, but would have a rethink on arrival. Eventually a large structure came into view. Our base for the day, the Platform was an exciting place to explore and enjoy. Marine biologists were at hand, and after a lecture on the wildlife and corals of this diverse ecosystem, I decided to brave it and have a go at something. It seemed ridiculous to come all this way and not get off the boat. Scuba diving looked far too adventurous, and snorkelling still meant getting my face wet, so I eventually decided on a sea bed walk. First, though, we had lunch. This was a huge affair, and offered a vast spread of seafood and tropical fruits which, in the Queensland sunshine and soft sea air, was particularly pleasant.

Before my slightly anxiety-inducing sea bed walk, we had time to look into the underwater observatory, giving Mum an opportunity to see marvellous corals and incredible numbers of fish species around the reef. I was so hoping to see a turtle but, similar to my South African elephant disappointment, I was out of luck that day.

Time for the sea walk arrived and Mum watched, taking photos, as I was dressed for the submersion. I felt a little nervous putting on various layers of protective clothing. First was a complete body suit, with just my face uncovered, to protect against the sun and sharp coral. Then a heavy belt was wrapped around my waist, followed by weighted boots. But the most alarming item was to come. A huge goldfish bowl-shaped helmet with shoulder rests was placed over my head. The weight of it all by now was quite something, and even walking was terribly difficult as I was led, together with my small group of fellow divers, towards a half-submerged platform. Standing on the platform, we were lowered into the sea as air flowed into my helmet. I realised the pressure of the air was the only thing keeping the sea out. This was not the time to have a panic attack. As we slowly descended into the depths, thoughts of a panic attack were soon overtaken by an excruciating pain in my ears. I was just beginning to think I couldn't bear it as the pain slowly subsided, and the platform came to rest on the seabed. Holding onto a rope, we moved in dream-like slow motion to a viewing area. Fish of all sizes and colours swam right in front of me, some close enough to touch, and once I forgot about the possibility of a small one swimming into my helmet, I relaxed and enjoyed the experience. At the viewing area we all stopped and objects were passed down the line. One was a living sponge that I dutifully examined and passed on. Next came a sea cucumber, which immediately proceeded to squirt a cloud of something from its nether region, making me jump – in slow motion, of course!

A diver armed with a camera positioned himself in front of us and made a show of waving until we all waved back, again in very slow motion, laughing inside our helmets. Fish food was thrown into the sea above us and a feeding frenzy commenced. Thick shoals of fish swept around, some barging into us, all unafraid in their excitement.

Our time was soon up, and we were slowly hauled to the surface. It had been a great experience and I felt quite brave, secretly wishing I had been even more adventurous. After changing, a lengthy business, and a welcome cup of tea, I suggested we should have a ride in the semi-submersible to give Mum a proper underwater look at the reef. Slightly claustrophobic for me, but exciting for her, and we managed to get on to one of the last trips before our return to Port Douglas.

Finally, I bought a video of my underwater walk (taken by the waving diver) to prove to family and friends I really had done it, and then it was time to leave. We felt happy and relaxed on our drive back to Trinity Beach, passing curved beaches bathed in evening light, and the wallabies feeding in their favourite spot, as night descended.

We were surprised to find Reception at Coral Sands still open when it was so late. Sue Willemse was waiting for us.

'I don't want you to be alarmed.'

'Alarmed?' I thought.

'OzTalk has folded. There is a fax for you and a phone number for you to ring.' She paused. 'We will do all we can to help you.' OzTalk were the seemingly very efficient firm who had booked us on to the next leg of our adventure – flying to Ayers Rock for four days and then a six-hour drive to Alice Springs. These kind souls had waited for our return to soften the blow. Internally I was panicking and thinking as quickly as I could. We had come this far, and I wasn't going home until we had seen Ayers Rock and Alice Springs, even if we had to pay again. For Mum's sake I kept very calm, but felt like a duck against the flow, paddling with absolute fury under the water.

The fax read:

Dear Mrs Fry and Ms Alvis,

As you may already be aware OzTalk has ceased operations. If you are travelling over the next few weeks, please call the Civil Aviation Authority.

The number to ring was given. It was a very long one, and no, we were not aware OzTalk had ceased trading. We had left home on 22nd March when they were still trading and expecting to hear from us on our return.

Luckily, our land arrangements had been taken over by ATS Pacific. We were advised to fax through to them all documents of the flights we had been booked on by OzTalk. This was the case with three further internal flights. I had these documents with me, but not the final ones which were to transport us from Newcastle to Melbourne on the last leg of our Australian odyssey. These were tucked away in Avenell's safe back in Warners Bay.

A lot of faxing followed that evening, with phone calls to ATS Pacific and to Avenell who called the CAA on our behalf. During this time Rob and Sue Willemse were close at hand, keeping their office open and staying around to make sure everything went as smoothly as possible for us. No charge was ever made for the multi-faxing and printing-off or phone calls. Such kindness and support at this time certainly softened the blow and streamlined all the new arrangements, although they always maintained they had never seen people keep so calm during such a crisis. I must be a good actor or naïve, but I really didn't want to alarm Mum any more than absolutely necessary.

New itineraries from ATS were faxed through from someone with the wonderful name of Janelle Ostergaard and, with Avenell's help, a kind Ella from the CAA in the UK telephoned to assure us that our flights would be honoured. As I had booked flights together with the tour the CAA covered them, but I wondered what would happen to all the folks who had booked everything separately. We were sorted for the time being, although vast sheathes of paperwork had to be carried around and relevant bits given up at each leg and tour of the trip. Stress levels slowly reduced, and we could now get some sleep before our excursion, the very next day, to the rainforest.

Our departure took a little longer this time, with various forms to be ticked and paperwork checked by our tour guide for that day. All was well, so off we went to the Skyrail Rainforest terminal. Once there, we climbed into a gondola and transported over four miles of tropical rainforest canopy in the stunning Barron Gorge National Park. It was an exhilarating experience, loftily sailing over this magnificent natural wonder. Below us lay a living museum, protecting rare animals, birds and plant life in what is left of a prehistoric forest which completely covered Australia many millions of years ago.

Arriving at Kuranda, we had half an hour or so before we were due to take our seats for an Aboriginal dancing display. It was only a short walk from the terminal to the village, and here I found my didgeridoo. We made our way past single storey shops, with several having forests of didgeridoos for sale. Which one to choose? So many sizes, curving this way and that, and with a variety of designs, this could be very difficult. One shop looked fairly business-like, so in I went with Mum following on. A young academic-looking assistant was already serving an Australian man with his two young sons attentively at his side.

'We would prefer a B flat,' he announced. Crumbs, time to go, I thought. I had no idea which key I wanted, so I decided to carry on along the row of shops to find one I liked the look and sound of, but I only had twenty minutes left.

Walking on, an open style premises looked quite inviting and an Aboriginal man was obviously in charge. I had by now noticed here how Polynesian the Aboriginal people looked, and remembered reading somewhere that didgeridoos originally came from Polynesia to this North Eastern area of Australia.

One quite large instrument kept catching my eye, beautifully hand painted and with a pleasing size and shape. The assistant was busy playing a didgeridoo as I walked around the store, and when he took a breather, and with time marching on, I approached him.

'How much is this didgeridoo please, and could you play it for me?'

He was such a pleasant looking man, and smiled broadly to reveal two missing front teeth.

'My uncle made this one.' He positioned himself and started to blow. The sound was marvellous. I need look no further.

He introduced himself as Greg, and his uncle, Dennis Undiji, had made and painted the didgeridoo.

The cost was about £200, so I agreed and, feeling the weight of it, realised there was absolutely no way I could carry this with me around Australia for the next month. It would have to be shipped. The manager appeared, I paid with my credit card, and a shipping form was filled out as I secretly hoped it really would arrive back in the UK.

Greg allowed me to take a photo of him with the didgeridoo, and I asked if I could take some close-ups of him to paint a portrait when I arrived back home. No problem, photos taken, and off we rushed to join the rest of our party for a walk around the Koala and Wildlife Park. Here, kangaroos and wallabies roamed freely, some with their joeys sweetly peeping out of cosy pouches. Crocodiles lazed menacingly on logs, luckily well away from the public, whilst sleepy koalas clung to tree trunks. An agitated cassowary ran back and forth as over-excited Japanese tourists, taking many photographs, approached too closely.

'Someone is going to get seriously hurt here,' called out an anxious keeper as she shooed the animal away. I kept my distance, knowing a kick from its vicious toenail could rip a person in half. I took my photo from behind a wire mesh fence, and even here the cassowary looked me right in the eye. It was quite unnerving, and not a time for poking fingers or camera lens through the wire.

An impressive display of spear and boomerang throwing, with an opportunity to 'have a go', completed the morning. A quick lunch was taken alongside a tropical lake before climbing aboard an army 'Duck'. This amphibious ex-army vehicle, (DUKW) dating from WWII, clanked away as it transported us through the rainforest on land and water. One enthusiastic ranger described various plants, birds and animals to his eager audience, who listened intently despite the rather uncomfortable metal seating and steaming climate. Snapping turtles, water dragons, kingfishers and butterflies were all pointed out, but the most fascinating was an innocuous looking plant with largish, morning glory type leaves.

'Never touch it,' we were told, 'or you will be suffering from pain and a rash for years!' I made a careful note; we still had a lot of Australia to see. Our drive-cum-voyage over, we heaved ourselves off the slippery metal seating and headed for our next experience, the Pamagirri Dance Troupe.

A makeshift theatre was the set for tremendously powerful tribal dances from Queensland's far north. We sat on wooden benches as a heavily painted didgeridoo player started the proceedings. We were then treated to a series of dances portraying various animals, such as cassowary, kangaroo and snake, and then the Sugar Bag Dance representing the search and chopping down of the Makor Tree for its sweet centre. Finally, the powerful Warning Dance.

The performers were athletic, authentic and sincere in their interpretations, and we watched in respectful silence, clapping only at the end of each dance. However, we had been joined by a noisy group of Chinese tourists. It took me right back to the incredible Peking Opera in Beijing in 2001. Here, the audience, mainly businessmen with their guests, displayed noisy and happy approval during the whole opera. This is quite the norm in China, but not in outback Queensland. Feeling they were not being taken seriously, the dancers became increasingly unhappy and agitated as the Chinese continued to voice their very obvious pleasure and clapped with abandon. Others in the audience turned to glower and shake their heads.

At one point the performance stopped as a well-built, highly decorated elder pointed to the offenders and put a finger to his lips. He was soon joined by others in the group. It only partially worked, but luckily the Chinese tour leader realised in time and managed to tone down the appreciation. Such are the cultural divides, despite a shrinking world!

It was a truly memorable performance, after which we were able to meet the dancers who willingly posed for me. One especially was an obvious candidate for a portrait, being very handsome, and he knew it. He stood confidently as I took several photos of him and another elderly man. This was to be a valuable record of two Pamagirri dancers for my work at home.

Our day at Kuranda was at an end, but a final treat was the ride home. Not on our Skyrail gondola, but the Kuranda Scenic Railway, taking us all the way back to Cairns. As we travelled through, we were asked to recognise the cultural and environ- mental significance of the region's indigenous Djabugay people. And what magnificence we witnessed on our return journey. The creeks, bluffs and waterfalls made me realise what a tremendous and arduous undertaking the making of this railway had been back in the late 19th century. It is so easy just to enjoy amazing scenery without appreciating the toil, and possibly some loss of life, of those who provided the opportunity to see these wonders. As we approached Cairns, swathes of sugarcane spread before us, and on our bus back to Coral Sands there were the wallabies, feeding in their favourite clearing, heads bobbing up as dusk fell. We felt quite at home.

We arrived in time for a barbeque dinner in the gardens with guest cook Phil Daniels. Phil was Welsh, an ex-rugby front row from Pontypridd now living and working in Queensland, and who was keen to encourage school rugby exchanges with the UK. A very good chef he was, too. We would have to speak to James when we got home. What a small world.

We headed for cover as tropical rain arrived at the same time as our delicious dinner, which we enjoyed in very good company. Especially good news that evening was the report that all our holiday arrangements were now sorted by ATS and the CAA. We could relax.

Our final day was free before the next leg of our journey, so we chose to bus into Cairns. We arrived in time for coffee and found a canopied open-air restaurant alongside Cairns Regional Gallery. It was so pleasant, watching the gentle city life of Cairns pass by, that we decided to return there for lunch after exploring the very modern gallery. Recently arrived from Perth in Western Australia was a travelling exhibition, 'Turtle Dreaming'. A fascinating collection of sound effects, paintings, artefacts and stories, both ancient and modern, celebrating the role of the turtle, the great ocean wanderer. The exhibition showed the turtle's journeying with the trade winds and southern equatorial currents linking Indonesia to Northern Australia. Coincidentally, my very special didgeridoo from Kuranda depicts a handsome hand-painted turtle, together with other lively-looking indigenous images representing man, boomerangs, a crocodile and kangaroo.

Bussing back to Coral Sands we looked out for the wallabies again, feeling sad to be leaving but also excited for new adventures to come.

Early the next morning we said our goodbyes to the Willemses, promising to keep in touch after their kindness, and made for Cairns airport and the 9.45 flight to Ayers Rock.

It is so easy to underestimate the vastness of Australia. The flight from Cairns arrived two and a half hours later at Connellan airport which serves Yulara, the Ayers Rock resort. With gorgeous weather all the way, the approach to Connellan gave us the most perfect view of Uluru and nearby Kata Tjuta, as they are now correctly called. Reaching majestically skywards, these massive structures stood out and alone in a flat red sea of spinifex and desert oaks.

'You are lucky today,' said the stewardess. 'We don't always take this route.'

We were soon picked up from the airport and transported to our 3* Hotel 'The Outback Pioneer', a slightly cheaper option to the luxurous 5* 'Sails in the Desert'. It seemed, and indeed sounded, more appropriate, and it certainly turned out to be lots of fun. On arrival, we glimpsed a Japanese lady walking near our coach. She was sporting a mosquito net completely covering her wide brimmed hat, head and neck.

'Slightly excessive, don't you think?' we tutted. However, within half an hour of leaving the coach, Mum and I were queuing up in the shop to purchase our own. Oh, the relief! This was the season for midges so small and numerous that open mouths, nostrils and eyes were fair game. They almost choked us.

We settled into our cabin and Mum had a look around whilst I, mosquito net firmly attached, visited the office to see what interesting extra outings were on offer. OzTalk had already organised a 'Sound of Silence Dinner in the Desert' for that night, then, the following day, a tour of the nearby 'Olgas', now named Kata Tjuta, and a sunset trip to Uluru. A very early morning eco tour of the Rock sounded just the thing for me, so I booked myself in for 5am the next day, knowing Mum would rather stay in bed. A camel ride in the desert sounded great fun, but as we only had two days here I decided against it.

Feeling peckish, we looked around for lunch. A poolside booth was open selling various wraps, and plumping for kangaroo and vegetable tortillas, we planned our afternoon. The Outback Pioneer is part of the Ayers Rock Resort, which also includes a Camping Ground, the luxury 'Sails' hotel, and central 'village' with a circular bus service to all points. I had picked up a bus timetable from the office, so we decided to make for the village and a cool drink.

The little bus arrived on time, and a few minutes later we were in the village ordering chilled drinks from a restaurant patio. Drinking out of doors meant risking a mouthful of midges, so we quickly learnt to negotiate straws underneath the nets for choke-free sipping. Refreshed and relaxed, we wandered around the little square of shops before bussing back in time for a swim and our exotic-sounding desert dinner.

We didn't know what to expect from the 'Sounds of Silence' Dinner. Would we be sitting on our own, or with others? Transport arrived as darkness fell and we, together with our fellow diners, clambered aboard for a ten-minute drive to the desert dining area with views of both Uluru and Kata Tjuta.

Candles and torches twinkled as we were allotted tables and settled down to introduce ourselves to the rest of our party. And what a party it was, all Australians and all determined to enjoy themselves. We struck lucky, soon feeling quite at home with Warren and his sprightly 90-year-old father, Maurice, from Melbourne, together with Tracy and Henny who were without their husbands and children for the evening. I almost remember the food and I know it was delicious, but it was the company that was the most satisfying. It was as if we had all known each other for ages. Such laughs and banter as a didgeridoo played, and our guide pointed the powerful beam of her torch towards southern hemisphere constellations.

Maurice took quite a shine to Mum. 'What a wonderful woman!' he kept saying, which led to much teasing, of course, and at the end of the evening we all said goodnight, looking forward to meeting up again for sunset viewing of Uluru the next day.

However, I had an early morning jaunt to enjoy before the day had even properly begun. At 5 am, when still dark, and leaving Mum happily tucked up in bed, I met up with our ranger and a small party of like-minded adventurers. Four-by-four vehicles bumped along to Uluru where, still in darkness, we tucked into coffee and flapjacks as we waited for the sun to appear.

Slowly, heralding the day, an orange light appeared on the horizon. This soon turned to a purple pink as we silently and expectantly stared at the Rock. Suddenly, it seemed as if someone was shining a giant torch at its base, turning it the most intense orange-red I have ever seen as light crept up to cover the whole of its massive surface. It was an incredible few minutes. We could hardly believe we were witnessing such intensity of colour. I soon appreciated how this amazing monolith came to be of such mystical importance to Aborigines, and especially the local Anangu people.

'Wow, what an experience!' we chorused, and so few of us there to witness it.

With the daylight, and in the cool of the morning, we were able to walk around the base of the rock, our ranger pointing out plants and places of significance. We came across a large clear watering hole serving both animals and man. To keep the water pure no animals were ever killed here, and so, with no taint of death to frighten them, they regularly used the pool. The hunting took place a little further away. It was fascinating to learn the wise ways of the indigenous peoples who had lived here for thousands of years. Some places were so sacred we were instructed to keep well away out of respect, so as not to violate them by intrusion. The Anangu people ask that Ulura is not climbed. It is so sacred to them and causes much sadness when accidents occur, and there are many, some fatal.

'Wanyu Ulurunya tatintja wiyangku wantima.' Please don't climb Uluru.

Continuing on, we were told, 'Look out for a bush with small black fruit, the Bush Plum. It is almost out of season, but if you find one we can have a taste. It is extremely high in vitamin C, which is essential for the indigenous Aborigines.'

Always one to ensure my intake of vitamin C, which had been rather lacking in our early morning breakfast, I kept my eyes peeled. Walking past scrubby bushes, I happened to spy a lone black fruit. 'Could that be it?' I asked.

'Yes, so who would like to taste it?' replied the Ranger. The party kept particularly quiet, and seemed to shuffle slightly backwards.

With no one else coming forward, I quickly volunteered. 'I'd like to try it!' The berry plucked and feeling rather bold, I put it in my mouth. The thinness of its flesh and intense bittersweet flavour quite surprised me. No one spoke, but everyone looked wide-eyed, half expecting me to keel over. Vitamin-packed, I remained upright, and on we marched.

Before returning to the resort, we had a brief stop at the isolated Aboriginal Centre. Here I found some beautiful hand-carved wooden bush animals and vessels. I bought a handful of interesting ones for the grandchildren, and then found boomerangs and spears lined up against a wall. These weren't the highly decorated type found in souvenir shops, but large, rough-hewn working tools. I so wanted Mum to see them and, expecting to be back there later when we were to watch sunset at Ayers Rock, I didn't buy any. Later, we could choose something special together to take home for the boys.

Before our sunset trip we visited Kata Tjuta, the beautiful 'Olgas', a continuous series of mountainous boulder-like structures, and these I found much more fascinating even than Uluru. Arriving there after lunch it was extremely hot, and Mum stayed in the shade of the oaks at the base, whilst the more intrepid of us walked the arduous Valley of the Winds. Only a mile in all there and back, it was a lot more difficult than I had expected. Uphill and over very stony ground, it was a very long half-mile to the viewing platform, and the heat was beginning to get to me. Perhaps this time I had bitten off more than I could chew. With frequent stops for water, and a quiet look around to get my heart rate back to normal, I started to take some photos when, to my horror, my camera jammed open. Thinking the battery had run out, I was cross with myself for not checking earlier. Now I would have very few images here, and indeed later of the sunset at Uluru. I would have to ask Warren to take some shots for me. What a disaster. Ah well, I walked on and eventually reached the platform. It was quite a relief to stop and scan the arid land.

It was then reassuringly downhill back to the oaks, although still precarious, but picking my way over rocks and boulders it felt a little cooler. Amazingly, as I reached the base and the shade of the trees, my camera zoomed shut with a gratifying 'bzzz'. Either the heat had jammed it open or the ancestors were taking their revenge on my intrusion.

Mum had enjoyed her quiet sit in the shade, and when I told her about the camera incident she said was relieved she wouldn't have to ask Warren and Malcolm if they could take some photos for 'those bloody Poms'. As it turned out, she eventually related the whole camera story to them plus the 'bloody Poms' bit, and they had a good laugh as we took our places in front of mighty Uluru that evening... and waited for sunset.

Evening viewing was on the other side of Uluru to the morning watch, and the rock formation is quite different. With pleasant temperature and banter we stared as the sun slowly disappeared below the horizon, and Uluru once more put on her display. This time the red was softer as the sun's power decreased. Crested doves came to roost on a large branch right in front of us, and the desert seemed to wrap itself up for the night. It was a peaceful end to a fascinating day, but there was a disappointment. This time there was to be no visit to the Aboriginal Centre. Those amazing boomerangs were out of reach.

Arriving back at The Outback pioneer for our final evening, we decided to give the Barbeque a try. This was a self-service open-air restaurant where you cooked your own supper. On offer were mounds of the fish barramundi, beef and kangaroo steaks, plus emu sausages and a vast array of salads. We joined the queue, feeling rather nervous, but bravely made our choice and, after carefully watching what everyone else was doing, soon mastered the art of the barbeque. This was fun. With our plates laden with sizzling onions and surprisingly tender kangaroo, hopefully cooked through, we looked for a table. Someone was calling us, and as we looked around who should we see but Malcolm and Warren, over from their hotel to enjoy the barbie. We had a great laughter-filled evening before we all went our separate ways. The next morning Malcolm and Warren travelled back to Melbourne, whilst Mum and I would be on the next stage of our journey.... to Alice Springs.

With paperwork successfully checked, we joined our coach and headed off on the Red Centre Way towards Lasseter Highway, eventually arriving on the Stuart Highway and a six-hour drive to Alice. It had seemed so close on the map! We settled back and looked in wonder at the expanse of seemingly nothing at all. However, we found the outback to be a fascinating place, and were quite transfixed by the red earth, dotted, as far as the eye could see, with tufts of spinifex grass. Passing vast salt pans, and with flat-topped Mount Connor in the misty distance, only the odd lone camel came into view.

On the Lasseter Highway, named after the man who had discovered a rich seam of gold, we stopped at Mount Ebenezar Roadhouse. This remote campsite and travellers' rest, owned by the Imanpa tribe, is a single-storeyed building topped by corrugated iron roofing and with an adjoining small café. We learnt from our driver that the roadhouse is part of a cattle station stretching over 2,000 kilometres, which for us, coming from the UK, is almost unimaginable.

A doorway from the café led to a shed, with its red dust floor and hessian-covered walls displaying local Aboriginal artwork. We had just half an hour here, so tea and cake was speedily consumed, then followed by an even quicker visit to the loo before a look in the rustic gallery. Small, typically Aboriginal paintings hung haphazardly on the walls, and more of the rustic carved wooden utensils and animals were dotted around. If only we had longer. Our time was nearly up as I chose a marvellous little painting and some carved wooded animals to complete my tally of gifts for the grandchildren. My beautiful dot painting depicts a woman with a bowl and digging sticks, sitting by a watering hole and surrounded by honey ants. The assistant wrapped it all quickly, but so carefully, with a photocopied sheet of the artist's name and history, plus another with the meaning of all the items in the painting.

On re-joining the Stuart Highway we passed an array of bleached animal bones, and a couple of mummified cows. Another diversion was a short stop at a wooden dunny, otherwise known as an 'aussie longdrop'; the one and only public convenience in the middle of nowhere. No water is allowed to flush, so this was a dry but amazingly odour-free lavatory. Outside was a small tap which, when turned on, dribbled a few drops of water onto our hands.

In the intense heat we had time for a quick stumble up some nearby red sand dunes, before returning to the coach for the final leg of our journey. I was so tempted to pocket a small handful of the very red dust, but thought better of it. As we continued north along the Stuart Highway, our driver switched on his sound system and we were mightily and unforgettably entertained for the rest of our journey.

The sound system clicked and sizzled until a recording started. We settled back, immersed in the outback landscape, listening to Len Beadell's incredible account of his survey of central Australia. This was obviously an after-dinner speech and he had his audience, including us, in the palm of his hand. His story of mapping the bush was so full of hysterically funny anecdotes we laughed almost all the way to Alice. Although he didn't know it at the time, Len was actually surveying an area for the most serious and quite unfunny of reasons, future atomic bomb testing. His book, 'Blast In The Bush', with accompanying CD, is a must.

As we approached Alice Springs, it dawned on me that, on this major highway, cutting right through the very heart of Australia from Adelaide in the south to Darwin on the far north coast, the only traffic we had seen during the past six hours had been a motorbike, a few parked cars at the roadhouse, two lorry trains and, during the final hour of our drive, four moving cars. Rush hour in Alice.

We reached the sprawling town of Alice Springs at 7.30 pm and settled into our hotel by the dried-out Todd River. It was a packed itinerary for one and a half days before we were due to fly back to Sydney.

A fax was waiting for us in our hotel room, apologising for cancelling a trip to the Cultural Centre the following morning. We were given the option of joining another group, as long as our flight out from Alice was after midday. Crestfallen, I realised our flight was at 11 am, and so it looked as if our much-anticipated morning of Aboriginal culture was well and truly 'off'.

'Right,' I decided. 'Let's get a taxi and go on our own. We can be back in plenty of time for this afternoon's trip.'

I hoped there was only the one Cultural Centre, but anything was better than moping in our hotel room, as pleasant as it was, and wasting an opportunity we may never get again.

A gleaming white taxi arrived, and after explaining our predicament to the kindly driver (we had yet to meet anyone in Australia who wasn't kindly, considerate and courteous), he whisked us off to Alice Springs Cultural Centre on Larapinta Drive, promising to return in good time to get us back to the hotel for our next outing.

Arriving at the sprawling Cultural Centre, I hoped it was the same place we had originally been booked into; but no matter, it looked marvellous. We immediately relaxed.

As the temperature rose, we quickly made our way from the taxi to the cool and welcoming main building. There in the art gallery, we were introduced to the distinctive paintings of Albert Namatjira.

His story was one of great poignancy. Born in 1902 near Hermannsburg Mission in Central Australia, Albert Namatjira was a member of the Aranda Tribe and earned his living as a handyman. However, his life changed dramatically in 1936 after an exhibition at the local Mission by the artist Rex Battarbee. Albert was greatly inspired, and when, two years later, Battarbee returned, Albert acted as his guide and camel boy in return for lessons. In a very short space of time, Namatjira was producing impressive Western-style watercolours, and in 1938 a full scale exhibition of his work was held in Melbourne. State galleries bought his work, which was then being sought in America and England. The portrait 'Namatjira the Painter' by William Dargie won the prestigious Archibald Prize in 1956. A book of his work and a film of his life followed, and Namatjira gained full Australian citizenship.

Just two years later, Namatjira underwent an eight-week jail sentence for supplying liquor to Aborigines. This destroyed him, and he died only three months after being released. However, his legacy is the most evocative work of the outback landscape and, for me, his depiction of the mysterious ghost gums with their startlingly bright white trunks is second to none.

Leaving Mum in the cool of the main building, I wandered around the complex and noticed an Aboriginal woman sitting in the shade of an arbour. I so wanted to photograph her, and went back into the main building to ask the staff if it would be permissible for me to ask her.

'Oh, that will be Tanya, selling her painting. Yes, of course, do ask her.' Out I went into, what was then, blasting heat. I approached Tanya, who had been joined by a middle-aged man looking for all the world as if he had spent the night in a ditch. He was rather dishevelled, with a deep graze on his forehead, and looked rather frightening, but was in fact a very gentle fellow. This was Tanya's husband, Wesley.

'Hello, excuse me,' I asked, rather tentatively, 'could I see your painting, and would you mind if I took your photographs?'

Tanya looked up at me and without changing her expression, which I have to say was fairly formidable, quietly spoke. 'Ten dollar.'

Her face was so strong I just had to ask if I could paint her portrait. I took several photos, mainly of Tanya, but one of her with Wesley, holding her own canvas. It was a colourful, bold and naïve oil painting.

'How much is your painting?'

'Thirty dollar.'

I opened my purse, took out $30 and handed it over.

'Can I put your name on the back and where you are from?'

'Tanya Nungari. I live in Papunya.' She casually waved in an indeterminate direction.

I wrote it out in pencil and showed Tanya to make sure she was happy. She nodded and then immediately stood up and, with Wesley, ambled off and disappeared amongst the gum trees. Taking my painting back to the main centre, I found the attendant who had told me about Tanya and asked if I could have some paper to wrap it. She was really pleased I had bought it. 'Bush Tucker,' she said as she carefully rolled it between sheets of tissue paper. Later I remembered the '10 dollars' for the photographs, but it was too late!

We continued to explore the Centre and Namatjira's paintings before the taxi came back for us. If we hadn't had the cancellation that day, I would not have met Tanya or bought my lovely Bush Tucker painting. What a great morning.

After lunch we had our grand tour of Alice. A small coach arrived and we joined a group of people already onboard to set off for the historic old Telegraph Station. Here, for sixty years from 1871, messages were relayed via twelve stations between Adelaide and Darwin, this being the best preserved. A series of buildings, now a museum complex, had also been a school for Aborigine children, and provided a fascinating insight into the working outback life of the 19th century. I wandered a little off the beaten track and, watching circling hawks, caught sight of a kangaroo bounding away ahead of me.

It was only afterwards Mum mentioned she too had wandered off but got very lost, only finding her way back in time for our departure! She had visions of search parties looking for her in the Outback. Luckily all was well this time, but I would have to keep a close eye on her from now on.

It was soon time to return to the coach and make for the School of the Air. Mum was particularly excited about this visit, as she was still involved with reading help at St John's Primary School in Worrall Road. It had become a late blossoming career for her, and she was much loved at the school.

The School of the Air headquarters had a broadcasting room, and we watched a film of outback children receiving quite superb education despite extremely remote locations on isolated farms and cattle stations. Before we left, we visited a lending library where the staff asked if anyone cared to donate a book. Mum and I couldn't wait to buy some for the school. I chose two very interesting picture books, one about music and the other on wildlife; both would have been enjoyed by my own boys. We were very surprised and rather embarrassed to find no-one else donated a book.

Next stop, The Royal Flying Doctor Service Museum, and an insight into medical procedures available in field conditions over the years. This was turning out to be such an interesting day, and it brought home how privileged we are to live in the West and to have such easy access to so many services. Back in 1928 a Reverend John Flynn was instrumental in literally getting the RFDS off the ground. He had seen for himself how important it was to provide rapid medical help in this truly vast country. His dream, to provide a 'mantle of safety' to outlying and difficult-to-reach areas, was indeed realised, and now over 2,000,000 square miles are covered by doctors and nurses in a fleet of airplanes.

A visit to the Reptile Centre was an unexpected addition, and clambering out of the bus we just followed the group. Making our way along a concrete path we passed a massive crocodile, luckily safely contained in a large pool and well out of reach, as he had, evidently, eaten twelve of his sisters! He certainly looked well padded.

After peering into various tanks and exhibits, we arrived in a lecture room and sat down in anticipation. A sparky young girl in work fatigues, cuddling a rather weird stumpy-looking lizard, proceeded to describe various Australian snakes, assuring us their bites were less dangerous than their African cousins. Something to do with shorter fangs, but probably best not to get bitten in the first place, unless there was access to an antidote.

The stumpy lizard was introduced as Martin, and he had the remarkable ability to bend sideways, almost in half, so that his tail, which resembled his head, could be used as a defensive ploy. If attacked by a predator, he could wave his head and tail around, looking for all the world like two lizards, in the hope it would frighten his attacker off. Martin was allowed to amble happily around the room as the lecture continued.

Out came an ice cream box full of tiny wire-like snakes. Our guide took off the lid to show us one or two, and they all seemed to shoot out like living spaghetti. This was fine until she needed to put them back, when they were completely out of control. As soon as she got a handful back in the box, another handful escaped. After lots of squeals and several attempts they were at last contained, and the lid snapped back on with just a hint of a tail or two peeping out.

Our next exhibit was a blue-tongued lizard, and we all had the dubious pleasure of a kiss from his colourful tongue. Finally, out came a female olive python, a beautiful and quite large creature which coiled around the girl as she spoke soothingly, stroked and kissed it. The snake's tail slipped out of her hands and hit the floor with a mighty wallop. 'Sorry, darling', she said. 'Who would like to hold her?'

After some hesitation a few brave souls volunteered, and standing in front of us all, with the guide by their side, they took turns in handling her.

Mum kept nudging me. 'Go on, hold the snake. I'll take a photo.'

'No. You hold the snake. Go on.'

This conversation was repeated several times, accompanied by increasingly energetic nudging. Eventually I gave in and happened to be the last person to hold the snake.

I was amazed at how relaxed I felt as I stroked her head and she quietly draped herself around my shoulders. This wasn't too bad after all, and I was actually beginning to enjoy the experience when a cry went up – 'Where's Martin?' Stumpy had disappeared. The girl left my side – left my side – and together with some of the group started searching the room on their hands and knees.

Suddenly abandoned, I didn't feel quite so confident, and sensing my nervousness and increasing heart rate, the snake started to get restless. How was I going to keep it calm? Would it strangle me? How typical of Mum to get me in this situation, and she probably hadn't even taken a good photo!

I smiled weakly and, stroking away, tried to look calm. At least the guide was still in the room. Beads of sweat were beginning to form when at last Martin was found under a cupboard, cuddled, and returned to his box, and to my great relief, the snake was put back in her tank.

Nonchalantly, I sauntered back to my seat. I had just had quite an experience, but sent a surreptitious scowl Mum's way. She just laughed it off. Typical!

As the sun went down, we finished the afternoon overlooking the sprawl of Alice and distant wide vistas from Anzac Hill – a typical Albert Namatjira view, I thought - and what a fitting end to such a memorable day. Tomorrow we were leaving for Sydney, where Avenell was planning to join us. The Southern Cross Suites in Darling Harbour beckoned. Our Outback adventure was over, but there was still so much to look forward to.

A morning flight took us to Sydney, and on arrival at our hotel we were ushered into a small two-roomed suite with the promise of a much larger one the next day. This accommodation was fine, Mum had the double bedroom and I had a 'cot' in the sitting room. At first, the mention of a cot was rather alarming. I wondered whether it was baby-sized and with bars. However, it turned out to be a huge folding bed, so all was well and we could enjoy our slumbers after a tasty supper in a nearby basement, where many booths offered a myriad of Chinese and Far Eastern dishes.

The following morning, our phone rang. It was James checking in on us. 'Has David been in touch?' he casually asked. He hadn't, but I wondered why James had mentioned it. 'No reason, just wondering.' Perhaps it was another baby on the way for David and Katie, as little Dickie was just over a year old.

We had two days on our own before Avenell joined us and so had excursions booked. The first, leaving that morning, was a coach trip to the glorious Blue Mountains. Our pick-up point was near-by, and we were welcomed aboard by the driver who was also our guide for the day. I couldn't help but notice he had a markedly nervous twitch and was on the move all the time, but he appeared quite unhampered by it and was an excellent driver.

Our first stop was at Bilpin, the apple growing area, where, joined by an army of leather-clad bikers, we had coffee before making our way to the Skyway across the Blue Mountains. Not for those suffering from vertigo, we were transported over tree-tops in the glass-bottomed Skyway. The beauty and expanse of this region has to be seen to be believed. Forested hills and mountains stretch far into the distance, where they appear a misty blue. Bilpin and this very area was to be ravaged by fire some years later. It was a sad sight to watch on our televisions as we remembered the innocent warm blue day we enjoyed so much.

Back on the coach we pressed on to the Fairweather Animal Sanctuary, but halfway there we were pulled over for a random vehicle check. An officer came on board to make sure we were all wearing our seats belts, and if not, fines would be administered. I became aware of some furtive clicking as he moved along the bus. This vehicle check took all of three quarters of an hour, perched over a viewing pit and inching forward every few minutes so the bus could be minutely examined. Evidently a common occurrence. We passed the test and our driver apologised for the delay, but his nervous twitch definitely increased. Sporadically, legs and arms jumped, and his head seemed to make involuntary left hand turns, but I have to say his driving was still magnificent!

The sanctuary was full of birds, and we walked amongst pelicans, kangaroos and emus, watched sleeping koalas and some log-like crocodiles. A ranger had a tiny, orphaned joey in his shoulder bag, and we all cooed over it as it snuggled in and looked at us with sweet dewy eyes. As we were leaving, I found the perfect boomerang for David. Not highly decorated but unpainted and etched, made by Aborigines indigenous to that area.

Everyone took turns to sit in the front, and it was ours as we returned to Sydney at nightfall. The illuminated skyline was a glowing panorama. By now our poor driver was obviously tired, and although still driving quite perfectly we couldn't help but notice how extreme his movements had become. Every few minutes he was almost jumping out of his seat. Poor fellow.

A city tour and lunchtime harbour cruise was scheduled for the next day, when, praise be, we were to move into a larger apartment. I had already dented my shin on the metal 'cot' as I tried to manoeuvre the two inches between its frame and a chest of drawers.

I must say, you cannot fault the tours laid on by enthusiastic Australian companies. Full, interesting, and always led by amusing and informative guides, and, true to form, that morning we seemed to visit every part of the city... and its outskirts. At a coffee stop at Manly Beach, we decided we much preferred it to the more commercial and busy Bondi. Sydney Harbour is vast, and as we toured various up-market suburbs with their luxury houses, all enjoying fabulous views, I tried to picture the scene centuries ago when the first ships arrived here. What would those exhausted travellers make of today's advancement and glamour?

Turning up at Darling Harbour for a lunchtime cruise, we wondered what was in store. Our rather swish 'Magistic' boat awaited, and as we boarded we glimpsed the dining room. It looked as if a banquet had been prepared.

The day was bright and breezy, but very clear. Perfect conditions to marvel at the sights of Sydney. It was bracing on deck, producing one of those amazing moments of realisation that we were actually there, sailing past some of the most famous sights in the world. The shell-like Sydney Opera House gleamed in the morning sun, and cruising under the Harbour Bridge brought back memories of Duncan House school days and my classmate, Susan Freeman. She was a talented artist, and a relation of hers had designed this impressive structure.

Lunchtime arrived, and indeed a feast had been prepared with seemingly non-stop service. A most incredible spread lay before us. I marvelled at the appetites of some of the visitors as they piled their plates with juicy seafood and delicious salads, soon returning for more... and yet more! The Sydney oysters were a tour de force, and available by the bucketful. Cautious at first, I eventually tried one before they all disappeared and could not believe how absolutely delicious they were. I have a photo of Mum, tucking into her oysters with gusto, as we passed the Opera House. Was anyone looking at it, I wondered – probably not. They were all queuing up for their second and third helpings!

After lunch, many retired to the deck to take in the sight of this beautiful harbour, as the water sparkled and an afternoon breeze gently brushed our faces.

We returned to the apartments in the late afternoon and were escorted to our new rooms. Standing at the doorway, we looked open-mouthed. Surely it wasn't all for us? There were rooms to the left and right of a very long and light hallway, which then led into a huge multi-windowed sitting room. This was more like it. Avenell was arriving the next day, and we had a bedroom each and space to spare.

Opposite the apartments was a Chinese garden. We could see the top of the pagoda from our new expansive sitting room, and tinkling music lulled us to sleep that night.

The next morning, I was determined to get to the Gallery of New South Wales and the famous Archibald Exhibition as soon as possible. Housed in a beautiful and imposing building, set in gardens overlooking the harbour, it was a delightful and enriching experience.

First things first. I made straight for the gallery shop to see if I could find those red t-shirts. My luck was in, but only just. There were very few left, so with some speed I bought one, hoping it was my size. Luckily, it proved perfect. How brave and quite wonderful of the gallery to reproduce such an honest and true statement: 'All I'll say is a lot of art teachers have a lot to answer for'. I would enjoy sporting that t-shirt back home.

As we entered the main galleries, we were surprised by an over-powering smell of curry. The source of this unexpected aroma turned out to be an 'Installation'. A large, bright room had, what looked like, many legs of nylon stocking or tights filled with spices and hanging as stalactites from the ceiling, dripping traces of their contents onto the floor below. It was actually rather impressive.

It was fortunate we had arrived in time for the Archibald Prize. A major annual exhibition of Australian Portraits by Australian artists, it is unmissable. It did not disappoint, and soon I was lost in portrait heaven. The 2006 exhibition was a mix of traditional and modern, with the winner, a massive canvas entitled 'The Paul Juraszek Monolith (after Marcus Gheerraerts)', a jaw-dropping work with hundreds of modern-day figures, all beautifully painted in historic poses, clambering over a monumental cliff carved as a face. Incredible, although rather unsettling, I thought.

I found it difficult to choose a favourite, as there were so many masterly works, but perhaps the one I remember most vividly was the portrait of Garry McDonald, 'All the world's a stage...' Here, with a rather penetrating look on his face, a man sat holding a smartly-dressed mannequin in his left hand as his right hand pulled its string. Another older mannequin stood by him, pointing a finger. Very revealing, and rather sad. I bought the small version of the catalogue and a postcard of the 2004 prizewinner – a mixed-media drawing of the award-winning indigenous actor David Gulpilil by Craig Ruddy. It is an incredibly strong representation of an ageing Gulpilil. I remembered well his memorable performance as a young Aborigine in the film 'Walkabout'.

On the frontispiece of the catalogue, the Gallery Directors state 'Sydney is a city that likes to prey on people. Portraiture is one of the most revealing and satisfying ways of exercising voyeurism.' So true.

We managed a few more rooms, including, of course, landscapes from the 19th and 20th century, as well as magnificent Aboriginal paintings on canvas and bark, before retiring, 'arted out', to the tea rooms for cake. We ended the day overlooking the harbour and its grand luxury apartments, some, we were told, owned by film stars such as Russell Crowe and Nicole Kidman.

We took a taxi back to the Southern Cross Apartments where Avenell was waiting for us. After she had recovered from the shock of the size of the place, we all came down to earth with a fish and chip supper.

The next day we checked out and, after taking our cases to Avenell's car, we walked around Darling Harbour, then took the water ferry to the arty, bohemian quarter of The Rocks, where we had a market stall lunch, bought some souvenirs, and where Mum found her own didgeridoo. Being shorter than mine from Kurunda, and undecorated, it was not quite so resonant, but a rather lovely plain wood, and a beautiful work of art.

Avenell and I climbed a few steps to reach a small souvenir shop. We both found ourselves looking at a bottle opener attached to a hard, round furry base. 'Whatever is this?' we asked the owner.

'Kangaroo testicles,' he replied.

We both shrieked in horror and ran out of the shop, nearly falling down the steps. How awful and disrespectful to the poor animal. We certainly wouldn't be buying anything there. Once outside, we nearly bumped into an American couple. After apologising, we struck up a pleasant conversation that, quite out of the blue, ended with the man saying sadly, 'Everyone hates us, except you British and the Australians, because of George Bush!' What could we say? We just smiled, said 'Goodbye, have a good holiday,' and went on our way, still complaining about the kangaroo's testicles.

It was now time to leave Sydney and drive the sixty miles back to Warners Bay. We were greeted by Bryan, who had bought a present for me, the CD I had previously enjoyed listening to in his car, 'Man in Black' by Johnny Cash. This was soon followed by some lovely family news. David and Katie telephoned to tell us they *were* expecting another baby in October. A good day. We broke open a bottle of Down Under best red.

We spent our last week with Avenell and Bryan under endless blue skies, visiting beautiful beaches, watching the monumental surf off Redhead Bay, and birdwatching in the garden. A family of lorikeets and the usual procession of king parrots, rosellas and sulphur crested cockatoos regularly swooped down to the balcony, arguing over the feeders that swayed on the gum trees, and at around 5am again, that gang of raucous kookaburras... To think we would soon be leaving this fascinating place.

There was still time for one more coffee at Bill's bakery, overlooking Lake Macquarie in Warners Bay, an evening or two of Scrabble, and a last visit to Audrey Wilkinson's Winery in the Hunter Valley. On a beautiful balmy day, we sipped rosé wine and picnicked on the lawns, overlooking endless grape vines and lakes down in the valley. Rose bushes stood sentinel at the head of each row of vines. They are the coal miners 'canaries' of the wine world, and the first to show signs of disease, giving warning before it reaches the vines. It was a pleasantly tranquil moment, and we made the most of it.

A supper visit to the local Teppanyaki Restaurant was our final treat. I decided to look a little smarter than usual, and off we all set, Bryan, Avenell, son Joe, Mum, and me, but feeling a little subdued as we were soon to leave.

If only Avenell had told me! I was expecting a civilised Japanese-style supper, but we were seated around a huge hotplate where the food was cooked right in front of us and with great panache. Not only cooked, but thrown around... and we had to catch it! At one point I saw an omelette lying, Dali-esque, half in and half out of Avenell's handbag. If only I had worn old clothes; but I soon warmed to it, and we had an evening full of laughter and gymnastics.

The morning of our departure arrived. Avenell took us to Newcastle airport for our onward flight to Melbourne and waited as we checked in and passed through the Customs area. She strained to see us as long as possible, crying hot tears and calling out

'Goodbye Auntie' so intensely so that the Custom officers, and all around for that matter, took pity on us. When I was asked what the shape of a smaller bottle of liquid was – I had already declared the bottles of wine from our memorable wine tasting day – I said tearfully, 'Mulberry vinegar from Pokolbin'. The lady Customs officer looked at me with compassion, as Avenell was still crying, and said, 'That's fine'. She could have asked me to unwrap it, as it looked for all the world like something much stronger, but no doubt she wanted an end to the sad scene and waved us on through.

Four hours later we arrived in Melbourne and there to meet us was dear Helen, who I had first met in the Ukraine, with her partner David. Night had fallen and the city was marvellously illuminated. Instead of taking us straight to our hotel, they gave us a grand tour of all the major sights before dropping us off at the Mercure by the Treasury Gardens, promising to collect us in a couple of days for an outing to the Dandenong Ranges. We had two excursions already booked, one to Phillip Island and the other for the Great Ocean Road, but we still had to fit in a meal with Bryan's brother Michael, visits to art galleries, and explore the city in daylight! We were in for a busy time.

Our first morning was spent enjoying coffee and cake with Michael and his son Nicholas in the atmospheric theatre café a short walk from the hotel. It was full of 'actorrrs'. There was just a little time to relax before our afternoon excursion, a coach trip to see the penguins of Phillip Island. I was a little dubious about this, thinking it would be very touristy, but never wanting to miss an opportunity, we clambered aboard our coach and off we went.

En route we pulled into a café for tea and cakes, followed by a visit to an animal sanctuary. Walking around, I was alarmed to see a large pelican writhing on the ground, its beak opening and shutting. 'Aw, he's ok. Just finding something difficult to swallow,' said the unconcerned rangers looking on. I wasn't at all sure, but pressed on to the next spectacle. Kangaroos and geese roamed around, whilst above us, kookaburras sat and koalas slept in the gum trees.

It was dark when we arrived at Phillip Island visitor centre, and I have to admit, it looked very touristy indeed; but as we queued up to enter the beach, and after buying the obligatory fleece blanket, I was impressed with the organisation. Specially designed buggies transported less able visitors to their beach side seating platforms, and Mother was soon whisked away in style.

Sitting quietly on rows of wooden benches, we awaited the penguins. Straining in the dark, did we see something on the foam of the incoming tide? Eventually, a white straggly line of penguins appeared in the gentle surf, and then immediately disappeared. This mysterious ritual was repeated several times, until it was obvious that the tiny penguins had decided it was safe enough to finally come out of the water and approach their burrows.

This performance was repeated until all the penguins were ashore and, chirruping away, they waddled past us, quite unconcerned by our presence as they made their way to the dunes. It was a delightfully moving scene, and I must say the blankets were invaluable on that clear chilly night, and have proved useful ever since. As we left, we were instructed to check for penguins under vehicles before driving away! Ooh, that could be nasty!

Soon after breakfast the following morning, Helen and David arrived for our Dandenong adventure. Breakfast was becoming a marvellous event. The Mercure possessed an impressive juicing contraption, a piece of machinery of industrial proportions, which made light of huge fresh carrots, branches of celery and fruit, all washed and piled up ready for action. Accompanied by the sound of an airplane taking off, and with shakes and rumbles, the most delicious juice poured forth. Not for the faint-hearted, or those of a nervous and shy disposition. However, it was my first port of call before slicing off chunks of honeycomb and catching the precious drips from a large wooden frame. This feast prepared us well for the day ahead.

It was a wet day, but this only served to make the swathes of monumental trees covering the hills all the more fascinating. Water dripped from giant ferns and lofty gums, all pressed close together, as we made for a coffee stop. Unexpectedly, we arrived at an art gallery tucked away between trees and houses. In we went, and found ourselves surrounded by Aboriginal art and the most incredible artefacts from Papua New Guinea. Strangely, there was no one around, so we just kept looking, and for almost half an hour, when a man approached us. This was Neil McLeod, the charming artist owner, who proceeded to escort us around his own western style paintings, and an extended private tour of his office and basement store where a vast collection of artefacts from Papua New Guinea filled the rooms. Headdresses, some the size of a small room, carvings, paintings, and fearsome weapons were stacked in abundance. It was fabulous. Neil was well on his way to making a national collection. What a wonderful and totally unexpected experience. Papua New Guinea is one place I would love to see. Perhaps one day.

We travelled on through quaint craft villages, with curious names such as Olinda and Sassafras, where we stopped for lunch and then tea tasting in small specialist shops, before returning to Melbourne.

It was an early call for us the next morning. We had to be on the coach by 7.20 am for the Great Ocean Road and, disappointingly, the juicer wasn't in service at our 6.30am breakfast. The day made up for it, though.

We headed for Geelong and Anglesey along the scenic Bass Straights. Many homes in the Anglesey area had been devastated by rapid fires in the 1980s and, further along the road, a mighty wooden arch stood proudly over the highway, welcoming us to the Great Ocean Road. It had been burnt down many times. 'Ten!' the driver told us.

We passed impressive forests of eucalyptus, grey box, stringy bark and turpentine trees on our way to Lorne Beach. Here we stopped for traditional Billy tea and biscuits spread with Marmite's rival, the much loved down under Vegemite, and Lamingtons. These little cakes, dusted in cocoa then covered in desiccated coconut, were supposedly made this way to keep ladies' white gloves clean.

As the morning progressed, the skies cleared. We were able to take full advantage of a brief photo stop at glorious Cumberland Beach by Mount Defiance, before moving on to Apollo Beach for lunch. Our driver guide took the opportunity to recommend a helicopter ride over the Twelve Apostles. 'Ah, yes!' I thought to myself, 'At a hefty price, no doubt.' However, the driver happily informed us that the company had arranged a special price of $30 for a 15-minute flight. 'Book us in!' I quickly replied.

The sky was beginning to clear even more as we arrived at Apollo Beach for lunch. Still feeling a little chilly, most of us tucked into fish and chips, which I accompanied with a most delicious spicy peanut Gado Gado salad.

So many trees, and passing a myriad of beech trees, myrtle, eucalyptus gigantus and the ubiquitous fast-growing blue gum, we soon arrived at a clifftop coach park. Miraculously, as we approached the stop for our helicopter ride, and with the Twelve Apostles coming into view, the sun began to shine. The helicopters were waiting for us, so in we climbed, and with headphones firmly on, up we went. The view all around was certainly quite magnificent. We flew so smoothly over the sea and coastline, with its impressive rocky inlets, outcrops, and the famous limestone pillars, and my view was perfect for photographs; but we couldn't help noticing there were only eight Apostles. Shouldn't there be twelve? 'Worn away by the sea,' said the pilot, although I believe there were only ever nine. Our fifteen minutes soon ended, but it had been a terrific ride, and what a bargain.

We still had time to explore before leaving, so I clambered the long way down to a beach as Mum safely wandered along a viewing platform above. At the water's foamy edge I found an Indian family, the Shahs, taking each other's photographs. I recognised them from our coach party. 'Would you like me to take a photo of you together?' I asked. Of course, they happily accepted but insisted they took one of me in return. 'I never look good in photos,' I told them. 'I take good ones,' said Asha. She was right.

On the long way back to Melbourne, we made several stops. An essential beachside ice cream, followed by a photo stop at London Bridge, and then a sudden stop in fairly open country.

'Just wait and watch that space', said the driver as he loudly sounded the horn.

Hundreds of wild kangaroo heads immediately popped up, then, in an instant, they took off like an army over a ridge. Obviously his party piece! Later, the coach pulled up alongside a steep muddy bank, close to eucalyptus trees. Those with sturdy shoes quietly plodded up through the mud to gaze into the tree-tops, and there they were, wild koalas looking like furry rugby balls clinging tightly to the trunks. What a rewarding day.

Night had fallen as we arrived back into Melbourne, with the lights of the city an attractive welcoming glow. Melbourne thinks of itself as a city of culture, and this proved true. The recently built Ian Potter Centre in Federation Square was a showpiece of modern and historical Australian art. The following morning, we spent many hours admiring fabulous Aboriginal work, carvings and paintings on canvas and bark, as well as a superior collection of Australian oils and watercolours. Extremely well-behaved young school children filled the galleries. They sat quietly on the floor, quite plainly enjoying the lectures, enthusiastically asking and answering questions. We stood close by for a while to make the most of the historical information from their tutors.

A circular 'hop-on hop-off' tram works its way around the city, and after lunch at the Ian Potter Centre restaurant we decided on a leisurely city tour, eventually alighting at Treasury Gardens right by our hotel. Mum went back to her room for a rest, but I, after a slice of pear cake at the theatre café, explored an art gallery shop specialising in Aboriginal work which was situated right next door to the hotel. The prices were extremely reasonable, and well within my pocket. I had to get Mum there before we left the next day. With some initial protest, she eventually gave in and loved the experience, taking ages to look around before leaving with two small paintings. On a display stand by the window, I had seen a beautifully carved, undulating wooden snake. It closely resembled the two life-sized serpents in the famous, heavily panelled Church of St Leonards, Old Warden, where David and Katie were married. It was irresistible, a masterly work, signed by the artist, and just right for David and Katie. I was so thrilled to find it, and especially for David as he had been a keen herpetologist in his school days, often regaling us with tales of axolotls and salamanders. We were living in the Beaconsfield Road house, which belonged to Grandpa Fry, when David badly wanted a pet snake. I would have given in but Grandpa was having none of it, imagining reptiles on the loose under the floorboards!

That evening, our last, Michael and his son Nick took us to the trendy seaside suburb of St Kilda's for a Mexican supper, and here, together with tostadas of crab and prawns, we found 'bugs' on the menu. Mum had been intrigued by the sound of these for weeks and wanted to try them. They arrived as small flattish lobsters, looking rather like giant pink woodlice, and quite delicious.

We decided on pudding from one of St Kilda's famous cake shops, and munched away on luscious cakes and chocolate with our coffees before returning to the hotel.

One full day still lay ahead. Decisions, decisions. After a walk in the Treasury Gardens opposite the hotel, we decided to look for the Immigration Museum. What a fascinating place it turned out to be, with galleries dedicated to every stage of immigration into the country, from the earliest convicts and those escaping poverty, to the Ten Pound Poms and beyond. It was a marvellous and important human record. One moment, which remains with me forever, was the sight of a pair of leather and wood children's clogs nestling on a glass-topped shelf.

'They are just like the ones you wore when you were little,' exclaimed Mum.

Something stirred deep inside me, and I felt close to tears. Surely, I couldn't really remember my little red clogs, worn before I was two years old... but, there was something about them?

We returned to the hotel to collect our luggage. David and Helen arrived soon after and drove us to their home in South Yarra. In this up-market leafy suburb we enjoyed supper with these dear friends, but all too soon it was time to leave for the airport and our long journey back to the UK.

Farewell, Australia. How we had loved our stay, and how I hoped we would be back. John was waiting for us at Heathrow, and we were home by 6 pm the following evening. Just like that, it seemed!

After a couple of days spent recovering from the long-haul flight, John took Mum for a 'big shop'. Off they went to Asda in Bedminster. In the meantime, I called in to see Sandy Brown who was recovering from pneumonia and administered some judicious percussion to his lungs. He rapidly said he felt better and didn't need any more physio! When I returned home, I found my phone flashing with five messages, and then I realised I had also missed some calls on my mobile. Scrolling through, I found they were all from John, except one from his wife Liz who was also trying to reach me.

John, sounding panic struck, had lost Mum in Bedminster. I called him back.

'I need you here at the supermarket so I can drive up and down the road to see where she has gone. Can you ring the hospitals first?'

'John, have you heard an ambulance siren?'

'No.'

'Well, she can't have gone to hospital. Did she hear what you said? She is deaf.'

'I told her I would meet her in the fruit shop, but she isn't there and that was about an hour ago. Can you get here quickly? Can Sandy bring you down?'

'Sandy is ill. I'll get a taxi.'

It took twenty minutes for the taxi to arrive, and another twenty minutes later, after struggling through heavy traffic, I arrived at Asda only to see the pair of them standing at the rear entrance, trollies full to bursting.

I wasn't too pleased. 'Someone owes me £9 for the taxi! Come on, what happened then?'

As I had thought, and it was no surprise, Mum hadn't heard John mention the fruit shop, speaking too quickly as he rushed off, and to cap it all she hadn't even got her hearing aid switched on.

'So, you mean you've got me all the way down here for nothing. I have just brought Mum safely back from six weeks in Australia, and within two days you've lost her in Bedminster!' They kept very quiet on the way home.

Little Harry was born in October that year. A really beautiful looking child, he was David and Katie's second son, and was soon to become the boss. Always smiling and joyous, it was easy for him to get his own way without anyone realising it.

My Bazaar was held that October, and Motivation used 'Robin' again for one of their Christmas cards. It was always a best seller. How that sweet funny little bird took only twenty minutes to complete, and seemed just to appear on the pastel board, was always a mystery to me.

On one of my many visits to the Browns', Mollie had a request.

'Sandy, Louise and I are going to India again next year' she announced, looking eagerly straight at me. 'September this time. Do you think you might come with us?' They had invited me to join them in the previous October, but it was the wrong time for me with the Christmas Bazaar to organise. After some pondering and serious studying of their especially prepared itinerary, there could only be one answer. 'Yes, of course.'

BROKEN BONES AND INDIA (2007)

BY 12TH JANUARY WE were longing for the rain to stop. It seemed to have poured for ever. After a visit to the Museum and Bristol Guild I hurried home, and by ten past five, in the dark, I quickly crossed the road just thirty yards from my front door. I didn't see the muddy puddle, and before I knew it I was performing a high-speed skid as my feet flew from under me and I crashed against a newly-built low wall. 'Ooh, that hurt!' My right arm felt dull with pain. Across the road a passer-by looked over anxiously as I popped up, feeling embarrassed, and quickly made my way to the front door. Oh, just to get in and sort this out, and I desperately needed the loo. However, as I reached the door, I realised my right arm was completely useless. I must have broken it. There was absolutely no way I could get into the house.

Feeling a little wobbly by then, I went next door and rang Judy and Derek's bell. 'Judy, I think I have broken my arm and I can't get into the house.' Her sweet smile as she opened the door quickly disappeared, and she called Derek to take me to hospital.

It dawned on me that I might be admitted, so I persuaded them to let me into my house first to have a wee, shut the curtains, and set the security lights for the night. They had to open the door for me first, of course. It would be three months before I could open my own front door.

'Just give me ten minutes.' I was beginning to feel rather ill, but willpower kicked in and I managed to prepare the house before the front door bell rang and there was Derek, waiting to take me to Casualty. As I left the house, who do I see but Mollie walking up the road towards me.

'I am coming with you,' she announced firmly. 'There is no need,' I protested weakly, but we were all in the car and setting off before I could say any more. Derek was especially jokey and light-hearted. A bit much, I thought, when I am not feeling at all hilarious. What I didn't know was that I looked so awful, poor Derek was trying to keep me alert and deliver me to help as quickly as possible before there were any further dramas.

Things didn't improve. As I sat in A & E with Mollie, awaiting my turn, together with other sad cases sitting glumly around, I suddenly felt faint. I never faint! A wheelchair was whizzed in. I was haemorrhaging inside my arm, which ended up looking like a bag full of blood. 'If you are going to break your wrist, you might as well do it properly,' said the registrar as he examined my X-ray. The bones of my wrist looked spectacularly out of kilter.

I was prepped for an operation, but a reduction of the fracture was attempted first.

'We'll just have one go,' said the registrar.

A tourniquet was applied to my upper arm and strong anaesthetics injected below it. Reassuringly I was informed the heart machine was close by, in case any anaesthetic escaped through the tourniquet. The drug was powerful enough to stop my heart. Nice. With quite a crowd now gathering, including the consultant, a plaster technician and nurse, one doctor pulled on my hand in one direction as the registrar pulled my elbow in the other.

'We are now using all our body weight,' they announced. But did I really want to know? I could tell it was quite an exertion for them, as red-faced and with beads of perspiration on their foreheads, they continued to pull. Suddenly, there was a massive *click*. The bones were back in place. I was later told by various doctors and nurses that this was a miraculous achievement in the circumstances, and after being plastered up I could go home.

The following week, after a lot of pain, I attended a routine clinic appointment only to be told, 'We are looking for a bed now. The fracture has collapsed.'

'Now? You mean I can't go home for my toothbrush?' Really I was thinking more along the lines of hairbrush and wrinkle cream.

No bed was immediately available so I was allowed home for the night, but with strict instructions to be back there by 7am the next morning for an operation!

At 7 am the next morning, as requested, I arrived, and was about to be taken to theatre for the operation when a kindly doctor approached. 'We aren't sure yet whether to plate or pin the fracture, but will make up our minds during the operation. As you are an artist pinning would be best, but we'll see.'

'Thank you.' Actually, I couldn't wait to go under the influence and get sorted out. A porter with my trolley arrived, and I was soon being wheeled on my way; but as we moved along, I couldn't help but notice I seemed to be slowly sinking.

'There's something wrong with this trolley,' the porter announced as he pumped away at the hydraulics, and up I went again. However, a few yards further on, down I went once more.

'They aren't going to let this in,' he said, frantically pumping away. He was right, and as we arrived at the operating suite, out came the theatre orderly.

'We can't allow that into theatre.'   .

Surely they can't cancel my op now, I thought.

Down on the ground again in the anaesthetic room, and feeling rather lowly, I waited to see what would happen next. The doors of the operating theatre opened and out came the anaesthetist.

He was charming. 'I am so sorry about this, but would you mind walking into the operating theatre with me? I can administer anaesthetic there.'

'Of course,' I answered cheerfully. What else could I say? He carried on to tell me his wife was also a physio, and as he took my good arm he guided me into the operating theatre. I suddenly felt considerably less joyful. There in front of me was the empty operating table, with a side panel awaiting my outstretched right arm, and over by the far wall stood two surgeons, masked and gowned, arms up, ready for action.

'Hellooo,' I said, in a rather casual way, and as they nodded back, I thought, 'This is a NIGHTMARE!' I felt as if I was entering the executioner's den.

Operation over, wrist pinned as it turned out, I awoke in the recovery room and began a long recovery.

After I left hospital, I had many unscheduled visits to A & E and the fracture clinic because of intense pain. Thinking it was the plaster causing the trouble, it was changed many times. Eventually the final plaster came off and was replaced with a splint. 'You will need intensive physio,' I was told.

Surely, I could do it myself, I thought, and no doubt there will be a long waiting list, but said nothing. The very next day, my phone rang. 'Physio Department here. We have an appointment for you.'

Expecting a wait of at least several weeks, I was told to be there in two days' time! On my first visit, physiotherapist Gail removed the splint. 'Oh dear!' she exclaimed. 'You have got the symptoms of Complex Regional Pain Syndrome.'

In my day it was called 'Sudek's Syndrome', and I remembered reading about it. Sprouting from the back of my red, swollen and painfully stiff wrist and hand were *black* hairs. The indignity of it; I wondered if I was turning into a monkey. They could at least have been white hairs to match my head! I had lost my lovely auburn hair in my thirties.

As well as deep neurological pain, and those embarrassing black hairs on the back of my hand, my nails were growing very fast – all because my brain was in over-healing mode. One very good thing came out of this. Gail told me that when someone presents with continual deep pain after a wrist or hand injury, they now realise it is possibly CRPS rather than an ill-fitting plaster.

After the hour's intensive treatment once a week, I always took myself to nearby Marks & Spencer for a very large cappuccino and gluten free double chocolate muffin. I became a familiar face to the ever-helpful staff, and was eventually able to carry my own tray to the table. Slow but sure progress.

'Why don't you paint with your left hand?' someone suggested. Quite frankly I felt ill as well as in pain. Painting was the last thing I wanted to do

I know, I thought, I will write a 'pamphlet' for my class. I had been able to continue to teach my pastel group with only a few weeks' interruption, and I would write something about how and when I started to paint, plus a few tips. Buoyed up, I set to.

After ten computer pages and some family history, I realised I was still in the 1940s! The little pamphlet was becoming a book!

I carried on with weekly physio and writing, but painting still felt out of the question. I just couldn't seem to put my mind to it, until I realised it was April, and 'BRACE', the Bristol-based Alzheimer's research charity, might need another Christmas card. They had approached me a year or so previously, and I was only too happy to let them use my designs. After some thought, and a few strokes here and there, 'Robin's Request' appeared on my easel. It looked good enough, so I offered it up and Brace chose it for their 2007 selection. As I slowly recovered, I kept the image of Aunty Lily in my mind. Brave and rarely defeated, she was my inspiration as I dragged the washing basket down the garden steps and heaved the rotary washing line up with my shoulder and pegged out washing using my good hand and teeth. The only thing I couldn't do was chop an onion, and Judy, ever smiling and always wanting to help, did that for me. We can't do without onions!

Mum was now keen to return to Australia. She wanted to see Avenell again, but there was something else she wanted to do.

'I've seen this train journey from Sidney to Perth. The Indian Pacific. Let's do it. I love seeing lots of outback and nothingness!'

My heart sank. Three days and three nights stuck on a train. As much as I love train journeys, I definitely like to get off at night. With this one, covering the width of Australia, east to west, it could be a nightmare. However, I wasn't going to be difficult. Mum would be 86 by then, and she had her heart set on it.

The Indian Pacific had two classes, Red Kangaroo and Gold Kangaroo.

'We'll have the Red Kangaroo,' announced Mum. This was cheaper than the gold class cabin, of course, and with only a reclining seat for the whole journey, I put my foot firmly down.

'Fine, by all means,' I replied. 'You sit in the Red Kangaroo, but you'll find me in the Gold Class!'

She didn't argue, and we booked our cabin for our 2008 trip.

We discussed the itinerary, and I suggested we had a look at New Zealand as well. It was too good an opportunity to miss, and would Mum be able to make this trip again? She readily agreed to a coach trip around the North Island, and I decided to do something more adventurous myself. I liked the look of Darwin, and booked myself onto an outback camping trip on Aboriginal land, and a visit to the more remote Tiwi islands in the South Pacific. This was going to be so exciting, and would make up for a three day and night incarceration on the Indian Pacific!

September soon came, and the Browns and I left for India with Mum's parting words ringing in my ears. 'Don't go anywhere on your own in India!'

We were met at the airport in Delhi, and as we made our way out we experienced the unfamiliar hot smell of India. Circling hawks screeched above the city, adding to the continual honking of car horns and, of course, the hub-bub, the masses of people... and such colour. It was immediately easy to understand how travellers fall in love with such a country.

The city was positively seething. Wide-eyed, taking it all in, I loved every minute of the drive on the Janpath to our hotel, the very grand Imperial. Two white-clad, red-turbaned men dashed forward to take our luggage. The hotel doors swung open, and the fragrance of jasmine overwhelmed us. I was soon to find that florists from Paris came every two weeks to arrange new blooms. This was the beginning of a marvellous adventure, and one in which I would experience for myself the remarkable diversity of great India, where huge wealth and privilege sit so easily alongside incredible poverty and deprivation.

My room was enormous, cool, fragrant and luxurious. I could really get used to this! Even the bed was the most comfortable I had ever known.

Asking at the hotel desk for details of my city tour, I found I had forgotten to confirm it with our tour agent; but no problem, it could be arranged. That very afternoon I arrived in the foyer to find my guide sitting on one of the many sofas, engrossed in his English newspaper. A dedicated Anglophile, this delightful, cultivated man ushered me to a large, shiny limousine where a chauffeur opened the door for me. Sitting on the spacious back seat, still a little jetlagged, I didn't think anything of it.

The next few hours were filled with the most interesting conversation, covering politics, literature, and, of course, Indian history. I marvelled at the sights of New and Old Delhi enjoying tuk tuk and cyclo rides, as we visited markets, temples and tombs. The richness and joy of my tour was quite unexpected. At one tuk tuk stop, a snake charmer sat cross-legged on the pavement, circling his flute-like instrument as cobras weaved from side to side. I was as mesmerised as the snakes. The charmer waved me away as, in my enthusiasm, I was getting too close! We walked through Chandni Chowk, the teeming bazaar, where every possible trade was displayed. Finally, the limo was waiting at the other side of the bazaar, and in we climbed, hot, but exhilarated. We had stopped at traffic lights when a little boy, no more than nine years old, tapped at the window, smiling and putting his hand to his mouth. There I was, the seemingly rich white lady sitting in the back of a huge, shiny black limo.

'We don't encourage begging,' said my guide. 'It is best not to give money in the street, as it prolongs what is a family profession.' I felt guilty as we moved off, and suddenly the boy stopped begging and just waved to me, smiling happily. I felt even worse. He had been smiled at by a white lady in a big black car.

Back at the hotel I thanked my most wonderful guide and courteous driver with the expected tips. I had experienced a very special afternoon.

The next morning, I was surprised to find a few stalls set up in the hotel foyer. Indian ladies, obviously not well off by the type of saris they wore, were selling embroidered linen goods to support poor women and children in Southern India. Here was my opportunity to buy lots of light, easily-packed presents for back home, and I made the most of it. The rest of the day we spent visiting the local bazaar, and later swimming for hours in the hotel garden pool, sipping drinks as the hawks circled and screeched above us.

The following morning, we left for Shimla. Our local agent took us to Delhi station, where crowds seethed in the morning heat as they headed for their various platforms, past beggars or the homeless sleeping on the hard concrete. Little boys ran along the tracks as a man, who had obviously just been run over by a cart, was being washed off and brushed down by a friend. The poor shaken man was at least able to stand. I noticed how red his hair was, although white at the roots. We were told that here, henna was the usual way to cover a grey head. Suddenly, our cases were grabbed by red-turbaned porters who seemed to arrive out of nowhere and sped towards the train. We squealed and rushed after them. Were we being robbed? But no, and what a relief, they were our porters and knew exactly where we were going. We arrived in the business section of the Shatabdi Express, found our seats and sat in comfort, with a nice breakfast and regular offerings of chai until we reached Chandigarh some hours later. Louise and I stepped off the train to stretch our legs for a few minutes, before setting off for the next stop, Kalka.

Here the process started again. Porters grabbed our bags and we rushed to the 'Toy Train' for Shimla. Expecting some comfort, we found ourselves in a basic carriage, sitting astride our luggage and with no real loo, only a 'squattie' at each end. This was how we spent the next five hours as we slowly travelled through many tunnels and the most spectacular scenery, ascending 7,500 feet to the foothills of the Himalayas.

At last, we arrived in Shimla. The hillside station was a wild melee of activity as our cases were grabbed by porters who seemed to know where we were going. Then, as we ran after them, our cases were deposited by a waiting taxi, which transported us to luxury again and the expectation of a comfortable loo - especially for one of our party who must have been absolutely popping. I had decided to brave the squatties, with the carriage continually lurching from side to side, thinking at the time, 'any port in a storm'!

Perched on a mountain in the lower Himalayas, the magnificent Shimla Oberoi Hotel is a glory of wooden panelling, balconies and light. Here we were ostentatiously welcomed with 'Namaste' and characteristic bows from all the staff. The cooler climate and easy-going pace of Shimla was so pleasant. Yaks, monkeys and roaming packs of dogs entertained us as we watched the world go by from our bedrooms. Advised to keep our windows closed, I soon found out why. Not being able to resist a peep out, I heard a frantic clatter and only just managed to close the window in time as a large troupe of macaques scampered by. Windows were kept tightly shut from then on. The thought of monkeys ransacking the room was rather terrifying.

One morning, as the early mist lifted, I could see some larger, more rangy monkeys in the trees opposite the hotel. These were langurs who, with their long tails and clever behaviour, took charge and tormented the local pack of dogs. The Temple of the Monkey God Hanuman was on our itinerary, and as we approached we were offered sticks to ward off monkeys and prevent them from taking our glasses, handbags, or anything they took a fancy to. Using the sticks, we walked up a hill to the small temple. We just peeped through the door rather than enter, as we would have had to remove our shoes and, quite frankly, didn't fancy losing them to the monkeys. As we left we returned the sticks, when immediately, in an instant, a monkey grabbed Sandy's glasses and made off with them. Stickless, there was nothing to do but buy a bag of peanuts to give the monkey, who immediately dropped the glasses and snatched the unopened bag of peanuts. A nice little earner for the stick man, who was duly given back the unopened bag, and then rewarded the well-trained monkey with a nut from his pocket! We were well duped.

A leisurely afternoon was spent visiting the Viceroy's Lodge and gardens, now converted into the Indian Institute of Advanced Studies. In an extensive photographic exhibition, I was particularly taken with a large, evocative photo of the Mountbattens and Nehru taken by Henri Cartier Bresson; Earl Mountbatten, bedecked in finery as usual, with Edwina very casual and obviously relaxed, enjoying Nehru's company as they both laughed together. Rumours abounded regarding their relationship, and I found the image very telling.

Unfortunately, Mollie was taken ill one evening during supper. We had only just ordered our meal as she slid under the table. It was remarkable to see the change in the staff. The bowing stopped and they sprang into action. As Mollie began to come round, a wheelchair arrived and we were discreetly taken out of the dining room, through the kitchens and up to our rooms. We made an amusing party, the manager pushing the wheelchair, followed by the three of us, two waiters and the chef. A doctor was called as the staff, including the chef, waited in the room until he arrived. We decided it must have been protocol, as the chef's position in the hierarchy meant he had to be there.

A young, impressively efficient doctor arrived, and the correct medication was prescribed and delivered within the hour. Anti-thrombotic cream was regularly applied to Mollie's now discoloured legs which, thankfully, slowly improved as the days went by, and we were able to continue our journey. We laughed many times as we remembered the incident, and especially the chef standing discreetly to attention in Mollie's bedroom.

Our next stop was to be the newly-opened Kikar Lodge Spa, deep in the Punjab. Our local driver, Chetram-ji, arrived, and off we went in his heavily tasselled minivan with its plush seats, velvet curtains, and an image of a god on the dashboard. Air conditioning was a series of fans. It was novel but very comfortable, and Chetram-ji proved to be a courteous and safe driver.

This spa was extremely remote and we got very lost. Chetram-ji had to stop many times to ask the way, and so the journey took hours longer than planned. However, it was no disaster, with wonderful sights en route, the most memorable being a village wedding. A young girl, completely bedecked in an ornate, thickly woven outfit, and with her head totally covered, walked in procession with her family along the lanes to her wedding. Then an elderly couple passed by on the other side of the road, both dressed in white from head to toe, sitting atop a wooden cart pulled by buffalos.

We eventually arrived at the spa, but first impressions were not good. The supposed luxury establishment we had expected looked very untidy indeed. There had been some severe weather and flooding, but staff were then busily clearing up, and we were soon taken to our smart, individual bungalows, where in front of each door was a shallow bowl of water filled with beautiful floating blossoms. Prominently displayed inside was a list of furniture and furnishings *(Not To Be Removed)*, half of which were already missing. Despite the lack of a sofa (on the list), the bungalows were very comfortable and the staff very attentive. There were a few other guests, wealthy-looking Punjabi families, and an obviously important group of men, all of whom kept themselves to themselves.

Kikar Spa was fascinating, and unlike any spa we knew. from the camel in the garden to the pleasant pool and the bar serving only non-alcoholic drinks. This despite the walls being covered with Guinness and Johnny Walker posters. As we entered the bar, the television was quickly switched from lovely Indian music to, of all things, 'Keeping Up Appearances'. There we dutifully sat, perched on our bar stools, sipping 'mocktails', watching Hyacinth Bouquet! I wonder how she would have reacted in this surreal situation. The food was truly delicious, but everything was written in Punjabi and no one seemed to speak English so, despite asking, we never quite knew what some of it was.

The owner appeared on our first day, a highly educated young Sikh who had worked for Johnny Walker in Scotland – hence the posters. He briefly took us under his wing, and led us to the jungle for a mini safari as his 'man' chopped a path for us through the nearby jungle. We saw large deer and amazing butterflies as his 'man' scythed away. We were to ask if we needed anything at all, he told us, but we didn't see him again, the only English speaker during our two-day stay.

Louise and I thought we would try out the spa, but on entering we found two very quiet and submissive young staff who bowed and smiled sweetly. There was no price list and no one spoke English, so we couldn't find out what was on offer and decided against it. We have often said how silly we were, but we didn't want to receive anything extreme, and what was the cost? Perhaps it was 'all in', but we were never to know.

Our stay at tranquil Kikar Lodge soon came to an end, and with Mollie nicely rested we made for our next stop, the heritage village of Pragpur in the Kangra Valley of Himachel Pradesh.

Arriving in Pragpur, we found our hotel, The Judges Court, a country manor house built at the turn of the 20th Century by Bhandari Ram for his son, Justice Sir Jai Lal, the grandfather of our host, dear Mr Lal. In its lush grounds we found exotic spice and fruit trees, and a 300-year-old ancestral cottage.

Within reach of the mighty Himalayas, the village has heritage status and all visitors to Judges Court are asked to add 200 rupees to their bill (less than £3!) to go towards restoration of the buildings. It was obvious that many of the plastered, slate-roofed houses had been strikingly beautiful in their day, and some very ornate indeed, but were now in a state of serious decay and dilapidation. We were more than happy to add the 200 rupees to our bills.

We explored the quaint market with its traditional open-style shops, and in the centre of the village found a most unusual, large, ornamental 'tank'. Water poured into it from a highly-decorated porcelain spout shaped like a tiger's head. It was a fascinating and peaceful place. We settled in easily, and were charmed by the aristocratic Mr Lal. My room was rather dark and traditionally furnished, yet spacious and comfortable. A torch lay on the bedside table, in case of power cuts no doubt, and I found mothballs everywhere, even in the shower.

During our stay, Mollie felt a little unwell again. Rather than risk travelling further north, it was decided that Sandy and Louise would take her back to Delhi, finishing the rest of their stay in the comfort of The Imperial Hotel. Luckily there was a room for them, and Mr Lal drove them to Chandigarh and the Shatabdi Express for Delhi.

Sandy offered to pay for me to stay the extra week with them in Delhi, but I so wanted to finish the tour as planned, and continue on to Dharamsala and Amritsar with the kind and very considerate Chetram-ji. I had missed the Golden Triangle the year before, and Louise was with them so I knew they would be fine. We would meet up in Delhi in a week.

We said our goodbyes and, feeling rather sad for them, Chetram-ji and I bounced off in the minivan along the track towards Dharamsala, with Mother's words ringing in my ears, 'Don't go off on your own in India.'

I couldn't have been happier coursing along the Indian roads, where, although traffic should drive on the left, it was obviously optional. Chetram-ji skilfully weaved between the tuk tuks, herds of buffalo, overladen lorries, bikes, carts, and cars, all honking their horns continually. I soon realised you 'honk' to let everyone know you are there, so it was a perpetual clashing symphony of horns. I soon got used to it all. Not once did I have any regrets, or feel the urge to press my foot into the floor, instinctively trying to brake. Coming from the Himalayas, Chetam-ji was the most careful of drivers and used to all road conditions.

Every two hours or so we stop. Chetram-ji turns round and says 'ToiLET?' He knew where the best 'squatties' were, and I was never going to miss an opportunity. At one 'ToiLET' stop there was a roadside stall, and I bought a huge bag of crisps and a bottle of water. Happily munching away, drinking in all the gloriously strange sights and sounds, we headed for Dharamsala.

Just before reaching Dharamsala, we stopped again. 'ToiLET?' But this time we were alongside the extensive ruins of the derelict Kangra Fort. What an enticing spectacle! I enjoyed a peaceful twenty-minute ramble around ancient, heavily overgrown ramparts, with highly carved remains of steep walls. Set amidst lush scenery, this was a fascinating place, and I came across a gang of stone workers cheerfully chipping away at the renovations. These very scrawny, hardworking, men earned 73 rupees a day. They were, at least, in work, and it dawned on me that the very young children I had seen previously working with roadside stone-gangs would also earn that 73 rupees, supplementing family income but, unfortunately, not being educated.

We drove on through vast swathes of countryside and bustling villages. However remote, the villages always seemed to have a semi-open-air school, with industrious children in spotless white shirts, heads down, concentrating on their studies. At break times the boys played cricket, the national obsession. It seemed every spare piece of ground, however rough, had a group of boys or young men enthusiastically playing the beautiful game.

Women at open wells beat their washing with stone truncheons, while children leaned over walls to wave enthusiastically. We stopped briefly to say hello, and a group of boys in gleaming white school shirts came up to ask about Manchester United and Liverpool FC.

We moved on, and soon reached McLeod Ganj and Dharamsala at the foot of the Himalayas. Clinging to the side of the mountain was the pink-walled, traditional hill-style Grace Hotel. As we pushed past cows and motorbikes to reach the entrance, the young manager came out to meet us and bowed, hands together as if in prayer.

'Namaste. This is your Home.' I was the only guest.

The Grace is a 200-year-old manor house, and was once the home of the First Chief Justice of India and the Prime Minister of Kashmir, Mehr Chand Mahajan. An illustrious history indeed, and the walls were decorated with many old photographs recording its important story, as well as small, original Kangra paintings. I asked about the famous Kangra School of Art, which I knew to be in the town and would love to visit.

'I will take you. We can walk through town. The Master is my friend,' the manager told me. I couldn't wait.

Communications obviously hadn't been too great. The Grace had no idea how many of us would be arriving, and I could easily tell this by the amount of food laid out before me at each meal. It was lunchtime and a multitude of hearty Himalayan dishes appeared, not all recognisable but interesting and tasty. I was hungry and did my best, but was eventually defeated and lots had to be returned to the kitchen. The half-glazed kitchen was alongside the dark, heavily-panelled dining room, and I could see heads bobbing by, regularly peeping over to see at what stage of the feast I had arrived. It was a strange scene with just me on my own, seated at the huge carved table, wondering what the next few days would bring. As my eyes grew accustomed to the low light, I could see some of the typically small but fine Kangra paintings on the back wall of the Dining Room. One was especially lovely: a simple design of a landscape, and a veiled young woman playing a stringed instrument with a pretty deer looking up at her. I couldn't wait to visit the art school.

To reach my room I had to travel a somewhat tortuous route. Up some stairs, then outside onto a very narrow winding walkway, canopied against the weather, but with only a low wall on the mountain side. I looked out and realised it was a sheer drop. I was then mightily relieved Mollie had gone back to Delhi. It would be all too easy to topple over, especially in the dark. The view was fabulous though, a wooded vista overlooking a school, and across vast plains stretching endlessly below. I had a huge key to open the ornate wooden door, and on entering found a very spacious room with traditional furnishings and wall hangings. Lots of mothballs, as usual, which escaped with an unruly clatter and bounced all over the floor when I opened the wardrobe door. Luckily there was a television, and a kettle with an assortment of teas. I would settle in very comfortably. The pleasant young manager showed me a bell to push if I needed anything, and then left me to settle in before our walk to the art school.

I looked out over the small school way below, amongst the trees and surrounding countryside. A dog caught my eye. It swayed from one side of the path to another as it made its way up the hill towards the town; it obviously had rabies. I made a mental note not to touch any dogs.

True to his word, the manager called for me. He took me through the busy main street to the edge of town and a modern-looking building, the art school. He introduced me to the master and then left to return to his duties at the hotel.

'You will find your way back?' he queried. It seemed to have been in a straight line, so I said I would be fine. The master escorted me around the museum and a small gallery displaying Kangra paintings, some very ancient, dating back hundreds of years. He was from a long line of artists and masters based at the school, and was very proud of his lineage. We walked through a quiet classroom where I met students sitting cross-legged on the floor, their heads down, diligently working. I learnt how it takes years to master this art, and indeed months can be spent just perfecting a jawline or the fold of a sari. I couldn't fail to be impressed.

'You can buy the students' work if you wish,' I was told. I was definitely very keen to own a piece of this exquisite art but, as it was almost 4 pm and the school was about to close, I said I would return tomorrow afternoon after my planned tour of the area. We shook hands, and I started back.

My return route wasn't quite so easy. I turned left and walked through the town, but it suddenly looked rather confusing. Realising I could get lost in this strange place, I had a mild panic as the crowds thronged noisily about me. The small open shops were very busy and I rather fancied a look at some of them, especially the cobbler with his enticing strings of colourful leather shoes and sandals hanging outside. I stepped gingerly over the open drain running the length of the town, and into the dark shop. There was an overpowering although not unpleasant smell of leather. The cobbler sat cross-legged, stitching a shoe. We smiled as he gestured for me to inspect his wares. They all looked rather small for my large western feet, but I eventually found a pair of very traditional white-gilded leather sandals which actually fitted. I gave him the few rupees required, the shoes were wrapped in newspaper, and off I went to resume my search for the Grace Hotel. I passed a policeman, but as he was wielding a stick and busily beating some passers-by, I decided not to ask the way.

I reached a crossroads and initially carried on; then, realising I had gone too far, turned back, and there, just on my right, was a side road and the Grace Hotel. I was home. Two small children, obviously a brother and sister I had noticed earlier, came running up to me. They were so sweet as they smiled and chatted away.

That evening I was the only guest at dinner, and again a substantial array of dishes spread out on the table before me... and, to my horror, they kept coming. I noticed the usual peeping over the glass screen and diligently ploughed on, eating as much as I could. The manager appeared to ask if all was well and had I enjoyed the art school? I didn't mention how I had almost got lost, but assured him I would return there tomorrow after my tour to buy a small painting. I hoped I would find one similar to the lady and the deer hanging in the dining room.

Off I went to bed with a herb tea, and what would become routine watching of CNN News, Old Bollywood movies, and an ancient guru. I couldn't understand a word of what he said, but he was fascinating and quite hypnotic. His appearances were quite frequent, and some programmes were obviously more recent as he seemed to have aged enormously in just an hour or two!

I slept well, and the next day, after a rather late breakfast, I gingerly descended the outside stairs, where a pleasant young man in smart-casual clothes jumped up to introduce himself: 'Arvind Sharma' – my guide.

I apologised for keeping him waiting, but he said, 'No, we have all day.' All day! My itinerary had stated a half-day excursion. Would I be back in time for the art school? He was so enthusiastic I didn't like to say, and Chetram-ji was waiting; so we set off, the three of us, on another adventure.

Looking back now, it is incredible how I just went along and took it all in, appreciating and loving it, but not realising then how special that day would be. Dharamsala became a refuge for Tibetans escaping Chinese repression. With women in traditional clothes, wearing distinctive aprons if they were married, selling

Tibetan artefacts and weavings, it could have been Tibet. In several booths, men were selling the unusual singing bowls. These decorated iron dishes, in all sizes, hummed as their rims were circled by accompanying metal rods. The larger the bowl, the deeper the mesmerising sound. They were so very heavy I didn't buy one, but regret it now, of course. How I would have enjoyed playing the bowl at home!

We entered the palace and temples of the Dalai Lama, who was due back that very day. Many hundreds of maroon-clothed monks and pilgrims filled the huge central hall of the palace, holding prayer rattles, chanting, and awaiting the appearance of their beloved leader.

We moved on, visiting temples to admire huge Buddhas and rotate the richly painted cylindrical prayer drums. Wood and glass cabinets lined many of the walls, and these were full of prayer bundles. It was all so fascinating.

I was getting rather hungry and told Arvind we should have something to eat. He was reluctant to join me, but I insisted and asked where his favourite eating place was. He took me to a canteen-style restaurant on the main street. Here was his favourite Tibetan dish. 'I love Momo,' he told me. 'I must try it too,' I thought, not having the faintest idea what was coming.

Momo is the whitest of white dumpling, obviously made with highly refined flour, filled with either meat or vegetables, and boiled to within an inch of its life. Arvind chose the meat, and I had the vegetable. Arvind suddenly disappeared, and when he came back he told me he had asked the chef to boil mine well. I was very grateful! The unappetising-looking dish arrived, and Arvind tucked in. 'I love Momo,' he murmured. I did my best, but was defeated after one and a half dumplings. 'Very nice,' I said, 'but filling.' I was pleased Arvind enjoyed his meal so much. He was obviously very hungry.

During lunch he told me about his proper job. He had founded the Himalayan Nature Society, which rescued stray dogs and assisted farmers whose animals needed treatment. He was passionate about vaccinating and neutering stray dogs, with so many suffering from rabies, putting many local children at risk. He was hoping to get government recognition for the problem, but was dismayed by their lack of interest and negligible eco awareness. Poor Arvind was going to have an almighty struggle, but one he was prepared to continue.

After lunch we visited the Norbulingka Institute and Tibetan Art School, where we found dedicated, commercially minded students producing most impressive work. I could see it being sold abroad, and indeed met one enthusiastic young man who was already a successful artist. We took tea in its peaceful garden surrounded by prayer flags. I stood up to take a photograph, but was startled by a very loud splashing as a multitude of nervous frogs jumped into the nearby pond!

After our tea we drove out to tea plantations within sight of the Himalayas, and there I photographed an old man sitting alone on a low wall as he looked out towards the magnificent mountain range. Unfortunately, four o'clock had come and gone, so any visit to the Kangra Art school was now impossible. I hoped I would be forgiven, but how could I complain after the riches of that day.

I was determined to buy my Mother a Yak wool shawl, a typical Himalayan hat for my nephew Timothy, and some Himalayan tea for me; but first Arvind wanted me to meet a friend who owned a gallery. When we arrived, I was immediately offered a delicious sweet milky chai which, despite the heat of the day, was the most refreshing drink. However, the art in this gallery was much too powerful for my taste. Fearsome, brightly coloured gods with too many arms or oversized heads seemed to be the main subjects. As hard as I tried to like them, and I really tried, I just couldn't see one on my wall at home, and they were quite expensive. I thanked the gallery owner for his hospitality, and told him how much I had enjoyed the experience, but left empty-handed. Another regret.

Time to find the shawl, hat and tea, which I did. Arvind, ever-diligent, found the best places and the fairest prices, and then, with my precious items stowed, the three of us, Arvind, Chetram-ji and I, headed back to the Grace Hotel. It had been a very long day, and as we left the town I noticed how tired Arvind looked. He had put his heart and soul into making this day so wonderful.

When we said goodbye at the hotel, I took his contact details and promised to hold a coffee morning at home to raise some funds for the HNS. I also gave him an extra amount in his tip, some for him and some for the animal charity. He was genuinely reluctant to take it at first, but I was insistent. Arvind Sharma was the kindest and most charming of young men, and thinking back now I realise how lucky I was to meet him that day.

Back at the hotel, it was almost time for supper. I apologised to the manager for missing the art school, and as we would be leaving at 9 am the next day there would be no opportunity to go. It was disappointing, but I was grateful to have been at least once. I asked him to explain to his friend, the master.

'Please,' he said, 'you must choose one of my pictures from the dining room. I have others.' I couldn't believe it, and sought out the delightful picture I had so admired throughout my stay – the lady in a pink sari with the sweet deer.

He took it off the wall and dusted it off. 'I will bring it to your room.'

'How much shall I pay you for it? He asked the equivalent of £20. I had such a treasure, and whatever the true value it was worth so much to me.

After another substantial supper, off I went to watch the Guru on TV and await the arrival of my picture.

Very soon, the manager arrived. The lady was playing a musical instrument, so I asked what it was. 'A star', I thought he said. 'Pardon me, a star?' But then I realised he was saying *sitar*. Of course!

I passed over the rupees, the picture was carefully wrapped, and we were both happy.

That night I had one of the most terrifying experiences of my life. I am rarely afraid, but on this occasion. I most certainly was. It was getting dark and, settling down to the Guru, I heard a distant rumble. Looking out over the valley, I could see an approaching storm. I didn't think anything of it until the thunder and lightning started. The storm suddenly became ferocious and, sweeping across the plains below, it hit the side of the mountain with gigantic force, thunder and lightning together. The noise was unbelievable. It was as if I was in a theatre, with intensely bright lights and someone in the wings hitting a huge piece of metal, and with unnecessarily dramatic force. Suddenly, the lights went out. All I could hear above the crashing storm were doors banging and a dog barking. I reached out for the torch, but it wasn't there. Of course, that was in Mr Lal's hotel; here I found a candle, but where were the matches? I was beginning to feel frightened, and certainly couldn't risk the narrow walkway and a possibility of being blown over the side of the mountain. Would I be rescued? Surely we would have to evacuate the hotel... no one came.

I grabbed my backpack with my passport in anticipation of a rapid exit and, wearing my jacket, lay rigid on the bed and waited. Feeling very alone, I wondered how this would end. For an hour the storm raged, floodlighting the room with lightning; and then, as the hour passed, I thought I detected a slight pause between the stupendous thunder and continuous lightning. The short pause between thunder and lightning gradually lengthened as the storm subsided, and gradually passed on to frighten someone else.

The next morning, all was calm and normal at breakfast; the sun was out and no one said anything. The storm, which would have hit the headlines back in Bristol, must have been a regular occurrence here. I was greeted by a smiling Chetram-ji, and with suitcase stowed, we said our goodbyes to the staff and headed for Amritsar.

On the six-hour journey from Dharamsala to Amritsar, we had the usual stops for 'toiLET' and enjoyed many more fascinating sights. We passed unusual dome-shaped charcoal burners by the roadside, and then great strips of paper or plywood lying in long tidy rows; and once, when wondering what the hundreds of dark cannonball shapes were, we came to a sudden stop. A turbaned Punjabi policeman got in the passenger seat of the van. Young and serious-looking, he had a few words with Chetram-ji as it dawned on me the 'cannonballs' were chunks of buffalo dung, drying in the hot sun and probably being used for fuel or building. I wasn't really concentrating until the policeman got out of the van and was furtively putting some notes into his pocket. Chetram-ji turned to me and, shaking his head, said, 'Punjabi Police!' I knew what he meant. The policeman was corrupt, and wanted $50 before we could progress. Poor Chetram-ji had done nothing wrong, of course. He didn't ask me, but I made a mental note to reimburse him when we stopped. The vehicle was Chetram-ji's own, and he would be responsible for all expenses incurred.

The roads continued to be chaotic with pedestrians, dogs, buffalo herds, tuk tuks, and cycles, as large, highly decorated lorries passed us with the slogan 'BLOW HORN' on their rear. Horns were, of course, continually blown. We continued on through towns rejoicing in the names of Pathankot, Dinanagar and Gurdaspur, passing sugarcane fields with processing machines industriously chugging away as we made progress to Amritsar. Gurdaspur seemed extra chaotic, and was noticeably full of young people, with policemen keeping a close watch and brandishing the now familiar sticks.

The Sikhs' holy city and largest of the Punjab, Amritsar, came as quite a shock. In intense heat, the town was absolutely jam-packed with people. However, the hotel was off the beaten track a little and quite cool, so I patiently waited in the foyer for my room. I needed to be patient, as I was one of several tourists waiting, some of whom had been waiting for hours. Their patience gave out soon after I arrived, which I thought a little unreasonable, but as the time went by and I was still waiting for my room key, I began to feel the same. I was hot, very tired, and in need of a drink and a rest. I was given a salt lassi and some chai, with the promise of almond cake that never appeared, probably scoffed by the first tourists. After several hours, a key appeared. I had a room at last. It was large, pleasant and cool, and I enjoyed a much-needed shower before supper.

Refreshed, I found the dining room and sat at a table near a young couple. They looked pleasant enough and we started to chat. This was to be embarrassing. The couple, ex-pats working in Amritsar, could have been living back in the days of the Raj. They were pompous, loud, and extremely rude to the young staff.

'This is how you have to treat them,' said the young man. His imperious voice made me jump. 'They are lazy.'

I wished I had sat myself somewhere else, but they obviously felt they had a willing audience in me. Another English couple came in. I recognised them as the earlier complaining guests awaiting their key in the hotel foyer. They were cornered by the young couple, but seemed happy to join in. I would make sure I kept out of their way for my few days' stay. We ordered pudding of kulfi, a delicious cardamom-infused ice cream.

'Just watch,' they instructed me loudly as the young waiter wrote it down. 'He will be off to the shops to buy it.'

Twenty minutes later, the man sidled in with a plastic bag. Smirking, they called out, 'There it is. Told you.'

What an uncomfortable meal. I couldn't believe people still behaved like this. I soon realised the staff were all young and obviously quite disorganised, so the hotel was inefficiently run, but it could have been worse. It was clean and safe.

That evening, I decided to find the famous Lawrence Bazaar and left the hotel to hail one of the horse-drawn carts waiting outside. There were quite a few there and, all smiling, hoping I would choose them. I quickly hopped in the nearest and asked for the bazaar. The driver seemed to understand me, and off we went. After quite a long time, now in darkness and with no bazaar to be seen, I felt a little concerned. Perhaps this wasn't the most sensible thing to do? No-one knew where I was, and I could easily get lost in a strange new city. I signalled for the man to turn round and go back, which he did, and when I found the nearest thing to a bazaar I got off.

I don't think I found the Lawrence Bazaar, but it was a bazaar and I eventually bought an ankle bracelet for Emily and, by accident, a pair of sandals. I had spent a lot of the week in robust Crocs, which were cool, comfy and easily washed in the shower after various visits to dubious 'toiLETs'. I had stopped to look at a display of sandals in front of an open-style shop, only to find I was being ushered inside by the manager. My mistake was to pick up an interesting pair, and soon I was attended by the manager, his assistant, and, of course, the box boy, who would run off to get various boxes of sandals. Looking at my feet, the manager assured me he had the right pair. The box boy carried them in while the manager and his assistant helped me put them on. In fact, they were quite nice, and certainly smarter for hotel wear than my dusty old Crocs. They even had a small row of mock diamonds on the strap. I paid the very few rupees needed, when the assistant came close and asked, 'How old you? You 50?' I could have said yes but had to admit to 60, which quite shocked the man and caused some discussion between the staff. By now I realised this sort of enquiry was not rude but quite normal. Evidently Westerners are difficult to read.

Now to get back to the hotel. I left the bazaar, and who do I see outside but another carriage driver who I recognised as one who had smiled at me back at the hotel gates. He looked an intelligent, kind man. He had followed me and was ready to take me safely back. What a relief.

I slept well that night, and after breakfast awaited my guide for the promised day tour. No one arrived. I waited and waited. Oh dear, a pattern was emerging! Chetram-ji was quite upset to find me still there and, after many phone calls and stern talks with the young counter staff, managed to re-arrange another guide.

The delightful Mani, dressed in a beautiful cool sari, eventually arrived, and the three of us set off, with Chetram-ji wearing a headscarf for the first time. When we reached the temple area, the heat was excruciating. Mani held my hand so tightly our palms flowed with perspiration, but she was determined we would not be separated. If we had, I could have been seriously lost for hours. The dusty and rather scruffy streets were a roasting, thronging melee, positively teeming with thousands of people. As fascinating as this was, I soon realised Amritsar didn't have the charm I had found elsewhere in India.

Still clutching my hand, Mani navigated the seething crowds and we made our way to the wondrous Golden Temple. As we entered its precincts, we had to remove our shoes and walk through a bath of water that separated us from the main temple area. So many shoes and sandals, I wondered if I would ever find mine again. Luckily, I remembered the scarf Auntie Iris had sent just before I left for India. I wore it that day. Black, gauzy and decorated with glittering paisley-style motifs, her note pinned to it read, 'For ceremonial purposes.' How perfect.

Feet washed, and with our heads respectfully covered, we entered another world.

But first, we had to shield our eyes against bright and almost painful light. Above us, the clearest blue sky held a scorching hot sun; before us, a complex of gleaming white marble buildings surrounding a large rectangular lake, its glittering waters adding to the intense dazzle. At its heart, with one pathway leading to it, the gorgeous Golden Temple stands, its roof and dome upturned as a lotus. It is truly spectacular, and I stood still for a moment to take in the wonder of it all, thinking about its violent history. In 1984, the temple was occupied by Sikh extremists demanding a homeland. The Government, led by Indira Gandhi, proceeded to bring the protest to an end, resulting in the death of thousands, including the Sikh leader Bhindranwale, along with soldiers and countless pilgrims who were trapped inside this holy place. Indira Gandhi was assassinated soon after.

To purify themselves, men swam in the vast holy waters, and family groups in their best clothes enjoyed picnics and chatted together as children played happily. I was struck by the calm and respectful atmosphere. Despite the crowds of many thousands, it was an oasis of peace, and a million miles away from the dust and chaos of the scruffy city just outside the walls. Mani could now let go of my hand.

Walking wasn't quite so easy. The marble pavements were sizzling hot, and very slippery from all the wet feet. I hopped uncomfortably from one foot to another. The alternative walkway was coarse and prickly matting. Which to choose? On balance, the rough matting was the best option, as I could, at least, keep upright.

I came across a huge kitchen area, where enormous vats bubbled away with boiling dhal; and, nearby, rows of diligent workers preparing naan breads to accompany the stew. This was open-style canteen cooking and anyone could join in and, of course, have a sustaining free meal. Fingers only, but with all that water it was spotlessly clean. Basic guest rooms were also available for weary pilgrims. What a place, and what an experience. Michael Palin was later to make a BBC travel programme visiting the Temple, and staying in one of these simple rooms.

Making my way towards the dazzling temple, I walked through a group of smiling though quite fierce-looking Sikhs, with their long curved daggers firmly held in place on tunic belts. The four entrances to the temple lead to a richly decorated cornucopia of mosaics, panelling, religious paintings, artefacts, and all that gold. When inside, I found holy men reading from scriptures, their followers sitting in respectful silence.

I came across the ancient remnant of a tree, the Jubi tree, protected by fencing. Reputed to be almost 500 years old with special healing powers, it is said childless women come here for its blessing.

It was soon time to leave this holy place, and Mani took me a short walk away to the peaceful Jallianwala Bagh Memorial Park, where I was shocked to learn of a further massacre. Families quietly sauntered through the park, yet, despite the calm, I began to feel uncomfortable as I learnt its past cruel history.

In 1919 Mahatma Gandhi ordered a peaceful mass demonstration against an act which allowed the British to imprison, without trial, any Indian suspected of troublemaking and incitement. Thousands attended. Without warning, the Irish General Dyer ordered his troops to fire on the crowd, killing and injuring many, some in the back, as they tried to escape. I was shown a well where many died after diving in for safety. Bullet holes were still visible.

My mood changed as I entered a gallery displaying portraits of gurus and poets. Here I found images of Rabindranath Tagore, the Indian writer who had visited and loved my school, Duncan House, back in the 1920s. It was comforting.

It was soon time to return to the hotel for a rest and some supper before meeting up with Mani again. We were to visit Wagah on the Pakistan border to witness an Indian Army ceremony, the Beating of the Retreat.

Remembering a delicious pakora we had enjoyed in Shimla, I ordered one from room service together with a cool fruit drink. I waited and waited. No supper arrived. Time was getting dangerously close to leaving for Wagah. Eventually a dish arrived. Originally freshly cooked and piping hot, the pakora was now a cold, congealed mound of fatty vegetables stuck to the plate. The accompanying drink, at room temperature, contained the tiniest flakes of what had once been ice cubes.

I was starving and had to eat something before a long evening out, so I set to, but eventually had to give up, the solid pakora now lying heavily in my stomach. I wasn't going to have my evening spoilt, so just before leaving I swallowed some travel-sick pills, together with some crystalized ginger, put on my anti-sickness wrist bands, and stuffed a few bags in my pocket... just in case.

Mani and Chetram-ji were waiting for me, and on a warm, golden evening off we set in the dear old van, heading for the Pakistan Border. We weren't the only ones, and we joined orderly queues of thousands, with family groups, whole school classes, and some tourists. This was a mega event! Indian police in their dress uniform and high pleated headdresses blew whistles, to keep everyone under control and in the right section.

Flanking a central roadway leading to the border gates were rows and rows of wooden seating. I was surprised to be ushered towards the VIP section on my own, with Mani having to leave for her less salubrious seat, but with a promise to collect me after the ceremony. I sat where I thought I should, only to be whistled at by a very serious soldier. I obediently moved on and eventually found the right place!

It was a glorious evening, and as everyone settled down and the whistles stopped, a group of men in khaki shorts arrived and pranced about hilariously. This was the pre-ceremony entertainment – rather bizarre, but very funny. As the sun slowly dropped towards the horizon, a group of the bedecked soldiers marched in, accompanied by a band, and proceeded to perform the most extreme goose-stepping antics. They marched in unison in a military style, but their high kicks, twists and turns were absolutely remarkable, and possibly damaging to health. These men were more like acrobats and contortionists. At the same time, I could hear a military band from the Pakistan side of the border and soon realised this was a competition, both armies attempting to outdo each other before the sun finally set. The crowd clapped and cheered them on. It was quite a spectacle. (Years later, I heard this performance had been toned down due to back injuries!)

As the sun set and the sky darkened, we all filed out. Meeting up with Mani and Chetram-ji, we returned to the hotel for my final evening. My stomach had eventually stopped its rumbling, and in the excitement of the evening I had quite forgotten the almost indigestible meal. I had come to no harm, thank goodness.

Sadly, I had to say goodbye to dear Mani, who had been a most delightful companion. I was leaving early the next morning to catch the 4am train for a seven-hour journey back to Delhi.

Chetram-ji would be taking me to the station, so it would be goodbye to him as well. I finished packing, and was about to retire when I saw a shadow through the obscured half-glass door of my room. It looked as if someone was pacing backwards and forwards, and I could hear some mumbling now and then. Eventually there was a knock at the door, and a tall young man, unknown to me, but one of the hotel staff, proceeded to say, 'I am a fatherless boy. Can you help me?' My goodness, he was more than a boy! A great tall chap in his twenties who had been practising what to say to the English lady before she left.

I gave him a few extra rupees and he disappeared. I locked the door and went to bed, hoping I would actually get my early morning call. What a thing to happen, but soon I would be enfolded in the comfort and security of The Imperial in Delhi. My last week had been a tremendous, unforgettable and life-enhancing experience, but how lucky to be born in the West. However poor we think we are, it is as nothing and is luxury compared to conditions in a greater part of the world.

In the early hours I was woken by a knocking at the door. A turbaned porter proceeded to kiss my hand and, bowing, touched my feet. It was a respectful gesture, and one I certainly hadn't expected. He waited outside as I dressed and gathered my belongings. It was very dark and quiet, with no one else about other than Chetram-ji waiting by his van. He looked concerned. Where was my promised picnic? I told him not to worry as I would get something on the Shatabdi Express, but undeterred, he and the turbaned gentleman set off to find it. Everything in the hotel was locked and no one answered the bell, but they disappeared, soon returning with a bag of drinks, crisps, and fruit. I was not allowed to go without my snacks. They had obviously raided the restaurant.

The city was still asleep, and in the cool of the early morning we made our way easily through the deserted streets. The only people we passed were a middle-aged couple walking together in the darkness. What a difference to the chaotic hubbub of the previous day.

Chetram-ji had been a most caring driver and guide over the past week, and I was truly sorry to say goodbye to him. I had been so well looked after. Before the Browns' early departure, Sandy had given me extra rupees as a tip for him, and so I added them to mine when we reached the station. Chetram-ji made sure the porters took my luggage, and we raced along the platforms to the waiting train. We had to carefully pick our way over hundreds of sleeping bodies, dotted over the hard platforms, wrapped in grubby blankets with their poor bony elbows and knees protruding, all angles and lumps.

At last, I was on board. A comfortable seat awaited me, with a large bottle of water and *The Times of India*. Tiffin and chai would soon appear. I settled back for the long ride to Delhi, with much to think about and remember.

With so much to see the journey passed quite quickly, but just outside Delhi the train came to an abrupt stop, and there we remained for an hour. I would now miss the morning's 11am laundry collection, but perhaps I could ask the hotel to still take my rather scruffy clothes and launder them before we were to return to the UK the following day. Meanwhile, there was nothing to do but gaze out of the window.

We had stopped alongside a huge rubbish dump, and as I looked over it a young woman in a lovely sari came out of a hovel and started to brush a path to its door. Such dignity amidst such squalor. I was fixated by her calm and rather noble bearing, and felt quite humbled.

At last, an hour later, the train juddered to a start and we eventually arrived in Delhi, where I was met and driven to the hotel. Ooh, the luxury again! Although I felt a different person from the one who left its sparkling precincts nearly two weeks before, I fully embraced the comfort, cleanliness and abundance. At the end of the shining, chandelier-lit corridor, my ground floor room was a spacious gleaming suite. I couldn't wait to have a bath, and stripped off my travel clothes, which had the distinct and very strong aroma of curry. Oh, the glory of a bath, soft robes and slippers. A fruit bowl brimmed over, with one large kiwi on the top which I immediately ate. It was so sweet and delicious. I rang to see if my spicy laundry could still be taken and returned in time for my departure. It could, and within minutes a porter arrived and whisked away the offending articles. Was there anything else madam would like? Well, I had to ask, I would love another kiwi if possible.

Within minutes another bowl arrived, and this time it was full of large ripe kiwis. Refreshed and rested, I soon met up with Mollie, Sandy and Louise for lunch in the airy, palmed restaurant overlooking the gardens. How peaceful it was, and then I remembered reading how this very place had been overrun by protesters during the fight for freedom. It was almost impossible to visualise now, as smartly-dressed waiters silently moved about and guests quietly chatted, fine china and cutlery gently clinking.

I didn't need to see the menu. It would have to be Minted Pea Soup. This plain sounding dish was anything but at The Imperial. When I had first ordered it, along came a soup dish with three very large prawns arranged in the middle, surrounded by a thin stream of sauce. 'Nouvelle Cuisine,' I thought. And then two waiters arrived. One held a tureen, whilst the other, towel over one arm, removed the lid, and with a silver jug ceremoniously proceeded to pour minted pea soup into my dish. It was a revelation. I longed to sample it again, and I wasn't disappointed. I savoured every moment of the serving performance and the exquisite flavours, as I regaled the Browns with stories of all my adventures.

Mollie was feeling better now. They had found a marvellous bazaar close to the hotel, and we still had time for a visit. We bought a few last-minute gifts and a CD of Indian music. I had so many memorable photographs and would eventually use the music as a backing to a slideshow.

Early the next morning, we had to say our goodbyes to The Imperial, to Delhi, and complex but fabulous and fascinating India. Some are so drawn to India that it continually tugs at their hearts. Others wish never to go. I am firmly of the former. Whenever I hear Indian music, I am back, bouncing along the dusty roads in Chetram-ji's mini-van, accompanied by continual honking of horns with the lorries, herds of buffalos, tuk tuks, carts, and every two hours... 'ToiLET?'

I was back in good time for Christmas Bazaar preparations, and this year, despite the broken wrist in January, I had managed to produce another card, 'Robin's Reflection (Just looking!)', to be included in Motivation's Christmas range.

New Zealand and Australia
(2008)

M Y CAREER IN ART was steadily progressing, and by 2008 I was a regular fixture in the annual Autumn West Bristol Arts Trail. In my new studio gallery (the old garage) I had started an art class once a week, and this was thriving. Clifton Arts Club were using my images on their website, so I seemed to be set fair for the time being.

Spring arrived, and with it our second trip Down Under. This was to be the big one, and almost two months long. As before, we flew to Singapore and the Pan Pacific Hotel for a welcome break, before continuing on to Auckland in New Zealand's North Island. The Pan Pacific had some great shops, and we bought each other a present; a Polynesian napkin holder in the form of a crouching man symbolising a welcome for Mum, and a silvery Kiwi for me.

Landing in Auckland in New Zealand's North Island, we were transported to our central hotel, where we met our guide and fellow travellers, before a very full North Island itinerary with the AAT Kings coach company.

After settling in and leaving Mum to rest, I wandered off to find some art and to have a good look around. Unfortunately, the main city art gallery was undergoing renovation and many others were closed, but I did find a superb photographic exhibition with the most beautiful gelatine photos, silver gelatine, gold and platinum. The depth of mood in these photos was quite gorgeous, and I wondered if I would be able to learn this complicated, and no doubt expensive, technique. I have never got round to it, but always make a point of searching out this type of photograph in exhibitions. Inspired, I walked briskly around the centre of this pleasant and lively place, although, and rather endearingly, it seemed a little old-fashioned. I was to find this during our whole visit to New Zealand. You could have turned the clock back fifty years, and it was a very pleasant experience indeed.

Back at the hotel we greeted our fellow passengers, a cheery lot, and together we waited for our guide. Soon a tall and imposing Maori appeared. This was Marty, a very modern Maori of royal blood, his mother being a princess. We felt rather special.

The next morning, we clambered onto our coach and drove further north to stay in a resort hotel for the Bay of Islands tour. A sprawling but very friendly Paihia Hotel overlooked palm trees and the sea, which, I couldn't fail to notice, looked rather rough and grey. The weather had turned against us, and it didn't bode well for our boat trip to the famous 'Hole in the Wall'.

After breakfast, and some surprisingly, rather hard and un-ripe kiwis, we left for the boat. On the way, we came across a very strange bird. Almost cartoon-like, with long legs appearing to bend backwards, the fairly common Pukeko, or Purple Swamphen, strutted busily but awkwardly around open ground. Arriving at a small pottery, we found this very bird portrayed on its many mugs and dishes. It is a gift to producers of souvenirs. My brother still has his Pukeko dish from the Keri Keri pottery prominently displayed.

The boat trip was indeed rough, and with great relief we had to forgo the Hole in the Wall rock and return to calmer waters; just in time, where I was concerned. It was getting to be rather unpleasant, but I did see an albatross, and this made the whole uncomfortable experience thoroughly worthwhile.

The North Island may not have the sweeping beauty and magnificence of the South Island, but it has a rich cultural heritage. At the Waitangi Treaty Grounds we were treated to a full-on Haka, the challenging war dance. It is a terrifying performance, and I could understand how many of the early visitors to this island could misinterpret this strange 'welcome' and end up doing the wrong thing and losing their lives.

Waitangi is best known for the Treaty of Waitangi in 1840, resulting in British Sovereignty over New Zealand; and also as the place where the Declaration of Independence was signed by 52 Maori chiefs five years earlier in 1835. Here we also enjoyed a Hangi, a traditional feast cooked by heated rocks in a pit under the ground. It was delicious. It all looked pretty traditional, although plenty of aluminium foil was in evidence, and I believe gas fired Hangi ovens are now quite the thing.

The following day we visited the immense kauri tree forests. Maoris traditionally used the wood from these trees for their houses, boats and carvings. With girths of up to 16 metres, they are truly gigantic, and I had my photo taken, arms outstretched against a huge trunk.

Mum looked at a row of historic 'dunnys', and opening the door of one to look inside suddenly said, 'Oh, sorry!', thinking she had surprised someone sitting on the loo. Then she started laughing. It was a very realistic dummy.

Our day ended with performances of Maori dances. These involved wild facial contortions, and tongue protrusions of some amazing lengths. The most fascinating was the Poi Ball dance, performed by women with two wool or straw balls at the end of lengths of cord, which they swung around rhythmically and often at great speed. It was most impressive. We had a go, but it wasn't at all easy, and our poor efforts gave the dancers a lot of laughs.

Luckily, we returned to our Auckland hotel briefly before continuing on towards Wellington at the foot of the North Island. I had left my nightie hanging on the door of our room, and would now be able to retrieve it!

Our onward journey towards Rotorua took in the Waikato River and an unexpected foray into the Waitomo Glow Worm Caves. This involved a precarious walk in semi-darkness, down to caves and an underground river. We stepped very carefully into waiting boats and drifted along caverns in total darkness, straining to see some glimmer. And then we arrived at the glow worm caves, where ceilings glittered like a star-filled night sky. Glow worms were twinkling in their millions, making a very eery but beautiful natural spectacle.

Continuing onwards, we approached Rotorua and detected the smell of sulphur in the air. The closer we got, the stronger it became. How could people live here with this overpowering smell? Every few yards it seemed plumes of smoke erupted from the ground. These could sprout up in a field, or even someone's garden, and apparently quite at random. The earth's crust is so thin here that 'boilings' open up anywhere, releasing vapour and their distinct pong. I took an evening walk and passed many sulphurous boilings, including a 'Laughing Gas Pool'. Supposedly therapeutic in the late 19th century, the combination of hydrogen sulphide and carbon dioxide produced something similar to nitrous oxide – laughing gas – but caused people to faint, so swimming was particularly risky. Eventually a system was devised where the town could access the water safely and without danger to health.

We soon got used to the smell, and by the end of our visit hardly noticed it at all. The good folk of Rotorua were especially friendly, and absolutely in love with their town.

A list of restaurants appeared, for us to choose one to visit for our supper. I liked the sound of The Fat Dog. It looked appropriately quirky and fun, so we decided this would be the place for us. Teaming up with a few more of our party, we had a most wonderful evening and probably the best food ever. It was inventive, delicious, and so reasonable, and made for a long happy evening in very good company.

Mum was telling everyone about my planned Tiwi Island trip, and one of our company said, 'Oh, she won't get there!'

'She will!' said Mum.

No visit to Rotorua would be complete without a visit to the geothermal area where geysers spout impressively upwards. They were a little reticent that day, just small spoutings, so, disappointingly, we didn't see their full force. It was also raining again, so everything was just a bit too damp. New Zealand's Maori name is, after all, Aotearoa, Land of the Long White Cloud. Our next destination, the Agrodome Farm Show, was thankfully inside, and what great entertainment it proved to be.

New Zealand is unbelievably full of sheep, and the Agrodome show is a 'tour de force' of shearing and theatrical displays. I hadn't realised there were quite so many different breeds. Some appeared quite docile, but others had definite attitude. We sat in the auditorium as a large pyramid-shaped dais gradually filled up with the assorted sheep. There were many spectacularly handsome animals, some breeds I knew of and others I certainly didn't. The magnificent Merino, of course, and others such as Texel, and the English types - Southdown, Suffolk, the especially bear-like South Suffolk, the Leicester, and a smug-looking Cheviot resembling an English Bull Terrier. Most were impressively bouffant, and I don't remember seeing this fulsomeness on our hillsides back home. Obviously pampered, they must have enjoyed a full sheep-spa session prior to the show. The activity on the dais was being closely watched by a large sheepdog, the strong and intelligent New Zealand Huntaway, and when the performance was complete, with all sheep in place, he raced to the top and stood proudly on the back of the Merino. It was a fun day, and a great family occasion.

Making our way towards windy Wellington, we stopped briefly at Taupo, situated in a volcano crater on the shores of Lake Taupo. Here I came across a patriotic rugby shop full of New Zealand kit and bought a rugby shirt for each of the grandsons. Being loyal England supporters, I wondered what my sons would think. For the remainder of the trip, Mum and I sported silver fern brooches, given as a gift from the shop.

We made a brief stop at Huka Falls, the largest on the Waikato River where, foaming spectacularly, it bursts through a narrow gorge, then over a twenty-metre drop to form the river again. The Maori word *huka* appropriately means foam, and the falls are a great natural wonder.

Onwards to Windy Wellington, and it truly lived up to the nickname that day. Before visiting a steep hilltop overlooking the city, we should have been given a health warning. I was nearly blown away and had to hold tight to my coat, which was in real danger of flying off. I was amazed to see cows calmly clinging to the hill, happily munching away.

Arriving at our hotel, we had a final supper with the group before they left for the South Island ferry. Suddenly we felt rather abandoned and vulnerable, especially reading the instruction booklet in our hotel room. We were in a tsunami and earthquake area, and needed to know what to do in case of trouble!

The wind calmed down, and our stay in Wellington was lovely. Blue skies, clear waters in the harbour and, of course, the fantastic Te Papa Tongarewa Museum to visit, surely one of the world's best. There we spent hours reliving the history, culture and art of New Zealand and the South Pacific. It was a wonder, and worth the trip to New Zealand alone just for this. We spent hours looking at exhibits from prehistoric times to the present day. With an art collection, ancient artefacts, photographs, costumes, toys and jewellery, the items were wide-ranging and totally fascinating. Later, standing on the quay, with the sun shining, a bright blue sky above and the sea a transparent emerald green, I could clearly see shoals of fish swimming far below.

Arriving in Sydney, there was Avenell, once more in tears, so happy to see us again. By then she and Bryan had recently separated, and she was of course especially glad to have family with her for a while.

We enjoyed a relaxing few days together, visiting our old haunts around Lake Macquarie and Warners Bay, Charlestown and Mount Hutton. The gang of kookaburras still woke me up at around 5 am each morning, and I found their raucous cries quite reassuring. We also needed to visit a good picture framer as I had completed a pastel portrait of Avenell's much loved border terrier, Rufus. During our last visit I had taken many photographs of Rufus; however, the best image for a portrait was of him standing proudly on Redhead Beach. It needed a framer used to handling pastels, and we found one. I don't know why I should have been surprised, but the lady framer even mentioned using the important 'trap' which allows the inevitable pastel dust to fall between picture and mount, leaving the mount pristine and unmarked. All was well.

Before leaving for my outback travels, I had time to visit one of my favourite places in Newcastle: Darby Street, with its funky shops and cafés and the wonderful Newcastle Art Gallery. I came across a young artist working there. This was Lucas Grogan, who invited me to the evening private view of his solo exhibition at nearby Pod Space. Called 'Tell 'im He's Dreamin', I decided I would go. He warned me some of it would be a bit explicit, but based on an Aboriginal theme. It was exactly as he said, but most impressive, and I thought to myself, this young man could go far. Having looked at his website since, the list of solo exhibitions, group shows and commissions worldwide is indeed impressive.

I would soon be safely leaving Mum with Avenell for my solo outback adventure. They would have a marvellous time together, so I knew I could go away with peace of mind, and no little mounting excitement for this new adventure.

Avenell decided on a day out before I left for Darwin. It started wet and dreary but soon brightened up, and after about an hour's drive, we parked near a high sand cliff. Leaving Mum in the car, we went off to explore. Climbing the steep cliff, we gasped in amazement. Before us lay a far-reaching lunar style landscape of dunes leading down to the sea. We were the only people there, and it felt very special. We reached a fenced-off area, labelled as an ancient Aboriginal midden. There, in the shifting dunes, was important evidence of an early settlement. It was a privileged experience for us, and I later discovered this could have been a sacred site of the Worimi people of that area.

I was contacted by my travel agent with the news that I could only have one day in the Tiwi Islands instead of the planned overnight camping. This was a great disappointment, but I was assured it was for religious reasons, as well as floods on the camping beaches. I couldn't argue with that, and felt lucky I was going at all. A day trip to Litchfield Park had been arranged instead. However, I made sure I would still see the famous and quite distinctive Tiwi Art, and Pukumani, the unusual funeral poles. Luckily that was still on the itinerary.

The time had come. Travelling light, with only one backpack allowed, I caught the train to Sydney from nearby Cardiff. Coming from the UK, it is quite unsettling visiting towns with names like Cardiff, Holsworthy, Newcastle and Morpeth, all within easy reach of each other. Yet, somehow, they happily sit alongside names such as Kurri Kurri and Wagga Wagga. Comfortably settled on the train, I remembered thinking about this and how familiar, yet exotic, Australia is. Eventually arriving in Sydney, I made my way to another platform for the airport train. All went to plan, and I arrived in good time for the long flight to Darwin.

Four-and-a-half hours later we landed in a very hot and humid Darwin, my base for the next week or so. From here I was eventually to take the short flight north to the Tiwi Islands, followed by a camping trip on Aboriginal land just to the south, in Kakadu.

Darwin enjoys two seasons, The Wet and The Dry. I was visiting just after The Wet, and the heat was absolutely stifling. I was met at the airport and driven to my hotel, called the 'Saville on the Esplanade' according to my booking, only to find the name had changed and was now 'The Mantra on the Esplanade'. I settled in and ventured out into the heat of Darwin for a look around. The city still had a distinctive pioneer feel, with low buildings and a very informal atmosphere, although signs of huge expansion and development were underway. I liked the feel of the place very much, but was extremely relieved Mum wasn't with me this time. The heat was so humid and so intense she would never have left the hotel!

I felt quite at home and had a little walkabout. The sea absolutely sparkled as if a mass of diamonds had been thrown in, and as I approached I came across several Aboriginal groups just casually sitting and chatting in the middle of the paths. We acknowledged each other, and stepping round them I passed on by. I noted the many attractions Darwin had to offer, and was determined to see as much as possible. I may never get this way again, I thought, but in such oppressive heat I would definitely need some extra lightweight clothes. A little retail therapy was required.

Early the next morning, a taxi arrived to whisk me off to the airport and the flight to the Tiwi Islands. I was deposited by a cabin and checked in with a group of five others. A six-seater plane was on hand to take us to Nguiu on the smaller Bathurst Island which, with neighbouring Melville, forms the fascinating Tiwis. Time for take-off arrived, and we walked across the strip to the plane and piled in.

It was a small aircraft, and with no real shade from the blasting sun, but we had good all-round views. The sun poured in, making it stiflingly hot. Thankfully, the flight would only last half an hour or so.

'Leave the cabin door open for ventilation,' said the pilot to the burly Australian lass who had taken the front seat beside him. 'I'll tell you when to shut it, and when you do, make sure you do it with a good slam.' The girl was quite unperturbed.

We taxied onto the runway and started our take off. There was a very welcome cool breeze in the cabin, and then the pilot shouted, 'Shut it now!' With a very muscular arm, our sturdy 'co-pilot' slammed the door shut and up we went.

Goodness, at first, I had rather wanted that front seat, but I could never have mustered up the strength to shut the door against such a powerful airstream with my right wrist still a little weak from the fracture . Well done, that girl in the front!

As we approached the islands, beautiful stretches of beaches, mangrove swamp, dense forest and bush appeared before us. On landing we were met by some cheerful Tiwi guides, who took us to a small camp for a breakfast of billy tea and damper bread. It was delicious, despite the damper being a little gritty! A small price to pay for bread traditionally baked in a fire on the ground.

We watched in fascination as our hosts painted their faces, using natural ochres and clay, in preparation for their welcoming dances. Jilamara, or body art, is an important part of the Tiwi culture, and they explained how, in the old times, they would paint each other's faces. When mirrors arrived, they could do it for themselves, and each person took the utmost care with their own distinctive design.

Before the dancing began, we had to undergo a sort of exorcising ceremony. Hot smoking branches were taken from the fire and pressed onto our heads. This, we were told, was to ensure we hadn't brought anything unwelcome over from the mainland, and to keep us safe that day. Well-cleansed from anything untoward, we wondered what else this day would bring.

Energetic dancing began, with accompanying sharp intakes of breath and animal-sounding hisses. The Tiwi culture seems quite a complicated one. Each person has their own 'dreaming' and dance representing their family animal, such as a buffalo, wallaby or crocodile, for example. Dancing is passed on through the father's line, and each family has its own 'skin'. There are four types of skin, passed only through the mother's line, and intermarriage between people of the same skin is not allowed.

We sat under tarpaulin canopies to protect us from the heat and watched the most expressive dancing. Unlike the mainland Aborigines, Tiwi Islanders have been in charge of their own lands since 1978, and the atmosphere was definitely upbeat and purposeful. So different from the many, seemingly rather lost, Aboriginal countrymen over the water. I thought about the casual groups of Aborigines sitting, with apparently no purpose, on the paths of Darwin.

One Tiwi lady was especially sweet, and I have never forgotten her. Dear Philippa, so gentle and courteous. With permission as always, I took some photos of her and some other Islanders to paint their portraits when back at home.

The day was spent learning about bush tucker and bush medicines, with visits to various art centres. Ngaruwanajirri at Nguiu is run by a charity supporting local artists who suffer from some disability, and what a humbling experience it was. There I met Aboriginal artists who were keen to show me their work, and how the raw earth is prepared for pigments. One gentleman grabbed my hand to show me the pigments he used: raw ochres and chalk. They were such delightful people and, wanting to support them, I bought some hand-painted purses, a small painting, and an upright bird carving with a sharp pointed beak – 'Tipuamantumirri'. This was typical Tiwi art, with its distinctive geometric abstract designs that also decorate the unusual funeral poles, or Pukumani I had been so keen to see. Not only the Pukumani, but many of the buildings on the Islands are covered with these colourful patterns.

How I wished I still had the overnight camping trip. I could have learnt so much more about these truly fascinating islands but, happily, it was a very full and enriching day. After the earlier bread and tea our two rangers took us on a walkabout, pointing out the plants used as medicine and one, a soap bush, for handwashing. We all had a go and then, clambering into a four-by-four, we ventured further afield. The islands are so heavily forested we found bird and animal sighting almost impossible, but suddenly one of the rangers shouted out. The van came to a sudden stop and he ran out into the bush. Laughing, back he came with a large fringed lizard. However did he manage to spot it, camouflaged in the undergrowth, and with us still on the move? He was so in tune with his surroundings, nothing escaped him.

We moved on to visit the former Catholic mission, now a mix of Christian and Tiwi culture. The typical Tiwi designs decorate the altar and walls, and it was this very mission, used in the film 'Australia', from where the local priest sent first warnings of the incoming Japanese planes as they made their way to Darwin during WWII. The propeller of a crashed Japanese plane remains there as a monument to that time.

Much too soon our day came to an end, and we were back on the plane, not so hot now, thank goodness, and returning to Darwin. Tomorrow would be the replacement day to Litchfield National Park.

I was expecting a four-by-four vehicle for Litchfield, but as I waited outside the hotel a massive coach turned up. Surely this wasn't for me? It was and, hoping not to show my disappointment, I climbed on board and settled down. It turned out to be a good day with a happy group. We bonded easily and together enjoyed a cooling swim in a large rock pool with its own waterfall, and from where we could see, and definitely smell, musty flying foxes hanging from the surrounding gum trees. Finally, we enjoyed a nice tea under the expansive roots of a massive Banyan tree.

On our way back to Darwin we passed armies of gigantic termite mounds, together with smaller ones, all positioned in the same north-to-south direction. The wonders of nature! Someone took my photo against a huge mound. I was absolutely dwarfed by it.

With the following free day I was able to explore more of Darwin on my own. I caught a taxi to the Museum and Art Gallery of the Northern Territory on the outskirts of town and spent a glorious few hours admiring their exhibits, and having coffee and a very healthy cake overlooking the sparkling ocean.

The gallery is a gem, with a wonderful mix of Aboriginal art, archival film, natural history and palaeontology. Of great interest was the exhibition depicting the story of the defence of Darwin in WWII, which linked to my visit on Bathurst Island. A real curiosity though was the stuffed five-metre-long male saltwater crocodile, 'Sweetheart'. He had such a sad story. This belligerent Saltie kept attacking fishing boats, dinghies and outboard motors, and so the Territory Parks and Wildlife Commission decided enough was enough and planned to move this very fine specimen to safer waters. However, on the voyage, the rope around him became tangled in a log, and poor Sweetheart died.

Luckily for me it was Thursday, and that evening the famous Mindil Beach Sunset Market would be open. It was massive, and looked as if the whole of Darwin was there – family groups, young and old, tourists and locals. I arrived as large crowds were gathering along the shoreline and, with excitement mounting, the red gold sun sank slowly and gracefully into the horizon. It was party time.

Accompanied by the playing of many didgeridoos and delicious cooking aromas, stalls began to open and the fun began. I heard some loud 'cracks' and found myself a few yards from the taped enclosure of 'Mick's Whips'. Stockman Mick was cracking his leather whip for all he was worth. It was an extraordinary display of high-speed whipping! We all kept our distance.

The most remarkable performance was by a young white Australian, eMDee, who played four didgeridoos at the same time. He was obviously well known and soon surrounded by enthusiastic crowds, many dancing, as his audience continued to grow. It was masterful, and quite stirring.

Stalls selling hot food were in full cooking mode and I joined a queue at the 'Roadkill Café'. I couldn't resist it, despite the slogan 'You Kill It, We'll Cook it!'. There were pans of possum, kangaroo, buffalo, squirrel and wallaby. I chose a kangaroo kebab; fairly chewy, but hot and tasty.

It was dark and getting late for me, but there must have been thousands of people still milling around enjoying the atmosphere. I could have stayed on, but I had an early call the next day. My outback camping trip was about to start.

Five days of heat, dust and mosquitoes, camping in Kakadu with a visit to adjoining Arnhem Land was one of the toughest things I have ever done. Led by a wiry outback Australian, Kerry, we made up a party of five, including two young German men, Karl-Heinz and Mike, and Nicky, a young girl from Melbourne. Our rather smoky camp was on Aboriginal land, and the owner soon appeared to reassure us that the fires, or traditional 'burn offs', were quite close, but not enough for us to worry about. We soon got used to the pervading smell of wood smoke. For night use we were given rechargeable torches, with strict instructions to use them to 'sweep' the ground for snakes if we needed to leave our tents to use the bathroom. This was located some 200 yards away, but if you have to go, you have to go! My first experience of this was rather terrifying. At night the bush is so full of strange sounds with cracks and rustles, hissings and cane toads croaking, all of which seem so loud, as if almost inside the tent. There had to be a routine. The main thing was to keep mosquitoes outside, so all lights had to be switched off before leaving the tent. When reaching the bathroom, after careful sweeping of the bush floor, the door had to be shut tight before switching on the light. It was to no avail. Whatever we did, we were all bitten through nets and our camping clothes, despite liberal use of repellent, and soon came to realise this was a battle we were going to lose. The mozzies lived here after all. We were visitors.

Each day we set off in our four-by-four, Kerry at the wheel and Geoffrey Gurrumul Yunupingu, the blind Aboriginal singer, on the CD player. His wonderful songs haunt me still, and every time I hear them I am back in that vehicle being jerked and bumped along the cratered tracks, with red dust billowing in our wake.

In searing heat, our days in the outback were a mixture of heavy-duty trekking over boulders and under fallen trees, with the reward of a cool swim in a rock pool at the end of the trail, or a steep cliff to climb for viewing ancient rock art. Evenings were spent enjoying water and nibbles at the local Billabong, but without alcohol, which is banned on Aboriginal land. The waning light was always so dramatic, and as we sat on a rocky ledge above the water we caught the occasional glimpse of a huge 'saltie', a salt water crocodile, slowly surfacing then disappearing. We stayed well out of reach as the sun went down, until Kerry eventually cried, 'The mozzies are here!', when we all dashed for the safety of the truck and bumped our way back to camp for supper. Supper in the fully anti-mosquito screened dining tent was regularly punctuated by sharp slaps as one or other of us whacked a mosquito that, too late, had already drawn blood.

One especially tough day involved a drive over rocky ground, with no real track to be seen, eventually arriving in a part of the bush from where we were to trek for several kilometres to a rock pool. Streaked with red dust and sweat, in scorching heat, we ploughed on over rocks, boulders and under fallen logs, my feet actually grinding in my boots, until we came to the pool. It was really picturesque, with a waterfall at its far end.

'You can swim here,' said Kerry. 'Fill your bottles. The water is pure.'

I then happened to spy a rather worn notice advising, 'Beware of the crocodiles.'

'It's fine. They're freshwater crocs, not salties. As long as you don't disturb them, they won't attack you,' Kerry told us quite confidently.

Well, how would you know? I could disturb one by accident.

Kerry and Nicky plunged in. I waited till they were well in and swimming towards the waterfall, so that any croc disturbance wouldn't be by me. Karl-Heinz and Mike decided not to risk it at all. I decided I would be last in and first out, staying very near the edge. How cool and refreshing it was. Tiny fish circled my legs and I had to keep swimming, with them continually following, as the pool floor was so rocky it was too painful to stand. After a brave swim I got out and was about to fill my water bottle, when I looked across the pool to see this chunky water dragon – a big lizard, half in and half out of the water – slowly turning its head to look at us. My water bottle would stay unfilled now. The lizard lived in that pool. It was his home, and his loo, I'm sure!

The minute I dressed I was as hot as before, but what an experience this had been. I loved it all. Eventually we trekked back to the vehicle for our return to camp. On the way, with Geoffrey Gurrumul playing in the background, Kerry told us stories from the outback. One I will never forget. Two young men were driving through the bush when they came across a kangaroo lying by the roadside, apparently knocked down. Sadly, many are killed this way. To have some fun, they went over to the kangaroo and dressed him in a jacket and cap ready for a photograph, when all of a sudden the animal came to and hopped off. He was still wearing the cap and jacket with, unfortunately, a wallet inside! How we laughed!

That evening I decided to leave my wet swimsuit on a chair outside my tent. I knew it wouldn't dry in such humidity, but at least it would be an attempt.

As usual, in the middle of the night I needed to visit the bathroom. Feeling more confident now, I followed the usual ground-sweeping procedure, but found, on my safe return to the tent, my swimsuit had gone. It was nowhere to be seen. There was the chair, but it was quite empty. A wallaby had been roaming round the camp, and in my bleary state, and after Kerry's kangaroo story earlier that day, I wondered if it had hopped off with it. I kept on looking in the vain hope my swimsuit would miraculously appear, but it had definitely gone. Eventually I gave up my search. Well, that was it, no more swimming for me. I opened up the tent and went in, only to find it wasn't my tent at all, it was the German boys! Oh, the shock and embarrassment.

'We heard you outside and wondered what was going on,' said a very amused Karl-Heinz.

Luckily the boys just laughed it off, and we were the very best of friends after that. Making my abject apology, I looked for *my* tent. There it was, just twenty yards or so away, behind different bushes and with the chair outside, plus swimsuit; still damp, of course, but quite intact.

A memorable final day started with a visit to Arnhem Land, with an Aboriginal guide who taught us the laws of his people and their punishments. Swift justice appeared to include frequent use of spears and knives, some serrated. The rest of our time was spent cruising the Yellow Water Wetlands, a partially submerged area of great beauty. It teemed with wildlife. There were wild ponies and birds on the land, with crocodiles and water lilies surrounding our boat as we made our way through the spectacular sunken forest. Thousands of trees and bushes, pushing up through the water, created glorious reflections under the hot, clear blue sky.

It had to end, and all too soon a six-hour drive took us back to Darwin. On the way, red with dust, streaked with soot from the burn offs and decidedly sweaty, we stopped at Adelaide River township. It was a Sunday, and the locals, in their best clothes, were enjoying lunch at the pub. We trudged in, longing for cool drinks. Just before we arrived, a police van had passed us at some speed, and as we approached the bar a man told us that we had missed the excitement. An old man had been arrested at gun point!

Adelaide River certainly had some surprises. A stuffed, fully grown water buffalo stood proudly with its four feet firmly planted on the bar counter. We ordered our drinks as the owner told us how this fine beast had been a gentle pet, and was the very one, supposedly aggressive, subdued by the star Paul Hogan in the movie 'Crocodile Dundee'.

Arriving in Darwin we had to make some sad farewells, but with promises to keep in touch. Exhausted, but bursting with the memories, I made my weary, sweat and dust-stained way though the hotel foyer. This rather ordinary hotel suddenly seemed very upmarket with its smart and fragrant guests about to have dinner. I quickly checked back in and disappeared off to my room.

The following morning, refreshed, and with a little time left, I made a beeline for the music shop in town. I had to find that CD of Geoffrey Gurrumul's songs. I was absolutely entranced by his music as we bounced around the outback in Kerry's four-by-four. Geoffrey Gurrumul Yunupingu, blind from birth, is a unique artist. He taught himself to play guitar, although the wrong way round, and proceeded to write songs and music linked to his land which, haunting and moving, seem to reach such depths of emotion. I eventually found a rather pricey CD, but couldn't go home without it so paid up. I have since spent many hours listening to Gurrumul, immediately transported back to the billowing dust, heat and magic of the outback.

The CD had been my priority, but the next and probably most important destination was the pharmacy. I had a painful row of blisters on my feet from the 'grinding' and was covered in insect bites. The pharmacist produced paw paw ointment and a small dropper bottle of Betadine. I had never come across Betadine before, and decided it must be an Australian speciality. This strange and staining brown liquid, obviously iodine-based, certainly needed judicious application, but it did the trick and the blisters improved.

It was almost 9pm when I arrived back in Sydney. Avenell and Mum were at the airport to meet me, and by midnight we were home. I had so much to tell them, but first needed someone to apply pawpaw ointment to the bites on my back.

'Oh dear!' exclaimed Mum. 'I have never seen anything like it. You are covered.'

Luckily, I wasn't in danger of contracting malaria, but knew there was the possibility of Ross River Fever. I was fine though. No fever, but lots of itching!

Soon we would be heading back to the UK, but Avenell still had a few more excursions planned, and one was rather spectacular. We spent a breezy day at the picturesque Nobbys Beach on the Tasman Sea, and at that very moment southern right whales were passing through. As they breached and swam purposefully onwards, we felt rather moved. At the same time sunlight seemed to bounce upwards, fan-like, from the horizon to the sky. It was in the opposite direction to normal, and I had never seen this phenomenon before.

A day trip to trendy and rather chic Morpeth, a riverside town in the Hunter Valley area, ended on a balmy evening with another visit to the historic Audrey Wilkinson's vineyard. Audrey Wilkinson, despite the name, was a man reputed to have been the first person to produce wine in the Hunter Valley. As we overlooked rows of vines covering the picturesque valley below, we relaxed and leisurely sipped delicious wine on this soft and sunny final evening.

The gang of kookaburras woke me for the last time. We were leaving, and I felt rather sad catching my last glimpses of the cheeky sulphur-crested cockatoos, sweet rosellas and striking king parrots. Time for goodbyes, with another promise to return, as Avenell dropped us off at Sydney station for the Indian Pacific train to Perth. It was all quite well-organised, and the steward, a pleasant young English lad, introduced himself. His tiny cabin was next to ours, and I was pleased to notice we were in the middle of the train, although right at the end of the carriage. It was well-appointed, with a sofa that turned into two bunks, a minute bathroom with shower and, of all things, a foldaway lavatory and basin. You could just about turn around in the space, but it was at least a cabin and not the reclining seat Mum would have chosen. We eased out of Sydney station and settled in for our three days, three nights, and the 2,698 miles between the Pacific and Indian Oceans.

Our first stop was Broken Hill, an isolated mining town, where some of its inhabitants waited on the station to welcome us and sell some trinkets. It was a very quiet place that day, and we had a little time to wander along the main street and admire its handsome buildings, obviously paid for by the proceeds of mining precious metals. Back on the train, we were on our way to Adelaide.

The Dining Car was bright and beautifully furnished, and sharing a table we had a very good meal in pleasant company. It seemed as if the travellers were mostly Australians and out to have a jolly good time.

When we returned to our cabin the attendant had made up our narrow beds, and the top bunk, mine, was extremely high up. It reminded me of one of Dad's boats when little Fraser kept falling off the top bunk, and it wasn't anything like as high as this one.

'I can see your bottom,' laughed Mum as I climbed up the vertical ladder. Oh dear! This didn't bode well.

It was a long way down, and I wondered if I would fall out in the night. When I reached the top, I found the sheets so tightly tucked in, and only open on the wall side, that there was no danger of rolling out. However, there would be no sleep either.

As time passed, I realised we were in for a very bad night. We rocked, rolled, jerked and heaved all through the night, and the noise was terrible. There was no let up. It just went on and on and on. I then realised what a man in New Zealand must have told Mum. Make sure our cabin was in the *middle* of the *carriage*, not the middle of the train. We were positioned right over the couplings at the end of the carriage. It was a nightmare, and we didn't get a wink of sleep all night. Poor Mum was mumbling and groaning, and I felt as if my very aorta was stretching inside my body. I held on tight. This was a real danger to health, and I decided we wouldn't stay here another night.

Morning came at last, and poor Mum rolled out of her bunk, head turned stiffly to one side. Her neck was rigid and painful.

'The next time I have one of my bright ideas!'

The young attendant came in looking white as a sheet. He hadn't slept either. 'I have never had a night like it,' he announced.

I called for the manager and insisted that if we couldn't be given another cabin, we would have to jump ship at Adelaide, the next stop, and fly on to Perth from there. We couldn't go through another night like that, and 86-year-old Mum had been injured in the process.

Unfortunately, the train was full and there were no spare cabins. However, the rather aloof manager assured us things would definitely improve. Evidently the infrastructure between Sydney and Adelaide was poor, and the driver had been going faster than normal to make up time. He wasn't at all sympathetic to Mum's plight, and was the only person I came across in the whole of Australia who was rather uncaring. Luckily we stayed on the train and, with a staff change at Adelaide, things definitely improved.

Mum's neck was very painful. She took painkillers and I administered some gentle massage, so she felt just about well enough to take the coach tour of the city. If I had known about this first leg of the journey I would have planned to fly straight to lovely Adelaide, spend a day or two there and then join the train. Quite a crowd of Australians got on at Adelaide, so obviously they knew what to do.

Adelaide is a beautiful city and we had a good tour that day, although in hindsight a longer stay would have been best. With its historic parklands, open atmosphere and illustrious cricket history, Adelaide certainly deserved a longer visit.

The atmosphere on the train became quite jolly as we progressed on through the immense semi-arid Nullarbor Plain. Stretching between southern and western Australia, the red Nullarbor is over 1,000 kilometres of actually very little. Mum loved this. She had been longing to see 'miles of nothing', and certainly had her wish. There are a few scattered townships, the most notable being Cook, 'Queen City of the Nullarbor', with all of five inhabitants. We met four of them! Once a thriving small community with a school, hospital and even a gaol, it is now virtually abandoned due to the reduced rail service. The good folks of Cook enjoy some celebrity and make the most of the Indian Pacific's twice-weekly visits. In her homely office, Jan told stories of the town and sold us her hand-painted wooden spoons. They were charming, and how could you not give her the pleasure of a sale? I was hoping to catch a glimpse of the fabled wedge-tailed eagles that inhabit South Australia. With a wingspan of over seven feet, they are majestic and fearsome birds, the largest birds of prey in Australia. A very large statue of this eagle dominates Cook station.

Crossing the Nullarbor is, it seems, an essential rite of passage for many Australians, and the days passed easily between sociable meals, reading, and looking out of the window. I caught sight of a lone camel in the distance, and as we passed over a dirt road crossing over the tracks, a group of four travellers waved enthusiastically from their dusty vehicle. It was probably the only excitement they had that day, and they must have waited patiently for us to pass by. It caused some excitement on the train as well.

Everyone settled back in the lounge car or in their cabins, but I kept looking out for some sign of life. And then I was rewarded. Somewhere from that vast nothingness, two wedge-tailed eagles suddenly flew down to my side of the track. The moment passed so quickly I could hardly believe it, but I had seen them, and was possibly the only one to have this incredible sighting as no one else mentioned it. What a stroke of luck.

The intercom suddenly came to life and we were treated to another rendering of 'Blast The Bush', Len Beadell's magnificent after dinner speech, the same one we had heard on the Great Ocean Road Coach. It was just as funny second time around, and I noticed all the cabin doors were open as Len's words filled the whole train. Everyone seemed to be enjoying it.

Our big stop was to be in Kalgoorlie, a major gold mining town where we were to visit the huge 'Super Pit'. Arriving at night, the city tour would be in darkness so Mum decided to go to bed instead. I didn't want to miss anything, so I boarded the coach with several others and off we set. Travelling down the main Burt Street the buildings looked quite historic, but it was so very dark we didn't quite get the full experience. However, the driver had a surprise in store for us, and this was almost certainly the highlight of his day.

'Look to the left when I beep my horn!'

He 'beeped' his horn loudly several times, and we looked out to the left as instructed, when out of a well-lit arched building, a small crowd of scantily dressed girls ran towards us, then waved and 'hello-ed' enthusiastically. It quite took us all by surprise, but we waved back, and as the driver turned the bus around the girls scampered back into the building. It was the local brothel. We laughed in shock more than anything else, but it had served its purpose; the driver was happy and carried on to the pit. This was, of course, a major and very thriving mining town, but it definitely felt slightly 'wild west'!

We approached intense bright lights and the entrance to the Super Pit, the largest open-cut gold mine in Australia. It was certainly gigantic, and as we entered a viewing area the scale was mind boggling. It is said to be so large it can be seen from space. We peered down into its open, terraced depths, and right at its base huge dump vehicles appeared as tiny Matchbox toys. Here was mining on the grandest scale, and the area was positively buzzing with activity. The work never stops, and millions of tonnes of gold are produced each year.

Back at the train, it was time for the whistle to blow for our final leg towards Perth. Mum opened an eye and asked how it went. As I told her about the girls, she sat up and asked enthusiastically, 'Did you take a photograph?'

'Certainly not. It took us all by surprise, and it was dark anyway. I've got some of the Super Pit though!' She was disappointed and went back to sleep.

The meals and company were great, and at our last dinner I decided I would have a glass of wine, the one everyone had been asking for and enjoying throughout the journey – 'Traminer'.

I ordered my glass, and our table of four toasted each other and the Indian Pacific as we tucked into our meal. The wine was delicious. The cabin manager then appeared with a tin of Schweppes tonic water. Before I could stop her, she opened it and poured some into each glass with a look on her face that said, 'There you are, a treat.' She smiled down at us.

I couldn't believe it. My delicious wine was now bitter and un-drinkable. What was she thinking? Was this some strange custom? Well, whatever it was it ruined the wine, but being English, I said nothing!

Perth is very much on its own, closer to Singapore than to any other Australian city, and with a marvellous quality and unique life. We loved it from the minute we arrived.

Staying at the Chifley on the Terrace, a boutique hotel on a main bus route with the city centre and Swan River nearby, turned out to be a perfect choice. We couldn't have wished for anything better. More used to short stay guests, the staff were kind and friendly and obviously enjoying having us around for longer than normal. We settled in and planned our explorations.

With the weather promising to be fine, we decided to take the ferry to Rottnest Island. It was such a beautiful day as we sailed out of Perth, stopping in Fremantle to pick up a whole school of children with red jacketed teachers, hundreds of bikes, crates of bags and all. Embarkation was undertaken with swift military precision, parents waved goodbye, and off we sailed again.

Arriving in Rottnest, we soon realised what a very special place it is; no cars allowed, the only transport, apart from the odd official vehicle and small transport coach, being shank's pony and bikes. It was tranquil, beautiful, and very, very therapeutic.

We walked around the lush green island, admiring its coastline and gorgeous blue-green seas while hoping to spot the famous 'rats' of Rottnest. Early Dutch sailors named the island Rottnest believing the little animals inhabiting it to be rats, but they are in fact quokkas, pouched mammals, found only here. There were hundreds of them, and quite tame, often just standing watching us with the occasional 'squeaks'!

We mused on how we would love a holiday home here, and how wonderful it would be for the family. On the ferry back to Perth, we saw dolphins leaping at the entrance of the river and, passing under a bridge, caught sight of a portrait under one of the arches. This turned out to be the late Bon Scott of the rock band AC/DC. A Scottish-born Australian, Bon Scott died too early at the age of 34. As we continued to approach Perth, the attractive city skyline was silhouetted against the sky which, that evening, turned a gorgeous pink and gold.

We decided to catch the train to Fremantle the next day. Another sunny morning, and arriving in Fremantle we enjoyed a coffee at trendy Gino's before heading off to the harbour. Here we found the Maritime Museum with its fascinating exhibits, and especially relics of the Dutch ship *Batavia*, wrecked off Western Australia in 1629 on its maiden voyage. Looking at its massive rotten timbers, held together by metal ropes, it was obvious a lot of work would be needed to get it to the Swedish *Vasa* standard.

Walking to the shore, we decided we must sample fish and chips before finding the art gallery. 'I could live in Fremantle,' declared Mum. It certainly was a great place, but I loved Perth best.

The following day we woke up to rain, and with a morning cruise to Margaret River already booked we began to wonder if it was worth it. Gamely pressing on, we joined a most friendly group of fellow travellers, but spent most of the time chatting in the cabin as the views were decidedly grey. Things looked up when we were told there would be a wine tasting, and in due course bottles of a rather pleasant Chenin Blanc arrived. Our spirits suddenly lifted no end.

Thank goodness, the rain stopped that afternoon in Perth. We visited the Museum and Art Gallery and found the strangest sea monster, an extremely rare megamouth. This beast, a type of shark over five metres long and officially named Megachasma Pelagios, was washed up on a beach in 1988, causing quite a sensation. It was frozen and then prepared in formalin for permanent display in the museum. What a strange sight it is.

On one of our forays into the shopping centre, we came across the bookish Merchants Tea House, a cut above the usual and where serious types sipped coffee as they read papers and magazines. I became hooked on their chai latte, and enjoyed several visits during our stay.

On another rainy morning, leaving Mum to rest in the hotel, I made a second visit to the art gallery. I arrived with a monsoon and the rain absolutely pelted down, doors rattling with the wind as I quickly took sanctuary in the café together with many other visitors. No one was leaving and then, looking around, I saw an elderly Aboriginal lady sitting in a wheelchair. I recognised her from a recent local newspaper article. She was an artist and a long way from home, but staying in Perth for a lower leg amputation due to diabetes. Poor dear. I had a chat with her and her carer. She was longing to get home, and I often wonder how she is.

A small ad in the arts section of a local paper caught my eye. That very evening, The Bare Naked Theatre Company were performing 'The Canterbury Tales' with a twist. It was billed as 'a hilarious and fast paced' modern adaption of the tales, and certainly sounded rather intriguing. I had to go, and when the time came, leaving Mum to enjoy some rest in the hotel, I set off walking through the centre of town to the Chinese area on the outskirts where I found an art house style theatre. Taking my seat, I wondered what I was in for.

Six Tales were performed, each set in a completely different time and era. The Pardoner's Tale was in a Western setting, The Miller was as a 'Carry On' film, The Reeve's was a silent movie, The Wife of Bath mediaeval, The Merchant's Tale a Victorian melodrama, and finally, The Franklin's Tale in Star Trek style. It was a terrific show, and so hilarious I can't remember laughing quite so much in one evening. Bawdy, poignant, and tragic by turn, and my sides literally ached.

It was dark as we all piled out of the theatre, and I decided to find a taxi rather than walk back through deserted streets. I waited and waited, hoping one would pass by, but with no luck. Eventually I went back to the theatre and asked if they would telephone for one. Not only did they do that, but when the cast came out they waited to see me safely into the cab when it arrived. What an evening.

The Perth Mint seemed to be an attractive proposition, and we still hadn't visited Kings Park, so we decided to make those two our destinations for the next day. A bus took us to the Mint, and as we entered we were met by a charming volunteer guide, Robert. This delightful man was terribly disfigured, obviously from a severe fire that had badly damaged his face and arms. As well as his facial deformity, one hand was clawed and the other was just a hook, but you could tell he had been a handsome man. He offered lots of information which we gratefully took on board. During our conversation I asked him about his accident. As a young man he had been crop-dusting by plane, and it crashed. What a brave man.

The Mint was indeed a fascinating place, dating from 1899, charting the progress and history of Perth, its involvement in gold mining with exhibits of gold, and the smelting process. Perth is a burgeoning city and you couldn't fail to notice its wealth, stemming from the rich gold seams still being mined.

We decided to get to Kings Park for lunchtime and asked Robert for the best bus route. His reaction was incredible. He absolutely insisted on driving us there, if we would wait for the end of his shift in twenty minutes. We tried to protest, but he was having none of it. After the twenty minutes he collected us and took us right through the Mint to a secure garage area. We passed some men who said, 'These must be your VIPs, Robert.' Goodness, fancy being VIPs!

This kind man drove us all the way to Kings Park, and then offered to collect us as well. We declined, not knowing when we would want to leave, but felt quite humbled by his generosity. At one point, as we were being driven through heavy traffic, it dawned on me we were being chauffeured by a man with no functioning hands, just the metal hook and a claw. You would never have known he was disabled. I have often thought of Robert since, a true gentleman.

The view over Perth from Kings Park is astounding, and on its own worthy of a visit, but the park itself has a huge collection of exotic trees and plants like no other: rows of baobab trees, banksia, and the boronia bush whose fragrance has inspired perfumes and confectionery. At the opposite end of the scale is the roo poo tree. Correctly called the grasstree, Aborigines made a superglue from the gum of the trunk, although it had to be mixed with charcoal and kangaroo dung first. We learnt how the local Aboriginal community, making full use of their knowledge and respect of the land, had turned the bark of the scar tree into shelters, containers and shields. Signs described how the Nyoongar people traditionally gathered here, overlooking the meeting of two rivers, the Swan and Canning, which together form a vast expanse of water around the city.

Before popping into the café for tea, we visited the memorial for the fallen. Overlooking the city, this beautifully designed and peaceful area has an obelisk at its head and reflecting pool in front, from where a central flame continually burns. We took a few moments to ponder.

In the café, who do we come across but Marty of all people: Marty, the son of a princess and our Maori guide in New Zealand, was visiting a friend in Perth, and had chosen that very day to come to the park. What a coincidence!

Avenell rang that evening to say a last goodbye, and we promised we'd be back as soon as we could. The following morning, there was just enough time to pack and have a last riverside walk before being collected for our teatime flight. We had been away a long time, and still deep in my carry-on bag was the tightly wrapped carved bird from Bathurst Island. At airport security my bag was unpacked, and a Customs officer tried to unwrap the bird. It looked particularly sharp and pointed on X-ray. I explained what it was and showed her the other things I had bought on the island. Beginning to look red-faced and harassed with the effort, she eventually believed me and gave up. The bird was so well wrapped it was going to take a lot of uncovering, and a queue was forming!

As we progressed out of security, with not much time before the flight, two men approached: the airport security chief with his burly but smiling assistant. He was a most charming and courteous Englishman – from Kent, we learned – who seemed to want to chat about England, his home, and where we had been, and where we were eventually going in the UK. They walked with us to the departure area, where they left with cheery goodbyes. We felt like celebrities.

However, to this day, I am not sure whether he just liked the look of us, two well-spoken white-haired English ladies, or whether we had actually been escorted out of Australia! Me with my pointy parcel!

POSTSCRIPT (2013)

M UM WASN'T TO MAKE it back to Australia

There were to be two more European holidays, her choice: cruising the Rhine and Danube; but soon after, in May 2013, at ninety years old, she succumbed to age-related lack of blood supply to the digestive system and virtually starved to death. Mum, who loved her food so much, was eventually unable to eat at all and, in hospital, became desperate to die. However, the last good meal she had was indeed memorable.

'I want one of James's famous pies,' she insisted. We were in Suffolk during February 2013 and she had a large helping of pie, savouring every mouthful. James had lovingly decorated the crust of the meaty pie with Mum's name in pastry letters.

'Ee, that was lovely, our James.'

We think fondly of that occasion, but always hoped 'It wasn't the pie that done it!'

The following day Mum collapsed, and an ambulance was called to take her to Great Yarmouth Hospital. After a few days, she recovered enough to go home to Bristol, but over the next three months these episodes kept happening. In hospital she remained buoyant and positive for quite some time, but her health slowly declined. It was sad to see, but she was so brave, and always wonderfully cared for by hospital staff.

Mum had eventually been moved from the Bristol Royal Infirmary to the new South Bristol Community Hospital, with the hope of recovery and rehabilitation.

Six weeks in, my friend Jenny came along on our daily visit. 'Can we do anything for you today?' we asked.

'Just shoot me,' she replied.

ART SCHOOL, PORTUGAL

I was due to tutor a group for an art holiday with Art in the Algarve. This was in the fishing village of Olhao in southern Portugal, and I was to take my own class, as well as meeting up with other Clifton Art Club members. Mum's illness progressed, and as she started to decline I decided I would have to cancel Olhao.

'Don't you dare,' Mum retorted. 'You must go.'

The day before I was due to leave, I checked with the doctors.

'Is it really wise for me to go now?' I asked. They replied that Mum would be fine, and it was only a week. Ok, I thought, and told Mum not to do anything silly when I was away. I would soon be back with lots to tell her. I gave my brother's telephone number to the ward, and asked them to contact him if Mum needed anything.

'Bye, Mum. I love you. See you soon,' were my parting words. She smiled and waved weakly.

The following morning, my alarm woke me at 4am and the airport taxi arrived soon after. The early hour wasn't a problem, as my night had been disturbed and I hadn't slept much. At 2am I had woken suddenly and actually jumped out of bed. 'It's much too early,' I thought, 'why ever did I do that?'

I met my little group at Bristol airport and off we went, arriving in Faro a few hours later. A taxi took us the short journey to Olhao, where the eccentric but lovable owner, the Honourable David Clark, met us in School House, handed out our keys, and went through the art school's weekly routine. The sun was so warm, and we all looked forward to a really good week.

Eating lunch together, with David at the head of the table, his phone rang.

'Oh, there isn't anyone called Linda Alvis here,' he joked.

My class and I looked at each other in alarm. I headed off to a quiet room to take the call. It was John. Mum had died suddenly in the night! He had been phoned by the hospital at 2am, exactly the time I jumped out of bed, and was asked to come in quickly. He was too late, and poor John had to see lifeless Mum on his own.

'I didn't ring you before as I wanted to give you time to settle in, and anyway you wouldn't have got on the plane if you had known. Mum wanted you to go.'

It was as if Mum was waiting for me to leave before she could die. I remembered all the times she had told us she wanted to die, and I had always replied, 'Please don't say that.'

It was surreal. I shed a few discreet tears with my class, and then we just got on with our art holiday. Despite all, it was a happy and successful week, and one that would be repeated for many years.

Mum's illness had been pitiful and short, around three months, but one that she bore so bravely, and with such kindness and respect from hospital staff.

As a poignant reminder of our many adventures, the Polynesian Welcome napkin holder I found for Mum in Singapore now sits alongside the silver Kiwi she bought for me at the same time. My journeys and visits to Avenell in Australia would now be on my own, but it was comforting to know how much fun Mum had over the years, and how our travels had given her many wonderful experiences to talk about in her old age.

In a funny sort of way, and with some guilt, I felt liberated after we lost Mum, with no one else to worry about or to make arrangements for in life. It had never seemed a burden, though; just exciting over the years for both of us. We had made a new life for ourselves after Dad's untimely death in 1985. Almost thirty years of exploring the world together.

THE FRACTURE (2007)

"I F YOU CAN'T USE your right hand, why don't you paint with your left?' someone kindly mentioned. It was beyond me with the continual pain, and feeling ill with the after-effects of such a severe wrist fracture. This had led to complex regional pain syndrome lasting for about a year, with weekly visits to the Physiotherapy specialist Hand Department of the Bristol Royal Infirmary.

I know, I thought, I will write a 'pamphlet' for my class.

I became quite carried away with my pamphlet, and after ten computer pages I was still in the 1940s. This little pamphlet was becoming a book.

'I'm writing a book, Mum.'
'Ee, that's nice, our Linda.'

ALSO BY LINDA ALVIS

MEMOIR
Hoovering Up the Holy Carpet, Volume 1: The Accidental Artist

CHILDREN'S BOOKS
Worrall and Robin
Worrall, Robin and the Garden Visitor

POETRY
Dawn Rising

COVER IMAGES

FRONT COVER
Waterlilies and Sky
Uluru Sunset
War Dance, Alberta

BACK COVER
St Mary's Lighthouse, Whitley Bay
Robin
Cree Boy
Chrysanthemum Green, Xi'an
"Hello Sailor!", Sevastopol
The Bridge, Balloons and Hotwells
Bison, Elk Island, Alberta
Calgary Skyline
Little Owl, Kielder Forest
Totem, Ketchikan, Alaska
Kangaroo, Alice Springs
The Bread Lemon

Photographs relating to this book can be found on my website at www.alvisfineart.co
.uk/books/. My paintings and further award-winning poems, inspired by these travels,
can be found in the poetry book *Dawn Rising*.

ACKNOWLEDGEMENTS

Without the wonderful author and founder of Hawkesbury Upton Literature Festival, Debbie Young, my story would not have come to light. She has my undying gratitude. My thanks to Peter Moore who so patiently read through the manuscript and offered gentle and most valuable pointers. I will never look at a hyphen in the same way again! Thank you to Dan Gooding for his editing skills and to Jac Solomons for producing the cover so beautifully. Finally, to my friend Jenny Walmsley and my partner Mike Rome a huge thank you for continued advice, support and patience.